X

Withdrawn

Learning
Resource
Centre

The College of West Anglia

~~1/11/15~~

2 7 SEP 2017

Withdrawn

Call 01553 8152306 to renew your books or if you have any queries.
You can also renew or reserve books by going to
http://library.cwa.ac.uk/
The card holder is responsible for th
return of this item. Fines will be ch
items.

D1471042

THE COLLEGE OF WEST ANGLIA

The Goat Care Handbook

SECOND EDITION

Mary Turner Stille

McFarland & Company, Inc., Publishers
Jefferson, North Carolina, and London

The first edition of this work, titled
Goat Care: A Complete Handbook, by Mary Turner,
was published by McFarland in 1984

LIBRARY OF CONGRESS CATALOGUING-IN-PUBLICATION DATA

Stille, Mary Turner, 1946–
The goat care handbook. — 2nd ed. / Mary Turner Stille.
p.   cm.
Includes bibliographical references and index.

ISBN 0-7864-2315-3 (softcover : 50# alkaline paper) ∞

1. Goats.   I. Title.
SF383.S78 2006   636.3'9 — dc22   2005032526

British Library cataloguing data are available

Cover photograph ©2006 Photodisc

Manufactured in the United States of America

*McFarland & Company, Inc., Publishers
Box 611, Jefferson, North Carolina 28640
www.mcfarlandpub.com*

To both my girls,
Doni Watson and Debi Schwartztrauber,
who have given me my grandchildren,
all of whom help keep me young and laughing
and are tirelessly willing to help me
and accept me as I am.

Acknowledgments

Nothing about this book would ever have been possible if my oldest daughter, Doni Watson, had not been here to help with printers, discs, photos, and my moaning and groaning. She has always been there to pick up the pieces. Thankfully, she loves me enough to put up with the ups and downs that came with this endeavor.

Steven Miller has faithfully done my chores every day for over two months to give me time to finish this. And although I don't know if the goats like him, I sure appreciate him.

Daion Loe pitched in to help finish the typing.

Jennifer Martinez has been invaluable for teaching me how to work on a computer. Jennifer also was kind enough to help with photos.

Kyle Snow jumped in at the last minute to do the sketching, for which I am ever grateful.

All of my friends, and my long-distance youngest daughter, Debi, have been kind enough to be forgiving of my neglect of them.

Dr. Jarrel Irby did a fast job on my new lenses so I could cope with a computer screen.

And always, there was the innocence of my grandbabies, not having the vaguest idea of why Mama Mary was so busy but loving me anyway.

My most grateful thanks go to my goats. They actually behaved themselves and did not tear up the neighborhood while I was busy.

Contents

Preface

Even after 28 years of raising goats, I still do not consider myself an expert. But I do attack my problems with a lot more gusto than most people, and I have not gone bankrupt. Over the years, I have studied harder, learned more, and cut problems to a minimum. I wrote this book so that anyone could read it, buy goats and raise them with as few problems as possible.

Few goat keepers write manuals on goat keeping, and the best ones I have read are about homesteading, not herd facts. This leaves a lot of us hopelessly alone. Much is written about large-scale dairy herds and about one or two goats, but not for the ten to 20 we need. This book, full of hands-on knowledge, will help you solve plenty of problems and help you save more goats.

You'll learn the basics about breeds, milk, meat, buying goats, and the many ways to keep them healthy, well-fed and well-sheltered. I offer many options in each chapter so that the reader can decide which solution best fits the particular situation. Since the first edition of this book was published, I have had to do a lot of things alone and have included some of these new practices and routines. Tips for the handicapped also are offered.

I strive to simplify the basics of goat care so that anyone can take care of goats. I show that goats can be raised simply and inexpensively. I am no vet, nor is this book meant to take the place of one. My vet is a vital link between me and my goats' good health. My management practices are meant to prevent sickness, but I am the first to call a vet when I'm up against something I don't understand or cannot handle. Nor am I a salesman. I do not use brand names for most products, since these names may differ from one area to another.

My original goal was to have a goat giving milk all year. It took me eight years to accomplish that feat, and I could have done it in one if I'd had the information you will find in this book.

Goat keepers have to continually educate themselves. New diseases, new solutions, and new breeds keep right on growing while we tend to our small herds.

1

I still take my business of raising goats more seriously than most goat owners because I am still poor and can't afford to lose the herd. And I'm confident that my goat milk has aided in the health of my children, my grandchildren and me. It has helped many sickly animals as well as a friend of ours who had AIDS. He stayed stronger than he should have for longer than he should have, and his doctors attributed it to the goat milk.

Buying goats' milk from someone else can be difficult, since most dairies have to be licensed and few states allow licenses. Buying the store-bought stuff will really make your children say "yuck" and empty your pocketbook. Meat, milk and manure bought from others cannot be trusted to be clean and chemical free, so raising my own animals has always been the cheapest, safest alternative. And I can honestly say that just the process of taking care of the animals has kept me younger and stronger, even with my handicaps.

I still never pass up a chance to ask questions, and I still make plenty of mistakes. I have learned a lot the hard way. I still check for new reference books, ask questions of many vets (it is not with disrespect that I choose to use the more common and affectionate term "vet"), and I never pass up the chance to talk to new goat people. Be sure to get hooked up to an Internet goat-discussion group. Choose one that appeals to you and your management practices. That will be easier after you have read this book.

Finally, I cannot stress enough: If there is anything new, your goats will find it. If there is anything you don't know, the goats will teach you. And just when you think your patience is tried to the end, the goats will do something so endearing that you forgive them.

1

History

Knowing the background and breeding of your goats gives you a better idea of what they are made of as far as their constitution, eating, durability, and adaptability to the weather. Understanding is success.

Goats were far more appreciated in earlier history than in modern times. The animals played a major role with the supply of meat, milk, cheese and fur in older civilizations. Goats supplied companionship long before the trusty dog, a testament to the easy domestication of the goat.

Archaeologists have dated the remains of goats, or their early ancestors, as far as 10,000 years in central and western Iran. Domestication of goats has existed in other parts of the world for 8,000 years.

The Bible, too, holds some history of the goat. Proverbs 27:27 commands "And thou shalt have goats' milk enough for thy food, for the food of thy household and for the maintenance for thy maidens." Also, in Deuteronomy 27:3, God promises the Israelites that after they passed over Jordan, He would give them "a land that floweth with milk and honey." Exodus 12 tells another story. When the Pharaoh wouldn't let the Israelites go, God told Moses to speak to the congregation, saying that He would pass through the land of Egypt and smite all the first-born, man and beast. The Israelites were to kill a lamb or goat and put the blood on the door posts of their houses and eat the flesh wasted, with fire, and God would pass over them. Now, we have the present-day yearly observation of Passover.

Many of the first explorers who left Europe, including Captain James Cook, carried milk goats on their expeditions. In fact, Cook is thought to have brought one of the first descendants of the Arapawa to New Zealand.

Winston Churchill not only drank goat milk but promoted it, and the American writer and poet Carl Sandburg raised goats on his North Carolina farm, drank the milk, and included goats in his poetry.

Greek mythology gives the unicorn a cloven hoof, which would have made it a goat, but modern times have turned the mythical creature into a horse.

This Nubian kid and a La Mancha belong to Rene Mathews.

Goats still serve the same purpose they always have. There have been great improvements in breeds, size, and production, but the goat is still a great source of nutritious, delicious, healthy milk.

Modern goats bred and put in the show rings originated in Europe and Africa. The Swiss breeds include the Alpine, Saanen, Toggenburg, Sable and the Oberhasli, all coming from different areas of Europe. The Nubian came from

This alpine buckling belongs to Rene Mathews, who lives south of Texarkana, Arkansas.

different areas of Africa and got its name from the ancient African country of Nubia. However, in Africa, there are five breeds of Nubian, but the American Dairy Goat Association grouped them as one for the dairy goat purpose. They range from a small black with white or salt and pepper trim, to a huge red goat, weighing more than 150 pounds as a yearling. The grouping of the Nubians was done more to keep paperwork straight and has caused a breakdown of each separate breed as they are interbred in the States.

The Boer goat comes from Africa and is raised primarily for meat. In many areas, 4H clubs are only allowed to show the Boer goat in the meat divisions because that particular area isn't sanctioned for dairy animals. Because of the European breeds' backgrounds and breeding, it is assumed that they thrive better in colder, wetter climates, and the African breeds in the warm drier climates. (I cannot attest to a difference because I have had all breeds in both climates and find that the wetter the weather, the bigger the danger is to all breeds.)

The goat was first brought to America on the *Mayflower*. But it wasn't until the 1900s that goats were seriously imported. To this day, the United States doesn't put the goat to good use like Turkey and India, the largest goat-producing countries.

Biology

Caper (masculine) and capra (feminine) are the Latin words for goat; therefore, "caprine" means relating to the goat. The word "caprice," meaning whim, comes from the goat, and Capricorn is the constellation of the goat. For further research, the Latin scientific name for the goat is Orramnos bovidae.

Products, books, and foodstuffs carry the terms on their packaging, making it harder to recognize them for what they are unless you know what the terms mean. This is not meant for you, the goatkeeper. This is meant to fool the public, who might find it disdainful to be purchasing some part of the dreaded goat.

Goats, like cows, sheep, deer and deer-related animals, are ruminants, meaning they regurgitate some of their food to rechew (cud chewing) for digestion. (This is not just good for their general health, it shows an amount of contentment.) The four stomachs are included in the first, the rumen, which is a pouch to hold the other three. The second stomach, the reticulum, is called the pump; the third stomach, the omasum, means many piles; the fourth stomach, the abomasums, is the true stomach. Only the fourth is mature and operating at birth. The animal will start chewing its cud when all four stomachs are mature and functioning properly.

Either sex of goat can have horns. At one time we were waiting for a Spanish goat to surface, bred not to have horns, but that hasn't happened. However, the Arapawa first brought to this country was of a hornless breed.

The old wives' tale that purebred Nubians do not have horns is false. Horns on goats are hereditary. The goat will keep its horns for life if they are not removed by man. The goats use the horn for natural protection against predators and other goats, and for scratching and bullying their way in the herd.

Goats have the split, or cloven, hoof for ease in climbing. This is not a solid hoof; each side is identified as a toe. The toe is filled with a pad to act as a shock absorber for the jumps that goats use in much of their maneuvering. The pads are covered with a very hard surface and, along with the hooves, have to be trimmed on tame goats.

Beards are also not hormonal and will be found on any mature goat. The buck will grow a larger beard, and if it is not clipped, it can reach the ground with age. Does' beards are shorter, thinner and usually trimmed off. Many breeds of bucks will grow manes, much like the lion, and sport them proudly. Some bucks do not.

Goats are cuspids, meaning they do not have upper front teeth. They do have both upper and lower teeth in the back of the mouth. They use the lower front teeth for pulling their forage up against the gums, breaking it off, and then moving it to the rear of the mouth, where the teeth are sharp enough for grinding the food. This works well for the goat, since their upper front gums are tough. If goats pull something up that hurts, they know that this is not something they need in their stomach.

Unlike sheep, goats do not have a split upper front lip and cannot shear grass and crops too close to the ground, ruining the ground cover.

Depending on the area, the breed and the maintenance, mature goats range from 100 pounds to more than 200 pounds, but 130 to 190 pounds is more of an average, providing good growth is maintained in the first six months. If, for some reason, a goat gets stunted before six months, it will never grow to its true size. Goats, like deer, are constant nibblers (browsers) but are seldom fat. Only overfed animals will have a tendency to be overweight. It is their nature to stay slender and lithe, as it could mean saving their life.

Goats are vegetarians and will consume more than ten percent of their body weight in roughage a day.

All goats will have two teats, but only the doe will mature and fill an udder with milk. Extra teats are not uncommon but are considered defects for show goats. The extra teats will seldom have milk. A goat will give from two cups to more than two gallons of milk a day.

Natural habits and behavior

Bucks do well by themselves, but does are gregarious. They do well in pairs, but the preferable situation would be a herd of three or more. That way if one leaves, the other still has company. Goats will grieve the loss of a companion for about three days. Being gregarious, they will adopt other animals, people, and sometimes fowl to satisfy their need for a social life. Since goats' habits differ so much from other species, it is not always wise for them to adopt another. If goats are left with people for companionship, the animals will adopt the same privileges, which include access to the house, the car and the patio furniture. They will chase cars, if the pet dog does. Goats will stop browsing and settle down when their friend is a cow, which could cause weight loss. Goats will stay on their feet all day if left with horses; this would be hard on their legs and feet.

The largest misconception about goats concerns eating habits. People seem to think goats will eat anything and everything. We may wish that were true, but unfortunately, it's not. Goats are quite picky, wasteful and downright snooty. They don't care for grass and will browse through it looking for choice weeds. Goats like a variety in their diet and will browse large areas, eating tidbits here and there. Goats are naturally curious, so they will taste a lot of things.

The myth that a goat will eat everything, including tin cans, actually had a very good start. Goats do reach out to taste new morsels, and the hungry goats found out quickly that there was a paper label and glue on the can. Paper comes from wood pulp, and glue can be quite tasty. But, this is not a habit due to goats' tendency to move on and browse.

Being picky, goats will not eat anything that has been walked on or soiled. A lot of feed and hay can go to the mice, or mold, if not properly contained. If the goat doesn't like the hay (and if it's not starving), it will simply nibble and walk away. The same goes with old, dirty grain. Goats cannot eat mold safely, and though they will try to pick past it, it's a bad idea to put old grain with them because they could get mold on their coats and accidentally ingest it.

When allowed to roam, the goats will browse, choosing only the best treats the landscape has to offer, and what is good for them. This includes rose bushes and shrubbery as well as honeysuckle and hedge. Those of us who also garden sometimes think this is a spiteful attack by the goat, but it is only their best instincts. It is perfectly natural for them to browse and eat half the rose bushes, and it's our problem to keep goats out of our prize shrubs.

When browsing, goats will reach up for their feed first. There are at least two reasons for this action. First, reaching up rewards the goats with the tenderest parts of the weeds and briars, which would be an instinctual way they have of knowing that eating close to the ground is not good for them. Second, with the head up as they eat, a goat is more likely to hear and see its predators and have a better chance to run away.

Goats will eat their way from their barn (or you in your house), so that they can always look back and run to safety faster. We often think that the grass is greener on the other side of the fence, but the goat knows that the grass is unsoiled and safer to eat.

Goats are not nocturnal. They sleep from dusk to dawn and eat and exercise during daylight. When allowed, goats will sleep up and off the ground as a form of self-protection. Being off the ground is in their best interest since it protects them from crawly creatures and dampness. Goats would rather stand than sleep on wet or damp ground or bedding.

On warm dry nights, when there is a full moon for light, goats will graze for short periods. If goats are allowed some form of nightlight, they may stay out more at night. They will sleep outside on hot nights for more air circulation but never far from their normal bedding. Goats do take morning and afternoon breaks, sometimes napping, sometimes just lying about, and chewing their cuds.

Goats have a natural pecking order, like chickens. This means the goats have a herd "boss." The herd boss is usually the oldest goat but may also be the more aggressive one. The boss leads the way to browse and to water and will start the way back to the barn at chore time. The boss gets the first choice in bedding places, starts the afternoon siestas, and will be the first to "announce" the time to arise to start the day. If the herd boss is removed, there will be a time of confusion before a new one is elected and accepted by the others. A new goat brought into the herd will be bullied until it finds its rightful spot and frequently may just win the spot of boss. When this happens, the owner may experience a time of confusion because the new boss may change schedules and bedding spots, jump fences, and cause stress until it can be controlled.

Goats will change their habits with the weather. They won't go out into the rain but will head for shelter with the first few drops. Goats don't like to walk in tall, wet weeds and will wait for the dew to dry. This, too, may be instinctual, since goats are highly susceptible to pneumonia (and remember, parasites stay out in the wet grounds) and just seem to know to stay dry.

Goats will avoid walking in deep or wet snow and won't take too many chances of slipping on ice. If they do go into the snow, they walk gingerly, each following the leader. Once the path is made, they stick to it. They would prefer that a resourceful human shovel a path and carry them food. I have seen goats follow a dogs' path to avoid getting wet. Should a goat fall on the ice, it only has two choices. One is lie there until it freezes to death; the other is to fight to its death to get up. Both are good reasons to stay off the ice.

Goats are as clean about themselves as they are about their feed. A dirty goat is a sick or neglected goat. Goats don't like to walk in the mud and will avoid dirty bedding, preferring to stand. I've watched them spend hours cleaning themselves and each other, which is why bedding needs to be clean. Their own cleanliness can be a disadvantage, because they will ingest parasites by cleaning, not to speak of the dirt and germs and possible insecticides on the ground.

Goats will usually survive on good browse by eating approximately two hours a day. They split this time between morning and afternoon. Give or take 10 minutes, it will be an hour, if you watch them. At one time, when I didn't have fences, goats were led to a wooded area for an hour each morning and an hour each afternoon. I learned this tidbit by that experience. The rest of their time is spent sleeping, cleaning, or investigating new horizons. This will vary from herd to herd and pasture to pasture, depending on the amount of forage, the area to which they have access, and what's on the other side of the fence. Once settled, they will browse the same areas at the same times of day. This scheduling makes them easy to predict, and if they are escaping at a particular time, going out a little earlier the next day will give you a bird's-eye view of how they did it.

Younger goats (kids) can be frisky, running, jumping and twisting in midair. Older animals are more sedate, choosing to watch the others. The kids will often jump on the older goats, which doesn't seem to bother them.

To introduce themselves, goats make a habit of butting heads. This is also a habit of play. It looks painful but is natural, and their heads are harder than you would guess. Goats have to be taught that butting heads is not to be used on humans. A smack on the nose is usually sufficient. Being active, agile, and graceful, goats will jump unseen objects just to be in the air, and they will climb anything just to run back down. Given the opportunity, they will run across hard surfaces just to hear the rat-a-tat of their hooves.

When left alone, does will let the young nurse for six or seven months, but tamed goats are usually weaned by four months if they are growing well. Some goats are not good mothers and would just leave the infant to die. If the kid cannot get right up while she is cleaning it, the doe is likely to go graze, leaving it to the kid to be strong enough to find her. Some does may even try to stamp their babies to death, and if the buck is left in with the birthing mothers, he will mistake the process for a heat cycle and go back into a breeding (rut) mode. The frenzy of the doe running and him chasing will surely cause death to the newborn. (As a breed, pygmy goats are not good mothers and may have to be forced to nurse for a few days until they get the idea.) First-time mothers are the hardest to work with, and veteran mothers are little to no problem at all.

Goats are not afraid of fire and will walk back into a burning barn. They are curious about the flames and will stick their noses into a bonfire.

Generally speaking, goats are friendly and easily handled. Some breeds are more aggressive (Angora), and some are more docile (La Mancha–Oberhasli). When properly treated, goats will adjust to man's habits. Since goats are very scheduled creatures, they are easy to train to your habits. If you do the same thing for two to three days at the same time, that will usually train goats to do it on their own.

Wild goats are almost impossible to tame, and tame goats will revert to the wild faster than any other animal except the common house cat. But being creatures of habit and adhering to schedules as they do, goats can be housebroken or potty-trained to certain areas. Goats have been accused of being stupid, but their habits and history prove otherwise.

What other animal seems to be smart enough to know what not to eat, where to sleep, and how to keep itself clean for its own good health? Not even dogs can be trained and scheduled as fast and as easily as the goat.

Buck goats do not have the same need for companionship and do quite well in a setting by themselves. During breeding season, the buck will go into a rut and go through fences to get to the does. The rest of the time, he is quite content, and better off, by himself.

2

Feral Goats

A domesticated goat that hasn't been handled and is skittish and wary around people is considered wild. However, when a goat is born and survives and reproduces in the wild, without the benefit of man or medicine, this goat is considered feral. The largest number of feral goats is found in the remote areas of the Eastern world and is not common in modern society.

I was lucky to hear of a herd in the unpopulated hills of southern Missouri. I was fascinated that with all our experience, training and medical knowledge, we have to work so hard to keep our domesticated animals healthy and that the feral goats survive without interference.

I was anxious to see how well this herd was doing, so I made it a point to visit the area. Before the visit, I did some research on the area, the people, and on feral goats in general. I learned it was a hilly region, sparsely populated and remote. There were legends that Jesse James used the hills and caves for hiding spots. I was informed that several years earlier, these goats had been purchased by a local man who found he could not handle them and let them go. I honestly thought that I would find a herd of wild animals that were being cared for by sympathetic neighbors.

I found the area to be sparsely populated, and no one cared about the goats, let alone tried to help them. If anything, the people were helping the demise of the herd by trying to shoot them. Their theory was that deer would not roam the same ground as goats. The people were basically deer hunters. By experience I have since found that this is not true, as many times deer have been in my pastures with my goats, and I also know a man who raises them together.

The people admitted that the goats were seldom seen and didn't bother anyone. I called the original owner of the goats. He described them as scrub (having no recorded ancestry) and black and white spotted. He said there were two does and one buck. He had wrestled with the goats through one winter and gave up on taming them when they escaped in the spring. He really thought they would return for feed, salt and hay; but they kept their distance, protected their young, and did not return. The last time he had seen the herd, he hadn't recognized the original three and assumed they had died or had been shot. For six or seven years they had roamed free.

My guide was my brother, who had warned me that the goats lived deep in the hills and I wasn't likely to get sight of them. It was late June and the hills were thick and green with underbrush. I chose the hottest part of the day for my first visit, hoping to catch the goats cooling with an afternoon nap, as goats are prone to do.

As we approached the area, he cut the engine and coasted down a steep hill that paralleled the cave where the goats were known to bed. We quietly prepared to walk up the hill to the cave.

The pungent odor of the buck(s) was hanging in the air, and there was no doubt we were in the right place. The trees and foliage were so thick that we couldn't see the cave though my brother told me we were only 100 feet down from it.

I had followed my brother through many wooded areas and had no problem reading his body language to quietly start climbing. I was thankful for the bubbling creek coming down, as the sound of the water joined with the sounds of the bugs and birds to camouflage the noise we made. We'd covered about half the distance when I heard the goats moving through the bushes, and he helped me find a vantage point to watch as they retreated.

A very large black-horned buck calmly led the herd single-file away from us, through the brush, and up the mountainous hill. It appeared as though these animals were in no hurry and had made this trip many times and were simply getting away from us. I was able to glimpse another buck, which was white, and several smaller does in a variety of colors. Though I saw only a couple kids at their mothers' sides, I was sure that there were more hiding among the feet of the herd. I guessed there were 12 or 14 goats, including kids. Most were horned, all were shaggy, and all of them looked very healthy.

Once the goats disappeared, we went on to the cave. I was astonished at the size of it. The ceiling was 18 feet high, the opening was at least 60 feet wide, and the main room 80 feet deep. My brother told me that the cave tunneled into the hill, but the goats' tracks were never found past the main room. A creek came from within the tunnels, through the cave, and down the hill we had just climbed. The water was fresh, cold, and clean, and a good water source for the goats, as it flowed throughout the year. The floor of the cave was dry. Obvious depressions showed the goats' general bedding areas. I was surprised to see that most of the bedding spots were up against the damp ledges and in some cases, they were using the ledges instead of the dryer area in the center to bed down.

That area had suffered through an unusually rainy season, and I expected to find many droppings in the cave from the goats being restricted by the rain, but there were none. My brother told me there weren't any other shelters in the area, so I had to assume that either these feral animals did venture into the rain or that they indeed were housebroken, going out between showers to relieve themselves. The undergrowth did offer plenty of protection, and their shaggy coats would help to shield them from the rain, but the rains had been bad, and, knowing the goats' natural dislike of the water, I could hardly imagine them staying out too long. I marveled at their stamina to ward off pneumonia. Judging from the tracks in the cave, my earlier guess of a dozen or more goats was correct. All the tracks showed well-trimmed hooves, apparently from the rocks in, around and above the cave. Because of the heat and the underbrush, I did not pursue the goats or look to see where they went. My brother took me back two more times that week, but we did not see them again.

I made arrangements to return the next winter when the underbrush and foliage wouldn't be so thick. My brother agreed to keep an eye on the goats and keep me in touch with their progress. He let me know that a black buck and a couple kids had been found dead at the opening of the cave on separate occasions. They had either fallen or been pushed from the rocks above the cave, where they played. There was news that a couple of does had been shot, along with a couple of kids.

In late December, when I returned to observe the goats again, the foliage and underbrush were gone, and I had the opportunity to hike around the hills, following the goats' trails. The cave had not changed, and the depressions indicating bedding areas were the same. There was still a lack of goat droppings in the bedding area. Within a 100-yard radius of the cave, the bark on the trees was stripped up to four and five feet, but the goats left the young saplings alone, choosing to strip the bark only from the larger trees.

We hiked most of the trails, though some were too precarious for human feet. I found bedding areas, resting areas, and rocks beyond belief. I crawled on the rocks directly above the cave and could easily see how a goat could go over the edge and drop two stories to its death.

The forest around the cave was not large, perhaps 30 acres. It bordered a farmer's hay field on one side and the little-used road on the other. Several creeks ran through the area, which was a succession of hills. The trails showed that the goats were just as conformed to habits as our domesticated goats, choosing the same paths as they browsed from day to day. I found rocky ledges full of hair, where the goats had rubbed and scratched.

I was unable to find the goats, but there were several areas that I could not make it through to find them. I returned the next day and was luckier.

Once again, they heard us coming. Without underbrush for cover, I could see them better. This time a white-horned buck led the herd up the rocky ledges. Again, they didn't seem to be in a hurry. There were four does, another young buck and one kid; a couple were black, one was white, and the rest were spotted. I didn't see any more goats but hoped that the does would be pregnant and replace the ones that had died. I left the area with a plea to my brother to ask the people to leave the goats alone, but I had my doubts that the herd would be allowed to survive. One year later my brother let me know that the goats were gone. They had been shot by a person who lived close to the area and who firmly believed the presence of the goats was keeping the deer away.

Nature seemed to protect these animals from internal parasites by providing enough forage so that they had no chance of ingestion. Their shaggy, unclipped coats offered more in protection than the harm they could have been in aiding the external parasites. Though they were smaller, they seemed to be sturdier animals. Nature and inbreeding cheated them of full growth but made up for it in stamina and resistance. They seemed to get the needed salt and minerals from the water and forage and didn't look or act unhealthy. The horns provided them weapons against stray dogs, coyotes, and timber wolves. Even without man's interference the goats mortality rate would have been low, but I have no doubt the herd could have survived a long time had man been satisfied to leave them alone.

When people take over the care and breeding of the goat, they can improve production, size and mortality, but people pass on their own problems. When –people pen the goat, there is no more free choice of feed, and nature can't protect what it eats. The goat's hooves become overgrown on soft pastures; and vitamins, salt, and other minerals are not available in man's overworked and overused soil.

Domesticated goats will live longer, look nicer, show higher production, and afford us companionship. Man has to pay the huge price when he tries to take the place of nature's control.

3

Why Do You Want a Goat?

The first thing I hear when people find out I have goats is, "What are you doing with them 'blankety blank' goats?" Those people turn somber when I tell them just what the goats do for me.

But, why do *you* want a goat? Once you know your reason, then streamline your management practices accordingly. Quite likely, you'll buy a goat for one purpose and find out later the many other options open to you. Then your management decisions have to change.

Once you know why you are getting the animal, you'll need to have an idea of the type, the price you'll want to pay, and the necessary feed and maintenance involved. What I want to make clear is: It is your purpose that counts. The guy down the road feeding beef cattle or the woman in town spoiling a pet, have no business telling you how to take care of a dairy animal. This book will help you to be prepared and knowledgeable about keeping these detractors at bay. We have enough hassle within our own lives; we can't run a business on everyone else's opinions. For instance, there is no reason to pay for a high quality protein dairy feed if you have a pet. A meat animal, a milk producer, or a sire during rut deserves different care at different times of the year. Don't fall for the old advice that you don't have to be picky with "just" a goat!

Remember, you will need to have two goats, as they need each other's company. One goat alone isn't going to be happy and will be more apt to get into mischief trying to look for companionship. One goat will be nosier in its attempts to communicate with anyone or anything. The animal won't stay in, and sometimes a lonely milk goat will give bad-tasting milk, as well as have lower production. A doe with kids will be satisfied, and occasionally a goat will break all the rules and do just fine, but they are few and far between. Goats relate well with other livestock, and it's not unusual for them to make friends with others. However, when their "friends" go on about their own business, the goats do poorly. Your second goat can be a wether (castrated male). It will pay for itself in the companionship that it provides for the first and make a good pet for visitors. Should you decide to use extra goats for meat or sale, he'll pay again, thus making your goats worth two purposes.

People relate easier with the idea of having cows, so goats are often talked about in cow-like terms. The phrase, "poor man's cow" refers to the goat, and though it is meant as an insult to the animal and owner, it is really a compliment to the goat. Goat owners can be proud to compare their small efficient animals to the cow.

Six to eight goats can be kept in the place of one cow, and be easier to handle, as even a tame cow is not safe. (Not long ago, a woman was killed by a cow in Arkansas. This tragedy occurred when she accidentally got between a cow and calf. And about two years ago, a Texas rancher was feeding his cows and was trampled to death.) A goat may yank you around, scratch you, butt you, or smack you with a horn, but I've never heard of a death. This efficiency doesn't count just the acre of land needed per cow, but quantity of feed involved and the amount of water, time, and care. And, if you are handicapped, you cannot medicate a cow by yourself, unless you have been able to afford the expenses of chutes and holding pens. Cows don't make a good pet and a 2-year-old child cannot lead a cow around. Cows are messier in the barn. For small homesteaders, handicapped people, and practicality, goats are simply easier to have around the small farm. My 6-year-old granddaughter not only could milk at 2, but she thought nothing of going into the lots and getting the biggest goat I had and leading her in. None of the children have any qualms about going to the biggest buck they can find and bring him up, just to show off.

Milk

Milk goats used to be the most popular, but meat goats and weed eaters are catching up fast.

For many digestive reasons, some people cannot drink cow's milk. A lot of people have allergies, and drinking goats' milk seems to alleviate the symptoms. Remember, if you want goats' milk for allergic reasons, and you have to purchase it, buy it in your own area so it will have the local anti-toxins that are bothering you. Goats' milk is considered a nutritious food and not a medicine. Many people, including myself, consider it a pure health food.

My two girls spent the better part of their first years going from doctor to doctor and emergency room to hospital. Neither of them had any resistance to the common cold, brought on by their allergies. The allergies activated colds, bronchial asthma, and pneumonia. In their preschool years they were restricted to what they could do. An elderly country physician suggested goats' milk. Within six weeks my girls were stronger, healthier, and could play in an afternoon rain shower. My 5-year-old was able to help build a snowman for the first time, and my 2-year-old was allowed to go out and get her cheeks pink in the Iowa cold. Goats became a part of our life, and goats' milk a part of our diet.

When my daughters went off to college, I kept the goats and sent milk to school with them, sometimes making an extra trip to get it there. I kept the goats for many reasons, but knowing that I would probably have grandchildren and that they would need the milk was the biggest.

A lot of people think that goats' milk usually tastes bad, but that's because they drank milk that wasn't taken care of properly. Fresh goats' milk has no off flavor and is delicious. Because it is fresh, it naturally tastes different, just as fresh cow's milk does. My kids, once used to goats' milk, thought store-bought milk was bad.

The milk can be used to make yogurts, cheeses, gravies, butter, puddings, custards, and ice cream. Buying a goat for the milk means you will be looking for a dairy animal.

Pasteurized, canned or powdered goats' milk is available at many health food stores and drug stores, but can cost up to $16 a gallon or more. You may be able to sell your milk to a market in your area, depending on the size, quality and maintenance of your operation.

Meat

The meat of the goat is chevon — edible, inexpensive, and delicious. Many people find the idea of eating goat disgusting. That's too bad. Calves, lambs, fawns, and even baby chicks are cute, but that doesn't stop people from putting these animals on the dinner table every week. Chevon can be a major dietary source at a low cost. People of many ethnic groups purchase meat goats around Easter, June 19, The Fourth of July, and Labor Day for celebrations, rites and picnics. The meat is comparable to venison and can be as sweet as beef, and is usable in any recipe calling for beef or pork. Most goats are of dairy quality and not very meaty. It takes several years to realize a profit, provided that there is a market in your area. The meat conversion for goats can be as cheap a process as tame rabbits, when your kids are fattened on pasture. Meatier animals, such as the Boer, are becoming quite popular and can integrate into a dairy herd with out a problem; lesser quality dairy goats, older milk goats, and other extra stock can be and should be put in the freezer, as a final payment for their keep. This is no time to be emotional.

It is my regret to tell you that some people do not kill the meat animals in a humane manner. I don't mind selling a goat for butcher, but I want to know how it's going to die. I ask questions, and if I don't like the answers, I don't sell.

For the past 18 years, I have served goat meat on my table to my friends, relatives and other company. And they have never had any idea that they were not eating beef. I don't think it's important to tell them after the meal, either. It's important to me that they enjoyed their meal, not that I pulled a good one on them.

With the popularity of the Boer, for its meat, herds of 20 to 1000 are popping up all over the country. Boers will fatten faster and bring farmers a return on an investment faster. I think we will see goat meat become more popular in the next few years.

Pets

Of course, people still keep goats for pets. Some will keep a herd of 20 or 30 just for amusement. They like their goats! The elderly and children enjoy the antics of the goats, especially the kids.

The pygmies are great grass eaters, and many people will keep them just to keep a pasture clean or a large lawn mowed. In that case, they can be quite ornamental.

Petting zoos almost always have one or more goats for the kids, and most large zoos will keep goats in an area just for children.

A LaMancha is just one of many breeds that can make a great pet.

MC holds an Alpine buckling. (Courtesy of Rene Mathews)

A famous British goat named Taffy was the mascot for the first battalion of the Royal Regiment and was allowed to attend the royal wedding of Prince Charles and Lady Diana. The regiment has kept a goat for a mascot since the 1850s.

Mohair

The angora goats produce the valuable commodity of mohair and are also found in zoos. Mature angora goats can yield six to 18 pounds of mohair twice a year.

Mohair goats cannot be kept in a pasture with barbed wire or within an area of briers because the animals will lose some of their precious hair before you get it.

Hobbies and shows

Many goat keepers are fanciers, hobbyists and 4-Hers, and shows play an important role. Much personal satisfaction and many awards can be obtained through showing goats, not to speak of the prize money, experience in the ring, and socializing with other goat people. Children learn about responsibility and appearing in public when showing goats. Though a goat makes a great project the show circuit can be quite costly in entry fees and transportation. Breeding a show animal can be a real challenge to the goat keeper with the experience, knowledge, and time to do it.

It was my decision to stay out of the show circuit because I didn't have anyone at home to trust with the other goats, and I am terrified to be in front of people, let alone judges. Keeping track of pedigrees and health papers, plus my children and our doctors' appointments didn't work, so we decided not to show.

If the area you live in does not even hold sanctioned goat shows, you would be traveling farther. That was also one of our problems.

Weed control

Goats can also be used for weed and underbrush control. This can be a good idea, because goats do handle the job well. Many people rent their herds for the purpose. In this process, new seed is planted, and it is assumed that the goats will help bring the seed into the ground, while they fertilize and take care of the unwanted weeds.

A big problem with this setup is if the owner is allergic to poison oak, poison ivy, or sumac, they won't be able to handle their own goats for a while because the goats will eat these noxious weeds.

Large tracts of timberland can be kept free of underbrush, and more timber companies in the South (where pulpwood is one of the largest industries) are look-ing into putting goats on their tracts— to make tree cutting easier and to profit from the sale of fattened goats sold for meat.

One timber company in Arkansas stocks its tract with many breeds of deer, antelope, and Boar goats and charges hunters a fee.

Sheep

Goats are often grazed with sheep. We've heard of the "goat leading the sheep to slaughter." Goats are easier to handle, and easier to tame, and when kept with sheep, the sheep will follow the goats. Whether the sheep are going to slaughter or to the barns for medical treatment or shearing, goats ease the frustrations of herd-ing the restless, stubborn sheep. Remember, sheep eat closer to the ground, dou-bling their chances of ingesting parasites, so pastures have to be changed frequently.

Horses

For reasons no one can explain, goats seem to have a calming affect on horses. At race tracks, shows, and fairs, goats will be seen stabled with the high-strung animals. The goats have laughingly been called "baby sitters" for the horses, but some horse handlers don't laugh. Horsemen will buy a goat at the same time they buy the horse so the goat can accompany the horse home. I keep my goats pastured around my horses. I have even "rented" goats to people for a short time so they may be taken to an exhibit to calm a horse.

Calves

People raising young calves for slaughter will often use goats' milk to raise the calves for faster, heavier gains. Compared to cost of cows' milk or prepared calf formula, it can be less costly to feed them goats' milk.

I have raised one calf to 600 pounds on the hay and feed that goats will automatically waste. I even keep a calf in my goat pens to clean up the grass that the goats won't eat, therefore letting the pens restock evenly, when the animals move on to the next lot.

Hides

The goat hide is comparable to the deer in texture and quality and can be tanned in the same manner. The United States imports millions of dollars worth of goat hides from Southeast Asia for quality handbags, shoes and gloves. The United States does not contract hides from within its own borders, as there aren't any large quantity producers.

My mother would cure the hides of the more colorful goats, in such a way that the hair stayed on, and use them for rugs, something that I wish I had learned to do, as our floors were always quite colorful. Two hides will make a nice coat, and four will make a blanket that no Northerner would want to give up.

It's not the hunter's dream, but a friend of mine had two goats taken to the taxidermist and they now hold a prominent spot on her patio.

Beasts of burden

Goats can be trained to pull small carts and are a big hit for small children and parades, though the animals could never carry the load of a donkey. Since goats are smaller and easier to handle, they can also carry hay, feed, and water if the cart can handle your ground.

Fleas, ticks and fire ants

As easy as goats pick up internal parasites, fleas, ticks, and fire ants don't like to be around them. The only time I have ever seen ticks on a goat is when the goats were allowed to roam in a wooded area at will and were neglected. Fleas and fire ants don't care for the goat manure.

Fire ants are a particularly bad problem in the South. Even though they won't habituate in the bedding area, if a goat gets sick or goes down, the ants will be there faster than you, and it's practically impossible to save the goat. Call you county extension service and do everything you can to keep the fire ants under control. So far, the Food and Drug Administration has not approved any products that will really work on the fire ants.

Snake control

There is a theory that goats keep snakes away, or that snakes don't care to be around goats. This is unproven; but most goat keepers will admit that they have not had snakes in the goat pens. I haven't seen any snakes around my goats. On

Toulouse the goose helps the goats with snake control. (Courtesy of Rene Mathews)

the other hand, as with all things, there are exceptions. One of my younger friends fled his milk barn several times because of a large black snake.

It is assumed that goats keep the ground well mowed, not leaving cover for the snakes. As pungent as the odor of a buck in rut is, I have to wonder if that doesn't keep them away.

Excess hay and manure

Leftover hay can be fed to cows, but the mulch for pathways, gardens and crops is priceless. It doesn't have to cure for a year, like hog manure, nor is it full of chemicals like the store-bought stuff.

Whether you garden with the no-till method or till it in, it won't take three years to have practically new, healthy ground.

Many homesteaders keep chickens with their goats. The chickens scratch up leftover grain, seed from the hay and nutrients from the goats' dropping and help keep down the parasite population. In this manner, the chickens cost very little. There is some controversy that chickens will pass coccidiosis on to the goats; but, coccidia is a microorganism that lives in all animals (including humans) and each species has its own variety.

It used to be that if we kept chickens with any other animal, we took precautions by treating the goats' water. However, I have not had to treat for coccidia in ten to 12 years.

Watch dogs

Some breeds are noisy like the Nubian. This can cause the goats to be quite loud when strangers come around — and not just people. Other animals will cause them to raise a ruckus. Since I usually have more Nubians, and I do live alone, they can often be a warning system, letting me know when I'm in the back that someone is calling for me in the front. When my young grandson "disappears," I look to the goats before I do the dogs. They will generally be watching him, and I can follow their gaze to find the baby.

Trading power

Bartering is a lost art. When you have things that other people want, bartering is still a powerful tool. The various products that you have from your goats, other people want. How do we put a price on a bucket of manure? I traded it for plants. Milk can be traded for produce, and hides traded for other things you need.

I once traded a very large goat that I couldn't handle (after an injury) for three-home fed turkeys, a box of shrimp, plus a box of flounder from the coast. I had no idea what a delicious meal I was getting!

The craziest trade I ever made was two young does for a pig. I reared the pig, bred her, and she had ten piglets. The man came back with my does, full-grown and bred, and said he couldn't handle them, so he wanted the pig back. By now my sow and babies were worth more than the two goats, so he threw in an old, old truck and I kept five piglets and the does, both of which had twins. I'm a little mechanically inclined and I kept and used the truck for two or three years. Eventually, his sow came into heat and without a boar, he could not keep her penned. He was so fed up, that when he did catch her, he brought her back to me for nothing.

Now if you've paid attention to this story, I got a sow and five pigs, my does fed and bred, their kids, and a truck for nothing!

Recently I traded two wethers for a registered male dachshund. The trader wanted me to keep the wethers for another month to fatten them for a barbecue. The barbecue was called off and he told me he did not want the dog back. Now I have been selling puppies.

Now that you know the many uses for a goat, and what you want and are capable of doing, you can streamline you equipment and space to get the most from your venture. Often two goats can serve so many purposes that they can pay for themselves two or three times.

Why not to have a goat

I would not be doing you justice if I didn't give you the reason *not* to own a goat.

Goats are a daily responsibility. If you like to take weekend jaunts, you better have a trustworthy person to leave with your goats. No more vacations, either. There is a never-ending monotony regarding the day-to-day goat keeping chores. Many chores are repeated twice a day. I happen to be the kind of person who needs structure and sureness in my life, and the monotony is a relief to me.

Unless you enjoy working, worrying and playing with animals and staying at home to do it, you are going to get tired of goats. Most goat owners get a sense of enjoyment from the handling of the goats and would keep them for pets even if they didn't need them for anything else. I'm a testament to that, because there were many years from the time my girls left home till the time I had grandkids. If you do choose to vacation, leave four or five people in charge, and an extra one to double-check on them. A lot of people will say they will be there twice a day, but if they don't take your goats as seriously as you do, they won't. Don't test your friendships.

Unfortunately, there is an amount of adverse peer pressure to raising goats. Most of your friends will think you have gone loco. Your neighbors will immediately warn you that the goats better stay on their side of the fence. Your co-workers will ask you to ba-a-a at work, and may even greet you by ba-a-a-ing. A few of your friends may slowly stop visiting, and the new people you meet will be less likely to become friendly when they hear you are a goat farmer.

I'm still not sure where the term goat farmer originated, but to be sure, it's generally meant to be derogatory. All my dictionaries relate farming to agriculture and the tilling, planting and yielding of the soil. I personally prefer the term goat keeper, but I also don't try to change narrow-minded minds.

If you're overly sensitive about what your friends, relatives and neighbors think, you need to think twice about getting goats.

Goats will test every fence, every little hole, and every low spot to get out. It just goes with their nature. The first time they get out, it's usually an accident. The second time they have to discover how they did it before. But the third time, they've got it down pat and will make a bee-line for the weak spot every day at the same time.

If you can get past these distasteful side effects and are willing to work, you're off to an exciting career with these delightful and loving animals.

4

Breed Characteristics

There are many breeds of goat, and breeders differ in their opinions of which breed is best. Seven major breeds are recognized as dairy-quality animals by the American Dairy Goat Association. The last one (Oberhasli) was accepted in the last 15 to 18 years. Other breeds are recognized by other associations for their assorted qualities. Many veteran goat keepers are surprised to learn that there are numerous other breeds in other countries, especially nations in Europe and Asia. I would suggest checking web sites if you're interested, as I did, but this book is not about goats we can't get.

The Toggenburg was the first registered goat in America.

The **Toggenburg** is from Switzerland and was the first registered goat in America. This breed is considered the "Guernsey" of the goats with its rich milk and milking records.

The Toggenburgs tend to grow the shaggiest coat (excluding the Angora and some of the foreign goats) of the registered goats.

Toggenburgs are of medium size (115 to 150 pounds) and are sturdy, vigorous animals. Their color is brown with white trim. The brown varies from light to chocolate. The white trims the ears, down both sides of the face, all four legs and forms a triangle around the tail. Some white is allowed in the wattle area (under the throat). Cream markings are acceptable, meaning they can be registered and shown in the ring, but the cream is not desirable. The ears stand up and forward, similar to the deer. The face may be straight or dished, but never the Roman nose.

Toggenburgs will show up in black and white, and though they can't be registered or shown, they may still be perfectly good goats. Because of their coat, they do well in the cold; but in the South they do need to be clipped.

The **Alpine** is medium to large, graceful, and can be of many colors and variations of patterns. The hair is medium to short, the face is straight, and the Toggenburg coloring and Roman noses are not allowed.

The Alpine is a notorious climber.

Patches and Cupid are two Alpine does from Rene Mathews' herd near Texarkana, Arkansas.

The Alpine has several varieties: British, Rock, Swiss, and French, with the French being the most popular. The French carry many color patterns.

Cou-Blanc: White neck, white front quarters, black hindquarters, with black or gray markings on the head.

Cou Clair: Clear neck, and tan or gray frontquarters, with black hindquarters.

Cou Noir: black neck, black frontquarters and white hindquarters.

Sundgau: black and white markings under the body, and white facial strips.

Spotted or mottled colors.

Chamois: Brown or bay markings on face, dorsal, feet and legs and sometime coloring the withers.

Also, light front with darker or grey hindquarters.

Any variation of colors with a band of white in the midsection.

The alpine is a notorious climber and is jokingly called a "car cruncher" because if there is a vehicle around, this goat is more likely than any other breed to be on top of it.

The **Saanen** is a Swiss breed and is considered the "Holstein" of the goats because, as a breed, the Saanen have the highest milk production. These goats are white or cream colored, with white being preferred. A few cream

The Saanen has the highest milk production.

patches are fine, but are not preferred. The Saanen are medium to large with a rugged stature. The ears are carried up, and should be forward. The face should be straight or dished, but never Roman.

The **Nubian** is called the "Jersey" of the goats because the milk is higher in butterfat content. The Nubian is a relatively large and graceful animal, though some of the breed variations tend to be smaller. There is a great variety in size, color, and milk production. The Nubian is the only breed with drooping ears, like a hound dog. The ears are long, extending at least one inch past the nose. The face is convex with a Roman nose, and the hair is fine, short and glossy. The Nubians can be of any color, pattern of colors or spotted, depending on which background of various African breeding from which they originated. These animals are probably the most affectionate (except for maybe the Oberhasli and the Boer) of the breeds, and tend to be a little more vocal with their bleating. Since the Nubian is an African breed, it does hold up better in southern summers, both in health and milk production, though I did have one Saanen that would not dry up between breedings, no matter how hot it was. This is another exception to the rules that goats are fond of breaking.

The Nubian's milk has the highest butterfat content.

This spotted Nubian doe is from Emily Dixon's herd in the Ozarks. This particular breed is from the Zaire breed from Africa.

Nubian and La Mancha kids from Rene Mathews' herd near Texarkana, Arkansas.

Left top and above: Two La Manchas from Rene Mathews' herd near Texarkana, Arkansas.

The **La Mancha** has been toasted as the most docile of the breed, but if it is they are, I haven't seen it for myself. The goats are an all-around sturdy animal. They are known to have lower peaks of production, but hold up for long lactations. They have been shown to keep up a top quality milk record on less feed than other breeds. The distinctive characteristic of this breed is their ears, or the lack of ears. There are two types of ears in the breed. The gopher ear is a maximum length of one inch or less, with little to no cartilage. The elf ear is a maximum length of two inches or less, with the end turned up or down. Cartilage is allowed for shaping this ear. The face is straight and the legs are somewhat shorter than most goats, causing them to look a little blocky. Any color or variation of colors is possible, but brown seems to be most common. The La Mancha is the least finicky and easiest to care for of the breeds. They will even clean up the feed and hay from the other goats.

The **Oberhasli** is a medium to large goat from Switzerland, with smaller sizes not accepted for registry. The ears are carried up and the color is bay, ranging from light to dark, with the deeper dark being most desirable. Black markings run down the sides of the face, with a black nose and black belly and udder. The legs are black below the knees and hocks, and the inside of the ears are black. There is

Oberhasli owned by the author.

A La Mancha from Rene Mathews' herd near Texarkana, Arkansas.

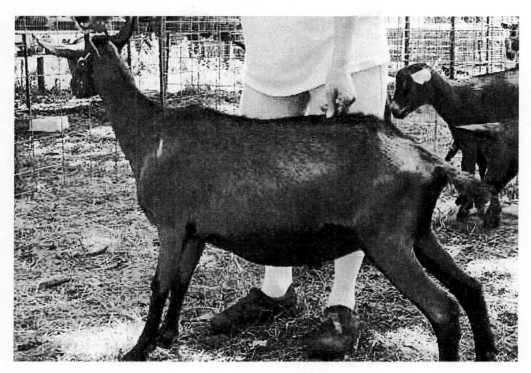

A fine Oberhasli doe.

black down the chest and a black dorsal stripe. Solid black bucks cannot be registered, but does may be, if the color is noted on the paper. These goats might be best described as black with a bay saddle and bay facial markings.

The **Sable** is a new "old" breed and is basically a colored Saanen with a large group of followers. The ADGA allowed registry beginning in January, 2005, and the Sable breeders still have their own association of registry. These goats may be cream, tan, brown, or black, and since they are a genetic throwback from the Saanen, they are of a good dairy quality. There is some speculation that the Saanen was always a goat with color, and somewhere down the line, keepers started breeding the color out to get the

The Sable has just been recognized by the ADGA.

solid white. If that does indeed prove to be the case, it will mean that the Sables should have been in the herd books all along.

There are many other breeds not of dairy quality, so I am only going to mention a few. These many other breeds are also not common in the United States.

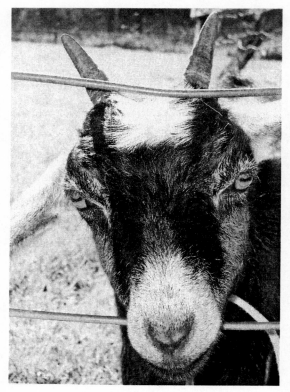

The author's pygmy doeling.

The **Pygmy** is as small as its name implies, with bucks standing not higher than two feet at the withers, and does being shorter. The pygmy is not known for its milk production and tends to be a meatier animal. Sometime when the pygmies are crossed with a dairy animal, the result is usually a smaller dairy goat, but sometimes breeders may get a larger pygmy with better production. The pygmy can be quite aggressive. It often is used to clear out briar patches. Unlike other goats, pygmies will eat any kinds of grass and earn the name of a "lawn mower." Their milk is high in butterfat. They tend to have two pregnancies per year with one or two kids. All body colors are expected. The most common is a dark salt and pepper and is sometimes referred to as blue, frosted or grizzled.

The **Angora** goat is most widely appreciated for its mohair. Angoras are generally shaggy and frequently cranky but can be profitable from shearing up to twice a year.

The **Boer** is an African meat goat. Its ears are floppy, although not as much as the Nubian. The goat is stocky, sturdy and attains a better growth rate in its first eight months than other goats. The Boer will be mostly white with brown around the head. The brown can be even, lopsided, or down on the chest. I've seen Boers with a spot on the side or flank. The Boer doe will have a pregnancy every eight months, having twins and triplets, as with other goats, and usually have enough milk to take care of all their triplets. When handled properly, they can be the gentlest and friendliest of all the breeds. There's a large market for goat meat and with the Boers being so prolific, they are quite likely to be *the* goat of the future. The breed may also be called Afrincander, Afrikaner, or South African common goat.

Since Boers are meat goats, they are stockier, with more meat across the chest and around the shoulders. They have more weight in the withers and rib area. The back and hips will be thicker and their all-around appearance will show a sense of meatiness. Some people are starting to breed some Boer into their dairy herds to get meatier kids, and, they hope, stronger, stable milk goats. This is still experimental.

Since the **Myotonic** were featured in media coverage, I feel obligated to include them. Myotonic means wooden leg. They were called the fainting goats, and people found it fun to watch them fall over. There are two main herds, one in Tennessee, and one in Texas, though there may be some smaller herds. When these goats become frightened, scared or fearful, their legs lock up and they fall over; giving the amused bystander the impression that they are fainting. It is expected that whatever gene applies to the "flight fright" response that most goats have is missing in these goats. They are very sturdy, and although rare at this time, they will make good crosses for the Boer goat as far as meatiness. The gene that causes them to fall over does not pass down to their young when they are crossbred with another breed. The animal humane service has deemed it "animal abuse" to scare these goats just for the fun of it.

Mixed breedings

"Scrub" or "grade" are terms used when the background of the goat is unknown or questionable. A "grade" does not necessarily have to be a bad goat. Many herds have started with the grade goat, and in many cases, up-breeding programs have a tendency to lower resistance and production, and the grade does not suffer as much from this man-made problem.

I deliberately crossbreed now, after I spent so many years upgrading, because in this area, a goat is a goat, and the crossbreeds are stronger; and my own up-breeding was weakening the strain and causing them to be less resistant.

The only real difference about owning a grade goat is that you have no papers and you do not have the advantage of knowing the past performance of its ancestors, so you won't have an idea how it, or its young, will produce and behave under different conditions. However, since papers don't make the goat, you really don't have much more of an advantage with a pedigree, because there is no guarantee that your goat will carry on the name, or production.

"Recorded grades" are animals whose backgrounds can be partially traced. When the grade doe is bred to the purebred buck, the offspring doe is a 50 percent recorded grade. The ADGA also allows for the grade animals to be recorded on either a standard of their appearance or on their productions (referred to as recorded on appearance or recorded on production). Many people will have the animals that qualify recorded on appearance or production so they can obtain the papers that are required for the show ring. These papers in no way help the up-breeding program and do not affect the papers of the offspring from the parents.

When the 50 percent recorded grade doe is bred to a purebred buck, the offspring doe (not bucks) can be recorded as 75 percent American. Then, when that doe is bred to a purebred buck the offspring does can be papered as American. Their offspring does and bucks will appear as American. They will never be upgraded to purebred. (For more information, read chapter 31, on Registration papers.)

It is very important to know that "breed" and "type" are terms that may describe the goat but are not the same thing. Breed refers to the kind of goats and the ancestry of those goats. In many cases, a goat can have the best of pedigree and not be worth one day's grain. On the other hand, "type" refers to what kind of quality to expect from the goat. Type can refer to any animal with meat producing qualities or more commonly, the goats that show dairy qualities.

Dairy type can refer to any animal, purebred or grade, that has the necessary qualities to produce and reproduce. Many times the breed may not matter too you, but the type should.

If you are breeding for meat, then you'll be looking for meat type, which is not thoroughly covered in this book.

5

Management

From the day the decision is made to buy your goats to the day the last one is gone, someone has to be in charge of all the decisions that will affect the venture. Ideally this would be a joint effort involving the entire family, with each member being equally capable and interested in the venture's success. But families do not always agree on everything that has to be done. Someone has to be willing to take the time to study, evaluate, and sort out the rights and wrongs to suit your situation and your purpose. The person in charge has to have the respect of the others involved, know that all duties assigned to someone else will be carried out properly, and the guts to periodically check the others to make sure the jobs are done properly.

I recall that when my youngest was 17, and because of my injury, she was in charge of most of the heavy daily chores. I was losing a lot of spring kids and could not understand why. I double-checked with my daughter on the amount of milk replacer she was using, the temperature of the water, and the cleanliness of the feeding pans. All answers were correct, and I was baffled. My oldest daughter came home from college one weekend and discovered the problem. The milk wasn't getting stirred properly (I had not asked about this) and was being fed in lumps. Young kids cannot handle lumps of dry milk very well and were dying of stomach infections. The problem was solved, and the rest of the kids lived. I should have been watching my daughter's chores.

The manager makes the herd. Goat keeping is a business. The majority of us accept it as a hobby because you do not expect to make money. Unless you're raising meat goats, you're going to be choosing *not* to lose money.

By the way, the Internal Revenue Service doesn't consider raising dairy goats a business either. They can't be insured, except as an addition to your homeowners' policy, and they can't be used as collateral, like other farm animals, unless you can prove you have enough for a dairy.

If the Boer goat's meat sales take off, and I expect them to, this may all

37

change, because meat goats will make money (and of course more money means taxes). The rest of us will get our money back in products and satisfaction and not cold, hard cash.

It is encouraging to know that there is a word for those of us who raise goats: **capriculturist**. So those of us who keep goats do have an occupation! I had it on my drivers' license for several years, but I got so tired of the questions that I had it changed.

As cruel as it sounds, that adorable goat has to pay for itself to earn its keep. Since some things can't be put into dollars and cents, you will have to put a value on them yourself. For a milk animal, it's simple to keep track of the milk, subtract cost of maintenance, and hope you come up with a plus. It was impossible to figure out how to put a price on the children's or my health. With a pet or a weed eater, you'll have to decide how much these services are worth to you and weigh the costs accordingly. Granted, I can buy some chemicals and get rid of weeds in a couple of days, but we are really trying to stay away from chemicals. I could also try to pay someone to regularly control the weeds, which would mean a stranger showing up from time to time, interrupting my privacy, not necessarily doing the job right, and taking my money. Safety is an issue, especially if you're alone or handicapped, so goats suddenly seem to be worth a little more.

Your job as a manager has nothing to do with chores or caring for the goat. Educating yourself and keeping up with all the discoveries and getting what's necessary applied to your herd is your first step.

Learning that you will need concrete floors with drains (in most states) to qualify to sell raw goats' milk is good information. But if you're going to keep two small milk goats in the tool shed for your own use, don't worry about the information you won't be using. Good management means applying the best of your knowledge to your own circumstances and not letting any of the problems get out of hand.

The number of goats you can handle, the time involved, the types of feed and forage, lot management, worm control, bedding packs, space, and unemotional culling practices all play a part in top production and quality products, with the least sickness, man hours, and cash.

It is difficult to make priorities, and from time to time they have to change, but here is a sample of mine.

1. This used to be my last priority, and now it has become my first because of my health. When to expand, delete, or keep the herd size the same is something to keep in mind, as each spring you get new kids. Planning helps distribute excess stock. Since it's almost impossible to keep the buck from the does, I have gone through a season without a buck to keep my herd the same; or have penned up younger or smaller goats and held them over for a year to keep my herd from growing.

2. The health of your goats has to be a top priority. Sick animals are costly, and dead ones are useless, not to mention emotionally taxing and a waste of the medicine you used trying to save them.
3. Quality of milk, meat, and hides is also a big deal. Three gallons of milk a day that is unfit to drink is almost worthless, or at best, pretty expensive animal food.
4. I have production down this far on the list because production is not just what your goat can do. Production is what your goat can do without risking its health, your budget, or the goat's happiness. **A top producing goat should keep at top production naturally, without extra feeds or chemicals.** The goat's best feature is that it is able to produce larger quantities of milk per pound of feed, and per body weight, to be efficient. These are called "easy keepers." They seldom get sick, they keep on producing and they don't require extra feed or attention to maintain good health. When you get a goat like this, you keep it, you breed it, and you pray it passes down its durability to the young.
5. This should be considered before ever getting goats—your health and your time. If you work a 12 hour day, you are doing it for the money, and then I would have to assume that you got the goats for the milk and meat to save money. If you spend too much time with the goats at home, it could prove to be fatal on your job, and if you have to spend too much time with your job, it could prove fatal to the goats. We're talking balance here.
6. The initial purchase, grain, worm medicine, hoof trimming, fencing, shelter, and watering is all a must for any goat and can cost money. Trade if you can, borrow if you know someone, but you will have to put out some cash.
7. Overlapping all priorities is that you have a host of other peoples' schedules to keep in mind — your own, your family's, and your neighbors'— as well as your goat's schedules. Everything must meld with the least inconvenience to everyone.
8. Breeding and upgrading used to be a big priority for me and may be to you. These are decisions that concern the future of your goats and improvement of your herd. This improvement plays an important part in profits and losses. (More in chapter 16, on breeding.) However, my personal priority has changed from upbreeding to breeding healthier.
9. Publicity: How the public accepts you, your goats, and your life style may not be of any concern to you now, but in the end it's important. The problems you don't have with the community will save you time, money, and many sleepless nights. (Refer to chapters 10 on public relations and 14 for fencing ideas.) I once sold a goat to a group that was having a public barbecue and in this state the meat had to be inspected by the Food and Drug Administration. I asked the packing house if I could be there to see what the FDA testers would do. Simply put, they check the insides of the goat for disease, worms, etc. My goat was stamped approved, and within days it was all over this town that I had the healthiest goats around.

A good manager lets the goats be a thermometer. Get to know them, be familiar with how they act, look, and even how they "talk." With experience you'll be able to tell with a glance if something is a little off-base. With goats, a "little off base" could mean death within six to eight hours.

If your goats are healthy and content, and producing to suit you, then your management practices are accomplishing what you want them to accomplish. This is not someone else's decision to make for you. You are the "boss" and your goats are the employees, and listening to the employees is the only way to find out what really goes on in any business. This is a twice-a-day observation, or more.

I like to get up and have my coffee on the patio before the goats get up. Watching them come out, on time, in line, and in order, helps me to know that they not only had a good night, but that they are all right to start their day.

Chore time is an hour or so later with closer observation and personal checks on each goat. Any time I'm outside, in my flowerbeds or on my lawn, I can take another look at the goats. I can also peek out a window. Frequently, I have to have help with the animals, so I have to keep up with things to leave the proper instructions.

Chore time at night is my last chance to check. I try to be around about an hour before dark to make sure they all went back to the barn, in line, and bedded down in the way they normally do.

6

Accepted Conformation for Dairy Goats

The conformation of the entire goat shows the ability of that particular goat, not only in immediate production, but in passing on good qualities to future generations.

Most books will give you a series of clues to help identify good conformation of the goat, and I'm going to do the same, but I do hope to make it simpler. When it's all said and done, experience is the only way to know for sure. This is one area where you do listen to everything the experts teach. Don't pass up a single chance to talk to those who know. Take the time to stop and look at every goat you see — this is no joke, because it takes a lot of looking and touching before you can spot a good goat. Eventually, you'll spot the worst defects at a glance, and the other points of conformation will be caught with a second, steady look. By being careful and studying, you will be able to detect the slightest flaws, like a show judge can. Talk to show judges, go to a few goat shows even if you don't plan to show. Watch for what the judges are watching for and see what wins in which class and ask why. Don't be afraid to ask questions. Judges and goat keepers love to talk.

You may think you don't need to know much about conformation. After all, for $50 you can pick up any old goat and get a couple of kids and some milk for a little bit of nothing. Right? Maybe. If you don't know what you're doing, there's a better chance that you will put a few paychecks into feed and hay, only to end up with a sickly goat, weak kids, and a dribble of milk. But you can pick up a good goat for $50 if you know what a "good goat" looks like.

Not everybody agrees on particular points of conformation. We are all looking for something different. Dairy type constitutes the ability to give a good quantity of quality milk, with the least amount of upkeep and care.

Assuming the goat presents a good general appearance and is healthy, you can start checking out its conformation for dairy type. Study the sketch carefully, to

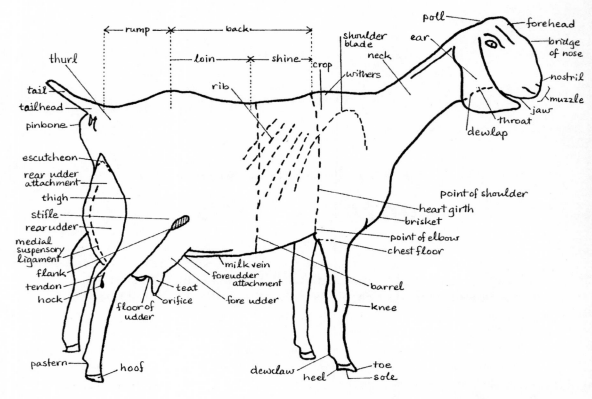

The conformation of a goat.

learn the parts of the goat. I was told several times to be careful about weak pasterns. When I finally looked up pasterns, I still had no idea what weak meant. Reading and studying did me little good, until I actually came across a goat with weak pasterns.

Watch the goat from a distance. It should move gracefully, unless it's in the last stages of pregnancy. It should not have a choppy, jumpy gait or strain under its weight. The goat should be alert but not nervous, relaxed but not lethargic. The parts of the body should move together evenly, presenting an impressive, proud animal. It should be aware that you're there and have a gentle curiosity about you, but should eventually go on about its own activities. A spoiled or overfed goat, and a goat that is accustomed to playing with people, may consider that you *are* their normal activities and stay with you. The animal should be sleek, not fat. The body needs to be long, to carry kids, with shiny, smooth hair, except for the Toggenburg, whose hair is naturally more coarse.

The neck should be strong and of medium length and blend smoothly into the body. The head should be large and bony, with good strong jaws for chewing. The nostrils should be large, whether the nose is or not. The eyes should be bright, clear, and alert, and set off to the side. Mucous membranes of the eyes and mouth should be a bright pink.

The withers should be well defined, meaning visible to the eye and to the touch. The withers should rise slightly above the shoulder blades, in a wedge, to the shoulders, should be strong, but blend smoothly with the body.

The withers are the area that is checked for extra fat. In a dairy goat, there should be none; in a meat goat, there should be plenty, and it should be firm. For a dairy goat you are looking for bony, with only skin and hair between your fingers and the bone.

You'll hear that the ribs should be well sprung. Sprung meaning that the ribs should bow out in an arc. The ribs should be apart, flat and long. Kids need not be so well sprung because this will develop with age. There is some controversy that if the ribs of a young animal are too wide apart it will have a short life. I have had a couple of these kids live to 8 or 9, so it's not a fact with all goats. The ribs have to be long to show a depth of chest wall. You should be able to lay a finger between the ribs. The rib area must be large, to allow for plenty of roughage, and to have room to breathe, as well as carry babies. You should be able to see the first two or three ribs on a goat that is not too fat. However, this does not mean that the ribs should stick out, with the hair and skin sinking between them. The whole area should be smooth and uniform. A good rib area means a good dairy temperament. A skinny goat will not be an easy keeper, because it will be sick more often and have problems. Avoid skinny goats and cull them.

The chest should be deep but not too wide. A real wide chest is desirable in meatiness, not in dairy. We're not looking for a narrow chest, either. There should be a good hand span between the front legs. The chest and legs should not look pinched or cramped but should blend well together with the body.

The flank should be deep, looking a little sunken, and hip bones should be prominent with thinner thighs. Thighs should stand apart from the rear, allowing room for the udder. A meat goat would have the same stance, only no sunken flank; and hips and thighs will be fleshier. Rear legs in all goats should stand apart and straight.

The skin should be soft, pliable to the touch, with fine hair, except for the Toggenburg. The skin should never be flaky, and hair should be even and shiny.

From the withers to the tail, and especially in the chine area, the top line should be a straight as possible. There will be some slope on most animals, from the top to the tail in the chine area, but the least slope is the best. The top of the chine will generally be lower than the wither, but this should be a very gentle slop and not a definite sway. From a side view, the straighter the entire top line, the better. Underneath the thurl and down to the tail are the muscles and birth canal area. Birthing is easier and safer if this entire area is as straight as possible.

If you do end up with one of these goats, especially a first freshener, try to be there for the birth. I avoid a really sloped tail when I can. Older does do all right with the birthing, but they pass down this defect in their daughters.

The barrel of the goat should be wide and deep. It has to breathe, eat, and carry kids, so they need the room.

Goat breeders will tell you "No legs, no feet, no goat." This is where we watch for those weak pasterns. I've seen goats in such bad shape that they actually were walking on their hocks. Some dragged their back feet, walking poorly on the next joint. These goats cannot carry themselves well, let alone kids; nor can they get around well enough to eat properly. At this point you have no choice but to hand-feed, till she has delivered, and then have her butchered.

Legs should be strong and straight, blending down to straight hooves, without the lumps and bumps of really knobby knees. When they get to age 7 or 8, goats may tend to get knobby front knees, and you may hear them crack as they walk. As long as it doesn't bother the goat, don't worry about it. When you see that the goat is having problems, think about putting her down before the next cold season returns. Knees will automatically be larger than the leg but should not so big as to look knobbier than what they should for the size of the leg. Saanens will have a tendency to have a larger knee, and this is not a defect.

Pasterns should be strong and straight in line above the hoof, with the goat walking directly down to the hoof, and not back on the pastern or the dew claw. Good legs, knees, and pasterns will cause the goat to stand squarely and well-balanced on all four feet.

Back legs should be straight, parallel with each other, and far enough apart to allow for a roomy udder. You'll hear the term "hocky," or "cow legged," relating to the poor conformation of the rear legs. This is when the back legs bow too close at the knees. This can be a light inward bow, or a definite coming together of the knees in the rear. Any inward bow of the rear legs in some degree is frowned upon. Some breeds, especially Nubians, are more prone to hockiness than others, and some goats with normally straight back legs will show a sign of hockiness when in poor health.

The udder receives at least one third of the attention on a show card. Since a goat is supposed to be a milking machine, this makes sense. Sometimes though, this is too bad, because the udder can be next to perfect while the goat has serious flaws. And other times, the udder can be awful and the goat gives more than the average amount of milk.

Unfortunately, a grand-looking udder does not mean the goat will give a good quantity of high-quality milk or that she will hold up her production for several years. Sadly, many goat owners will keep a goat with nothing but a capacious (large) udder to her credit, and they don't pay any attention to udder attachment or feet and legs. Large udders will hold up only a couple of years if not supported properly.

The udder should be of a relatively large size, when full, in comparison to body proportion. It should hang from between the legs and forward. A good udder should not bang up and down against the goat's legs or hang to the ground. This type of udder is called pendulous, and one tries to avoid it. However, I have to say that the best milk goat I ever had came from a goat with a pendulous udder. She gave me triplets for eight years and could feed them all. Her milk was good and she adopted other goats, if the younger mothers abandoned them. I wouldn't have taken $500 for that goat, as she did not hand down her bad qualities to her daughters when she was bred to a good buck.

The udder should not be so loose and floppy that when the goat runs, she has to jump over it or flounce it back and forth under her.

Teats should be evenly placed, pointed downward, or slightly forward and only large enough to hold firmly with four fingers. Larger teats are harder to grasp and milk properly, harder for the newborn to nurse, and harder to place in a milking machine, should you choose to use one. But larger teats do hold extra milk, and older goats will get larger just by age. Though larger teats aren't wanted in a show ring, I certainly don't discount them for my herd.

Smaller teats are simply hard to hang on to while milking, and harder for the newborns to find. Young first fresheners may have smaller teats, until they are broken in. You have to milk them to break them in.

Attachment ligaments at the front of the udder should be apart and not bring the udder up in a triangle. The udder should blend smoothly into the stomach on the belly, with no "pocket," or depression, between udder and stomach. Rear udder attachments should also be wide, holding the udder up and round.

When checking udders, don't automatically assume that larger udders mean greater capacity. Since the udder is supposed to be soft and pliable, it is difficult to detect the meaty udder. You need to discount the udder with lumps, knots, or hard bunches. However there is an udder that can be large and spongy. When it is full, it's hard to realize that it contains meat as well as milk. To be on the safe side, check the udder after milking, also. It should resemble an empty leather glove, empty of milk and meat. The spongy udder can be deceiving. It usually appears to be huge, and you have immediate visions of getting three or four gallons of milk a day. There is a tremendous disappointment when the squirts stop after a few quarts, and you still have your hands full of a very meaty udder.

Just as easily, the small udder can be deceiving. Check carefully to see how much the doe is carrying up inside her legs. Frequently, when you're touching it, the udder will be larger than it actually looks. This udder may also be spongy, so be sure you feel liquid swishing around and not just flesh.

First time fresheners should never be discounted for their size unless you know that their mothers and sisters were poor milkers. It often will take a doe a couple of seasons to put on size and quantity. Just as easily, I've had first fresheners show great promise and not do well in their second or third year. Older goats will start decreasing in milk quantity, which is the time to start thinking about culling.

Teat placement needs to be balanced with the udder. Extra teats are not common, and may give milk, but are certainly considered a defect. (Refer to papered goats). Goats with the extra teats should eventually be culled, including the bucks, as it is a hereditary defect. If this is your personal goat and she is milking well, I certainly would keep her and not her daughters. Extra teats can be clipped at birth, or surgically removed later, but this doesn't get rid of the heredity factor.

The teat orifice (hole where the milk comes out) should be of a size that is large enough to make milking easy. Milk should come out in a smooth, easy stream, but milk should only come out when being milked or nursed. Teats should not leak, as this is messy, a waste of milk, and a bacterial problem. Leaked milk can attract many pests you don't want or need, including the larger rats and some snakes.

Another problem I've discovered is the goat with two or three tiny holes. When you milk, it goes in several directions, including on you and the goat, and little makes it to the bowl. You have to get really inspired to keep this goat, let alone figure out how to get all the milk in the same place. This goat may actually straighten out the streams after several milkings, so patience is really a virtue to keep her.

When the doe first has her kids, her udder has a small plug in the holes to keep bacteria out of the udder. Strong, healthy kids can suck this plug with no problem and nurse, or we milk it without thinking. Sometimes the kids won't be strong enough, or the plug will be thicker and needs a simple pull to remove.

Meatiness is the opposite of dairy. Since I use and breed dairy, most of my writing is dairy. Though I have included some information about meat goats in this book, I still stay with dairy goats. When looking for meat goats, you will be considering the rounder withers and shorter, stocky necks. The meat animals need not be so long, but should have legs and feet strong enough to carry the added weight. Since defective goats are generally used for butcher and excess dairy stock is culled for butcher, meat animals are not commonly bred for dairy.

Does should always look feminine, even dainty. Bucks will be more rugged and masculine, with features being more angular, even "ugly." Bucks should show a larger sense of aggressiveness, whereas does will tend to be more affectionate. Well-trained bucks may be affectionately aggressive and should not be discounted for their gentleness. The doe that has been the "herd boss" may show signs of aggressive bossiness and should not be discounted if she is otherwise easy to handle.

I have culled at least one doe that was too aggressive. She was a good milker, had twins every year, and was easy to manage, but she would attack the others so much that they suffered injuries. I didn't have a wether big enough to take her attacks, so I couldn't separate her. I reluctantly sold her to a man who needed more milk than he was getting from his herd. I warned him of her nasty habit, and she beat every one of his goats, almost killing one, before he took her to the butcher.

Conformation can be complicated, but when checking goats, try to watch for the all-around appearance. Sometimes you have to choose the goat with the least offending defect, as opposed to the one with the best conformation. A good pro-gram of breeding can minimize and eventually erase some defects in the kids.

None of us have time, money or patience to waste on nonproductive, sickly, car-crunching goats that won't give enough in milk and kids to earn their own keep.

7

Buying

Before you start this exciting new life, you'll have to decide if you have the room, the proper fencing and housing for a couple of goats. If you don't already have goats, sheep or other companionship, you might as well set out with the intentions and money to get two animals. Unless you buy a doe with kids, you should get goats of the same size and approximately the same age, because they will get along better in the beginning. Remember, if you have other goats, you need to have a place to isolate the new ones.

Next, can you afford to feed the goats? Do you have excess cash on hand for feed, hay, and salt till the goats return your investment? Is there available browse, or will you have to scrounge for forage or hay and take it to the goats yourself? Are you physically capable? Are there ordinances against small livestock? Are your neighbors the type to complain? Can you protect the goats from dogs, wolves, coyotes, or vandals? And if you are in the country, you have to worry about reckless hunters. (I paint my goats purple during deer season.) Who will care for the animals if you get sick or have to be gone? Have you read this or any other book so that you know what you are getting into with this venture?

You need to have the equipment ready before you bring home the goat. It's hard on everyone if pens have to be erected and feed purchased at the last minute. Meanwhile, the goats wait, tied to a tree or the bumper of the truck.

A pet or a "weed-eater" should not have to cost the same as prime dairy. Don't be forced to get a goat you don't need. On the other hand, if you're after a good milk goat, be sure you come close to getting one. Most authorities advise that you shop around, check goat breeders, and check health certificates. I still get excited when I'm out looking for a new goat. It is really hard not to buy them all. Not having the money helps put a stop to my nonsense. Knowing I can't handle a wild goat cuts out a few more choices. Horns are a nuisance and harder to remove if the goats are older, not to mention that horns can hurt—and that's how my search goes.

Joe England's Big Mama, a starter doe, is of unknown origin. England raises goats outside of Hope, Arkansas.

Many states require health papers. You need to know that the vet goes to the property and glances over the herd, and if the animals appear to be in a good place, with generally good health, he signs the papers. If the goats have been checked for tuberculosis and brucellosis, it will be checked.

Health papers will not tell you if the goat has been wormed regularly, its age, whether it is malnourished, or even if it's lousy. You have to know how to look for these things yourself. Check out state laws before you leave the house by calling your county extension service. You will also find out if you have any extra responsibilities by owning a goat.

Prices will vary from area to area. I have found that in areas where the local 4H clubs are allowed to show goats, the prices will be higher. In places where goat shows are a part of county and state fairs, the prices will be higher. If you are in an area where there are buyers who ship goats out of the county, or buy and sell for a living, as I am, the prices go up.

Some goats can be obtained for nothing, and this does not mean there is anything wrong with them. People get rid of goats when they have to move, when they find out their "pet" is a real handful, or when the older member in the family dies, and they don't need the milk. They don't want to sell for sentimental reasons; they just want to make sure the goats get a good home.

Many people have bought a goat and found that it did not meet their expectations. Some people will buy a goat and realize that this just was not the pet for them. When the kids go to college, the goats usually get a new home. There are many reasons people will let a goat go for nothing.

A registered goat will cost more than a grade, and a purebred registered goat will cost even more, depending on the pedigree. In many areas, the breeding will have nothing to do with the price because no one cares.

Remember, reputable dealers did not become reputable by handling inexpensive stock. Be prepared to hand over a respectable amount of cash when dealing with them.

This is another time when papers may not be of any use. Registration papers give you a very good idea of a goat's background. If the parents produced well, you're to assume the offspring will also. This just isn't true. Papers show background, shows won, and blue ribbons, but not production records. Learn the conformation that is expected of the goats you are buying.

Don't be embarrassed to look them over very carefully before you buy. If you are willing to pay less than the asking price, don't be afraid to make an offer. In the South, especially, owners love to bargain and trade. While many owners will drop their prices, others will not. Originally, I didn't bargain for a goat. I figured if the seller said a certain amount, that's exactly what he meant. Then it was pointed out to me that all these people bought goats, and that they tried to get the best deal they could. Start a conversation with the seller. Maybe you have something or some service to trade.

If the goat is not what you want, don't buy, no matter how low the price, unless you have another use for it. If you haven't taken the time to learn your animals, take someone with you who has some experience with goats or cows. Qualifications expected are close for both. Don't be too shy to tell the seller that you aren't interested and ask him to refer you to someone else. You will find that goat owners are very friendly, very helpful people. Since you are about to become one, check out the seller's arrangements, the goats, and ask questions. Don't ever pass up these opportunities to learn.

In many areas, you may need to take a translator along, or learn to speak a different language, since many people from other countries, who have appreciated goats for more centuries than we, have set up herds throughout this country.

Not only do prices vary with the area, they will change with the seasons. Expect to pay at least $60 for a good grade doe, more than $100 for the registered does and up to and over $125 for purebred does and/or bucks, depending on their breeding. Butcher goats and pets will start at $25 and go up as the goats get older and bigger. Pedigreed goats from breeders, who take their breed seriously, can cost up to $500. Word of mouth may be the best way to buy a goat. If someone has earned a good enough reputation, you know they know their goats!

In some areas, kids will pay up to and including $175 for a weaned Boer goat to show. Goat magazines and the Internet carry ads on goats. They are not usually local, and you have to buy sight unseen. These goats are expensive and you have to be sure you get written guarantees on the health and shipping of the goat.

The want ads will list goats under pets, livestock, and good things to eat. When you answer ads, get as much information as you can on the telephone so you don't waste your trip. If the seller can't or won't answer your questions, don't waste a trip.

Some sale barns handle goats, which can be quite cheap, depending on who is bidding against you. Goat clubs often sponsor annual and semi-annual goat sales. Check with the owner of your local sale barn and get his or her opinion of the goats and prices, and if other clubs rent it from time to time. A word of caution is needed at this point. Not all sale barns and auctions are a safe place to buy a goat. They can be full of disease, full of disreputable sellers, and employ the worst kind of people to handle the goats.

Local breeders are usually helpful. If they aren't selling, they will be glad to try to help you find good animals.

When you go to the sale barn or an auction, don't sit and wait for the animals to come to you. Get there early and go to the back and check the animals for your-self. Frequently you can run into the owners, find out why they are selling and learn more about the goats' background. By stepping behind the scenes you'll find out if these animals are wild, mean, or otherwise bad choices. Buying a healthy goat is more important than buying a good goat. I have bought sick goats when I knew what was wrong with them, knew I could treat it, and knew I had a place to isolate them until they regained good health. Never wear the same clothes to the sale barn or an auction that you will be wearing around your own goats. Be sure to wash the clothes and disinfect your shoes so you will not carry anything home with you that you did not buy.

Take long drives on country roads and watch the landscape. You'll find goats. Look for good fences, sometimes sheep, and all too often, stacked-up junk and junk cars. You'd be surprised how many goats are out there.

Prices on does and kids will rise in the spring because the owner knows it won't cost as much to keep these animals through the green season, so he can afford to wait to sell. However, prices on bucks may go down in the spring because bucks are not needed until fall. Many owners don't want to bother with the bucks, or changing bucks and figure they will save money on feeding the older one. Buck kids will be cheaper, because if you are going to butcher them, they still have to be castrated. Wethers will cost more because someone has already gone to the trouble of getting them ready.

Prices are a bit lower in fall, except for the bucks, because owners don't want to pay the added the costs of winter feed on goats they are going to cull. Fall presents the problem that most yearling does will be bred, and maybe too early. This raises the price when in fact, neither she nor the kids may make it through delivery, and you have less chance knowing what buck has been involved in the pregnancy.

Bucks and wethers will cost more in the fall, the bucks because they are needed at that time and the wethers because they have gained weight. I have seen teams of matched wethers trained to pull carts sell for $400 — without the cart and harness. In the South, where festivals and parades are more commonplace, the trained pairs are great parade attractions.

When you first see a goat, its general appearance should be alert and interested. Don't feel sorry for the one cowering in the corner. This is not a puppy. Once goats are allowed to get skittish, they are really hard to tame.

The goat should be healthy and active, with the tail up, unless it's being handled. The animal should stand square, with the front and back feet placed straight down from its body. A goat standing hunched with its feet placed together under its body is not feeling well and could be dead in six hours.

Don't be afraid to touch the hair and skin. Check the gums and membranes inside the eyelids and mouth. They should be a bright pink. Check for signs of diarrhea, and don't buy any animal with such signs. Some sellers will tell you (very knowingly) the stress of moving, selling, and change in water will cause diarrhea. In healthy animals this is not true. Horned animals will cause you some difficulty, and overgrown hooves could take months to repair. Abscesses are a sign of an unhealthy animal and should be avoided unless you have plenty of experience in handling this problem. Not only does a goat with abscesses have to be isolated, the abscesses have to be drained, and all drainage cleaned and kept off the ground, because it can contaminate the whole area. It is possible for this goat to be healthy again, if you choose to keep it, build up its blood, give it vitamins and a special diet, and keep the abscesses clean and under control. The goat cannot go in with the regular herd until it is healed and free of all bumps for sometimes six months or more. All of that time, you must keep yourself and your clothes clean and away from your other animals.

Everyone sells a goat for a different reason. Try to find out why. Culls are someone else's castaways. They may be very highly bred and better than what you have at home, just not better than what that breeder has at home. The goat may be too old for the seller's purpose. The color, type or breed may not conform to what that particular breeder wants in his goats (such as the Sable). The owner may have excess stock and choose to cull by selling. To avoid line breeding or inbreeding, that owner may sell off good stock of his bloodline that is too closely related to what he's keeping. All too often, people will buy goats and not know what they are getting into with them. Within a few weeks, they give up and sell the goats.

Let your pocketbook and your main purpose be your guide. Don't be duped into buying a goat from someone who doesn't have your desires and circumstances in mind.

I have to remind you that papers do not make the goat. Thirty years ago I bought one of the worst looking does you'd ever seen for $17.50. She was black and white, and my imaginative girls named her Blackie. One of her ears tried to hang down, and the other one couldn't make up its mind if it should fold back or fly up. She had a hideous, pendulous udder that hit the ground toward the end of her pregnancies, with teats far too big for the normal kid to suckle. I continually bred her and her daughters to purebred bucks. She gave over two gallons at her peak, had a nine-month lactation, and kidded every year with healthy triplets each time. I had her six years, and she was the herd boss. Her daughters, as first fresheners, peaked at a gallon a day and improved their udders with each generation. I kept her descendants and each continually improved with up-breeding. When she went down in her knees, it took me two winters to get emotionally ready to send her to the butcher, at which time we still got about 80 lbs of meat. I can never complain about the price I paid for that goat. For several years after she was gone, we still went out the back door and called "Blackie" to get the goats to come in for chores.

I also bought a very well bred large, two-year-old doe, complete with papers and blue ribbons. She had a huge, well formed udder, and I felt fortunate to get her for $120 in the '60s. Imagine my shock when she kidded the first time with quads. My joy was short-lived. One of the kids died immediately, the other three demanded around-the-clock care to keep them alive, and her udder turned out to be very fleshy. She didn't produce enough to feed the remaining three and we had to purchase milk replacer until I had other does come fresh. She never did give over a couple of quarts a day and she slacked off so early in lactation that I dried her off after four months. This goat landed in the freezer the next year after she delivered more quads and did not improve on milk production. I burned the papers.

Once you get the new goats home, get them settled before calling in the friends, relatives, and neighbors. They will get so sick and tired of hearing you talk about your goats that they won't want to spend much time with them a year down the road. If the goat is welcomed in the front yard with the family, she may very well want to stay there and will make every attempt to get back to the fun place where she was most contented upon her arrival. Naturally, if you have goats, the newcomer must be isolated in a separate pen for at least 30 days. This is an important preventive measure to protect your entire herd.

I repeat this isolation because I neglected this when I agreed to take two young kids from someone who couldn't keep them 30 years ago. I assumed that their age and their pampered environment prevented them from having contracted any illnesses, and I put them with the rest of my herd. Within weeks, all my goats were badly infested with hookworms. I lost five kids, including the two new ones, and I spent well over $100 with the vet and medicine before the problem was diagnosed, treated, and under control.

If you know the owner and know that he has followed a strict method of disease prevention, then isolation is not so important. It's good to put newcomers on the other side of the fence for at least a week, no matter how well you know the background. This gives you a chance to know the animals, gives them a chance to adjust to their new surroundings and gives your goats a chance to get used to them before they start beating up on each other.

Anytime a newcomer arrives, the older goats are going to bully it. This is their nature. When you do put them all into one pen, do it in the evening after your last chores, as they are bedding down. They will not interrupt their sleeping habits to pick on each other for too long. By morning most of the newness will have worn off, and they will start the new day with fewer problems.

I never move goats to their new home at night. I don't think I would want to go into a dark strange place, with strangers, and try to sleep, so I don't do it to an animal. I move them at least a couple hours before dark, so they will have a chance to see what is around them, find the water, and recognize the smells when they get up in the morning. This may be an emotional matter with me, but I have had little trouble getting goats to settle down. If I have gone to the sale barn, I'm getting home after dark. I give the goats food and water in the trailer, leave a light on in the area, and move them in the morning.

A very strong word of caution is always in order when it comes to buying bucks. These animals can be quite dangerous when mishandled, and only gentle bucks should be allowed around people. Just as important, try to avoid buying grade bucks, as there is close to no resale value in most areas. Unless a grade buck looks really good, he's not going to improve your herd. Now that I live in an area where papers aren't worth anything, I will use grade bucks if their conformation will compliment my herd. If I ever move, I will immediately purchase a pure bred buck. I have found that in the South, the grade bucks are worth as much (or more) than papered ones, especially if they are large. They are going for butcher, and the weight counts, whether we like the idea of butchering a buck or not.

Even knowing what I do, I have made a couple of serious mistakes regarding bucks. One was a purebred 200 pound La Mancha that handled like a charm and was as gentle as a lamb, until he got in with the does. Rutting season or not, he turned aggressively possessive, and we not only couldn't get in to care for the does, we couldn't get in to feed. When he almost broke my daughter's arm as she was trying to feed through the fence, I sent him off. The other was a smaller purebred Nubian with a six-foot horn span. I knew he was wild, but figured I could chain him into the pen and take the does to him for one season. I did not have an extra shelter, so I dragged an old Chevette to him, took out the back seat, and chained him to a wheel hub, leaving the back hatch open for him to get in and out. Well! How dare I be so crude? Using his horns, he broke out every window, and then, quite for spite, I'm sure, he used his horns to tear the front doors off. I did have a witness when the second door went. I used the goat that one season, then tied a rope to both his horns, and two of us led him back to the trailer, and he went to the sale barn.

These are the kind of animals you do not try to pass off on your friends or colleagues.

8

Age, Teeth and Weight

Discerning the age of a goat is not an art reserved for the old-timers, though it helps to be one, or have one on hand from time to time. You need to have an idea of how old your animal is when buying, selling, breeding, showing or for reproduction records, and in many cases, for medication.

When buying a goat it's nice to know that the animal really is three instead of eight. Being able to confirm the age for a prospective buyer may just cinch the sale. You may not want to breed a 13- to 14-year-old doe, and if you do, you will certainly want to watch her pregnancy closely, because of her age. An older buck

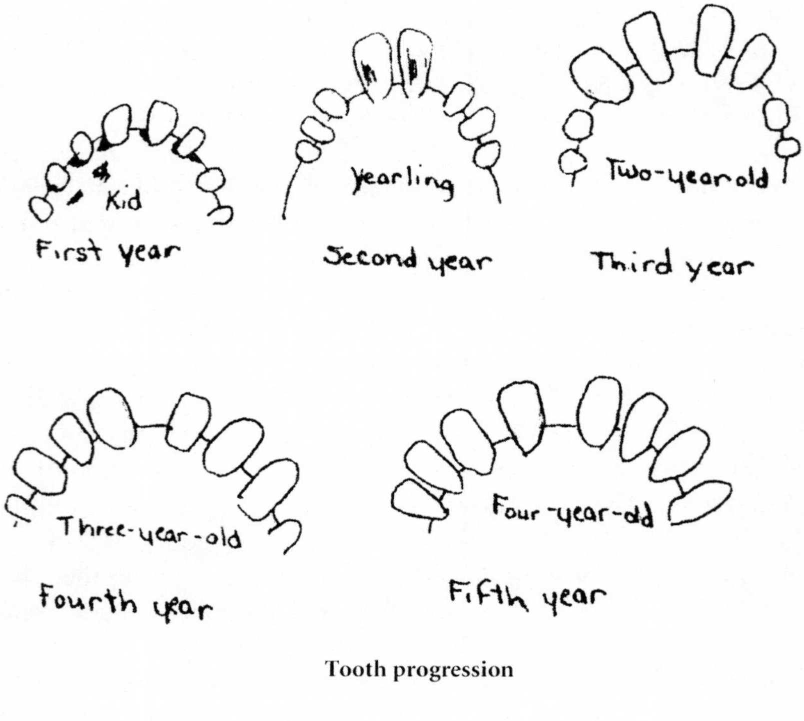

Tooth progression

54

may not be as fertile as a younger one, and knowing the age may help detect the reason for fewer pregnancies. As for butchering, the older the goat, the less tender the meat. For an older goat you would want it ground into summer sausage whereas a younger goat means the luxury of steaks and chops.

Most commonly, medication is given to goats by weight, but it's not unusual for a vet to ask the age. You should have the correct answer for him. The ideal way to tell a goat's age is to have it born on your property and then keep your own records. Second best is getting an animal with complete records. Papered animals have their age recorded with the other significant data.

You may have to tell the age by the teeth. They can be used to get a good idea up to four years of age. After that age, only experience can tell.

Remember, goats have no upper front teeth, so any age reading has to be done on the bottom teeth. Goats have eight incisors on the lower front jaw. These are the biting and cutting teeth and should meet the gums of the top of the mouth. The animal is not likely to bite you with these front teeth, but they are razor-sharp when approached at the wrong angle.

At about a year, the two center teeth will drop out and be replaced by two larger permanent teeth. About two years of age, two more teeth, one on each side of the first two, will drop out and be replaced by permanent teeth; this happens again at three, and again at four. Naturally, this doesn't happen on exactly each birthday, and it depends on the individual goat.

The four- and five-year-olds will have eight permanent teeth on the lower jaw. After that they can only be guessed by the wear on the teeth. As the animal ages, the teeth will spread apart and may loosen and drop out. If this happens, the goat cannot graze and eat properly and should be kept only if production is kept up.

The goat has 24 molars, six on each side, top and bottom, in the back of the mouth. These are the teeth used for grinding and regrinding food. If you have an older goat that has slowly started to fail over the past few years for no medical reason, you will want to check the teeth. If the goat is missing teeth or if it is injuring the inside of the jaw, the goat cannot maintain proper health.

A thorough examination of the goats' mouth is only possible under complete sedation, and goats don't sedate well. This is a job for your vet.

However, you can give the goat a preliminary examination by having someone quite strong and experienced hold the mouth open as you try to get a good look. Goats don't like you to mess with their mouths, and quite honestly, in some circumstances — your age, the age of the goat, your health, the health of the goat and the size of your herd — it may not be worth it.

The British are experimenting with false teeth for sheep and there seems to be possibilities in that area, though it may not be feasible for goats.

We don't normally pay much attention to the dew claws, but they get longer as the goat ages. A 12-year-old goat may have a dew claw four to five inches long.

Beards are usually shaved on does, but seldom on bucks or grade goats, so a long beard will mean more age. If left alone, a goat's beard may grow two to three inches a year.

If the animal has horns, they will grow five to six inches a year, and the bucks' horns maybe a little more, especially if there has not been an attempt at disbudding.

Except for when I'm buying, I seldom worry about age, because my goats' knees start popping and their production drops somewhere around seven or eight. This does not mean they are goners, just that I watch them closer, keep them warmer in the winter, and prepare myself emotionally to let them go.

Weighing and Measuring Goats

Knowing the goats' weight is most important, and the hardest fact to keep up with getting the job done, especially when you are alone. Medicines are generally given by weight. Knowing their weight is essential in getting a goat healthy faster, and knowing the weight helps to know how much feed and forage the goat will require.

Since most of us don't have, and really don't want, a scale big enough to lead a goat onto, there is a handy way to measure the goats and convert the measurement into weights. There are dairy tapes available that show weights right along with inches for dairy cattle that work well for goats. For those of us who haven't got the time to shop for a dairy tape, a regular measuring tape can be used, along with the conversion chart. To measure, wrap the tape around the goat's stomach up close to, but not touching, the front legs (heart girth). Bring the tape up across the withers, measure with tape lying flat against the goat. Not tight, not loose, just snug. This chart is not positively accurate, but it is close and accurate enough for butcher weight, dispensing medicines, and keeping up with growth gains.

Measuring goats should be a regular chore and will take less time and save more money than any other management practice. You can do this right along with the rest of the chores, but it is easier to do after feeding time, as the goats are most likely to stand still, especially the younger kids. I cannot stress this enough. Keep the tape measure, clipboard and pen in the barn.

When my daughters were home, I would measure and they would write it down, and all numbers went to the house and in the book. Now, I am alone and moving a lot slower, so I keep what I need in the barn.

This is really important for the kids, since they are more susceptible to worm infestation. The sooner you know it, the sooner you can catch it and medicate. Early infestation of parasites will stunt growth for life.

When measuring, make sure the goat is standing square, with the head held in a normal position, not bent down, and not stretched out, as the body position will alter true measurements. Should the goat have a heavy coat, try to tighten the tape to make up for the hair. Just the same, when goats are trimmed for the warm

Conversion Chart

Inches	Pounds	Inches	Pounds	Inches	Pounds
10¼	4½	21¼	35	32¼	101
10¾	5	21¾	37	32¾	105
11¼	5½	22¼	39	33¼	110
11¾	6	22¾	42	33¾	115
12¼	6½	23¼	45	34¼	120
12¾	7	23¾	48	34¾	125
13¼	8	24¼	51	35¼	130
13¾	9	24¾	54	35¾	135
14¼	10	25¼	57	36¼	140
14¾	11	25¾	60	36¾	145
15¼	12	26¼	63	37¼	150
15¾	13	26¾	66	37¾	155
16¼	15	27¼	69	38½	160
16¾	17	27¾	72	38¾	165
17¼	19	28¼	75	39¼	170
17¾	21	28¾	78	39¾	175
18¼	23	29¼	81	40¼	180
18¾	25	29¾	84	40¾	185
19¼	27	30¼	87	41¼	190
19¾	29	30¾	90	41¾	195
20¼	31	31¼	93	42¼	200
20¾	33	31¾	97	42¾	205

weather, take the measurement into account before you assume that they have lost an inch of weight, instead of an inch of hair. A goat's growth, or lack of it, is the first and greatest indicator of problems. Many illnesses show no symptoms other than a loss of weight or a lack of normal gains.

Kids should be weighed at birth and every week, up to two or three months, so that you know that they are growing according to their age. After a couple of months, if all is well, you can measure every other week, until six or seven months. Then, you'll want to measure once a month (six weeks in winter) thereafter. All goats should be measured every week to ten days through the worm season, which can be year-round in the South.

The normal worm season is usually from June through August but can be early or later, depending on what part of the country you raise your goats.

Any sick goat should be measured every week, even more, until healthy. Any time there is a feed change, or when goats are moved, they should be measured weekly, until you know they have handled the change.

This may seem like an extra hassle in added chores, but it is well worth the time and records to know if something is going wrong. Goats are hardy creatures and can be sick or lacking feed for a long time without any outward signs, save the fact that they aren't gaining or holding weight.

All animals should put on weight at the beginning of the grassy seasons, lose a small amount through hot spells, and put it back on through the fall. Goats should not lose weight in winter, though they won't gain as much on winter forage. If they do show a loss, feed more or better forage, until the goats gain weight — providing that's the only problem.

If you don't follow any other management practice, follow this one. Weight gains and losses are the biggest and sometimes *only* way you'll know in time to save a goats' life. When I found myself alone and grieving, this is the first chore I neglected, and I lost a lot of goats before I got myself back together to take the proper care of my animals.

For the handicapped, a folding chair with a plastic bag stuffed in it, needs to be hung outside the goat's shed. When you are ready, you can sit, and as the goats mill around you and your chair, you can measure. Stuff the tape back in the baggie, stuff it in the folded chair, hang it and go. I keep a folding chair at every shed and goat pen. Money bags that you get from the bank are handy to keep things in, and easy to slide into a folded chair. Zipper-lock plastic bags, canning jars with lids, or coffee cans with lids are all usable containers for this sort of thing. You will want tape, paper and pencil, and maybe even one of your own treats, in this container. Anything that does not have to be refrigerated should be kept in the barn, handy for the handicapped. Some of us have a hard enough time getting to the barn, and making a second trip may just mean that the chores won't get finished.

Even if this means getting two or three tape measures, two or three folding chairs and extra pencils and clipboards, do what you can to shorten your steps, so you can finish the job.

Having a radio in the barn is not only good for the goats, but may help you to relax and enjoy the job a little easier.

Anytime you can get someone to erect a banister, a railing, or even hanging chains for you to grab, be sure to take advantage of it.

9

Moving Goats

Once you've bought your goats, and even after you've had them for a while, you are faced with the problem of how to move them from time to time. People have moved goats successfully for years. Goats have suffered being stuffed into dusty trunks of old cars and crammed triple-decker onto trucks. Even years ago, they were put in the holds of ships. Some make it, some don't. The problems with moving goats don't seem to be with goats, but with the movers. Unless goats are crammed too tight and suffocate or get trampled to death, they seem to manage to survive the most abusive forms of transportation.

The more softhearted we are, the more we shudder at the idea of stuffing a goat into the trunk of a car. The inhumanities of cramming a load of several hundred goats on a triple-decker truck, with little or no bedding and no water, to travel thousands of miles, knowing full well that a percentage won't make it not only should pull the heartstrings of any tough guy, it should also be illegal.

Seriously, let's save the trunks for spare tires and leave the overloading to those who ship toilet paper or peanuts.

If you're going to move one or two goats for a short distance, it's simple to use the family car or station wagon. Just pull out the back seat, or cover it, lay down a large piece of plastic and put down some bedding. I save all my old electric blankets for this purpose. Take the goats anywhere, and when finished, simply unload the goats, roll up the plastic, bedding and all, and dispose of the whole mess. I throw the bedding into the barn, or on the garden, and hang the plastic or blanket to air out until the next trip. Generally, a goat will not make a mess until the vehicle stops, so unload it quickly.

Goats travel well in this manner, but you may want to take the precaution of tying them to the door handles. Give them enough rope to lie down, but not so much they'll tangle with each other.

I once moved my goats in the family wagon and still use my regular car.

Three does can occupy the back seat, 11 kids can fit in the back end of a wagon on a bed of hay, and newborns can have the prestige of a clean box in the front seat and floorboard. At every stop, the kids all had to look out the windows and "talk" to every passing person, begging for attention. When I got to my destination, I unloaded the goats, rolled up the mess and walked away from the car. There was no mess and no lingering odors. However, should there be an odor, baking soda or carpet fresheners work quite well.

Anytime you load the goats in a car, open the windows a crack so they can have air. Pickups are really handy. They need sideboards, and if it's raining, you'll need to put a tarp over the top.

For shorter distances, allow 10 to 12 cubic feet for adults, less for smaller goats. When you figure cubic feet, don't figure the top space that the goats don't use. I figure four feet for height, because that is all the goat is actually using. For those of you who have let your math slip by, you figure length times width times height. If your trailer is four feet by five feet and four feet for the height, the total cubic feet equals 80. You can safely load seven to eight goats.

For longer travel, I get a little more technical and actually measure the length and width of each goat to prevent overcrowding. Moving longer distances can be safe and easy. It's not more time-consuming, but should be done with a truck or trailer. I safely moved 11 goats over 700 miles in a stock trailer. Five were pregnant and within three weeks of their due dates. I'm happy to say that the trip went well. All newborn kids were fine when they arrived, and there were no adverse effects from a trip that totaled more than 24 hours.

I did make a serious mistake when I didn't take the seasonal changes into mind. I had transported them from the cold early spring of Iowa to the warmth of Arkansas. I had to do some fast clipping of their thick Iowa fur to make them comfortable. It stands to reason, that if you won't need your coat when you relocate, your goats won't either. On the other hand, if you move to a colder climate, you may have to supply extra warmth until your goats adjust to the temperature change.

Arrange for rest stops where you and your goats can walk about. Goats are not likely to get off their feet while the vehicle is moving, so plan two to three one-hour rest stops to give them a chance to lie down.

It's a good idea to pinpoint vets and sale barns at strategic points along your route. If you have car trouble on the road, you may have to stable the goats; and if a goat gets sick, you may need a vet. I didn't need my rest stops and vets, but after we arrived I sent each of the people postcards to thank them.

On trips of more than a few hours, offer the goats water every few hours, especially in summer. If at all possible, take an ample supply of their regular feed and hay. This is not only to get them through the trip, but to tide them over their first few days until they adjust to their new environment. Carrying extra feed and hay will also prevent any drastic changes in the goat's diet. Try to do your (on the road) chores at the same time you do them at home, so the goats' schedules won't be altered. Before the trip, trim the hooves to protect the legs from any unnecessary strain.

Keep your goats clean, change the bedding when needed, and ask permission at your rest stops before using the facilities. After you have received permission to exercise your goats, be kind enough to keep them out of the shrubs, roses, and other plants that aren't meant for goats to destroy. Be polite, courteous, and answer their questions as best you can. When you leave the area, leave it with a good impression of yourself, and your goats. Always remember to thank your host for his hospitality.

If you are lucky, you will be able to make the necessary arrangements for your goats' arrival at their new home before they get there. Unload them, give them feed and water, and leave them to rest and adjust to their new surroundings.

Goats that travel several times a year to fairs and shows do it like it is second nature, because it is. Don't be alarmed if your goats don't drink the water in their new home. It's new to them and they don't like changes. Give them a day or two and if they still won't drink, add molasses or honey to the water to help them adjust to it. Kool-Aid and Gatorade are also good additives to the water.

Some goat-buyers ship goats for a living and do not take these precautions. I have seen 30 goats come off a pickup with no bedding from a distance of 200 miles. Two were dead. The driver swore they must have been sick in the first place, because he had never "lost a goat before."

Remember, when you take your goats to a sale barn, there's a good chance they'll be bought and shipped by someone who has no interest in their health or comfort. I try to sell privately and only take the worst bullies or animals that have developed the worst habits and made me frantic to the sale barn. Some goats just don't let me get emotional, and some are not worth much more than butcher. I try to not let any of them get on those trucks, but sometimes it's my only choice.

Moving, traveling, and relocation need not be troublesome because of the goats. Take the extra time and consideration to see that the goats are cared for properly, and they will blend in with the rest of your plans.

10

Public Relations

All too often, I run across goat keepers who do not take very good care of their animals, and for a short time I was one of them. My own lapse brought me more understanding, so now when I see neglected goats, or their area, I stop and visit to see if the owners got stuck like I did, or if they just don't know any better. Most often, they just don't care, and it amazes me how well some of these animals survive. Mine didn't do that well.

There is always the person who scoffs, "Oh, it's just a goat; you don't have to go to all that trouble. They'll take care of themselves." And occasionally, he's right. And then there are the people who will tell you they had goats for 30 years and never trimmed hooves. They might be right, if the goats have played on the rocks for 30 years. And if you ask him how long his oldest goat has lived, he won't have the answer.

In every group of goat owners, there will always be the one person against good goat care, and he will have a healthy goat tied out behind the garbage to prove his point.

With proof like this, could we assume that conscientious goat keepers unknowingly inflict their goats with all the problems that befall them? Could we also assume that we weakened the strain when we domesticated these animals? Or is it possible that every once in a while there just happens to be a goat out there that is hardy enough to withstand the effects of poor management?

It's obvious that some goats just don't need much care. We call these goats low maintenance, or "easy keepers." Domestication has weakened some of the strains. But good management, conscientious care, and careful breeding will help to strengthen the lines again. The number of goats that do survive poor care are few. Generally they are scattered, one by one, and when they do die, no one knows it. When they survive in herds, the inbreeding and line breeding causes earlier deaths.

The whole truth is that when a goat is doing well, the owner brags about not taking care of his animals. When one of them dies, he keeps quiet.

Judy Ehrlich's goat in Alaska doesn't mind a little snow and may steal the next ride out.

As goat keepers, we have to make a decision. Do we want to risk our financial investment and emotional ties to take a chance on losing our animals? If we don't use good management, we take a definite chance of losing our animals. Even when we do our best, we may lose an animal. But the more we learn, the less our chance of failure.

Almost every problem with goats can be prevented if you know how. Learn the problems, plan for them, know the cures, know the causes and practice preventive management by not letting them occur.

There will be times when you can't avoid illness or accident and when you won't know what to do. Before you push the panic button and blow your savings, decide if your animal is worth it. This is not cruel, just practical. You are not going to get in and out of many veterinary clinics for less than $75. That doesn't take into account extra money in medical expenses, the time spent before the animal regains its health, and whether it will affect the rest of the herd. Once you've calmly weighed all the alternatives, call the vet and try to save the animal, or put it out of its misery as humanely as possible.

If you have no idea what is wrong with the goat, it's a good investment to take it to the vet. You definitely need to know what is wrong in case the rest of the herd has been infected. Any time an animal dies unexpectedly, take the body for inspection. The lab fees are nominal compared to the knowledge you need to protect the rest of the goats. Whatever you decide, do it quickly and calmly. Letting a goat slowly waste away from poor health is cruel, inhumane and dangerous to the herd. As for finding an interested, knowledgeable vet, that's another story. Most vets are good in their field. Unfortunately, there just aren't that many who chose goats to be their field. You'll find that some of them are willing to try and some aren't. Some will help, even if they don't know what they are doing.

Find a vet before you need one. Don't be embarrassed to tell him that you are checking him out. He would do the same thing if he were in your place.

Other goat breeders in your area can tell you their experiences with medical help. Chances are they can tell you whom you can depend upon. If there are no other goat owners in the area, you're stuck with the yellow pages. Call every single vet within driving distance. I've chosen 30 to 35 miles as a range I feel I can "rush to a vet."

Introduce yourself at the beginning of the call and explain that you are looking for medical service for your goats. Ask if they're interested and if not, could they refer you to another vet. Many vets will not hesitate to say they do not want goats near their office.

Some will agree to help you, even though they don't know as much about a goat as you do. I divide this group into two sections: vets who really would like to learn more and treat my goats and the vets who don't but still want the money. I can usually separate this group by a long conversation on the telephone. I ask how often to worm in my area, if they will sell me medicines in bulk, and if they mind if I do my own stitching. You can usually tell which ones give a hoot and which are out to get the money. A good vet won't mind teaching you. Even though he may lose a sale, he hasn't lost a customer.

If the vet you are talking with doesn't sound as concerned as you are, skip him politely. He'll be relieved. Once you've found a satisfactory vet, use him or her. Build a rapport.

Many goat owners have chosen to go into veterinary medicine themselves because of the lack of service in this field. I have chatted on the Internet with one group that is studying herbal medications so we can keep our milk and meat chemical free. Other people, like me, have chosen to learn as much as they can and treat their own goats for just about everything.

In 2004, our area was hit with a freak snowstorm, complete with ice, on Valentine's weekend. My best doe began birthing three days early. Every vet in the area was at a convention, and the ones who were farther away were not going to come out in the storm. Even with my years of experience, I lost the doe and three kids, because the first was a very large buckling with his head and neck turned back, and his feet protruding. He had apparently fought so hard to be born, or her fighting so hard in labor, it was actually too late when I tried to help. Since then, I have found a vet 45 to 50 minutes away who is willing to open his office at any time because he lives there. He said if I can drive, come on. I should have considered storm conditions and real emergencies much earlier than this year.

With any illness, be reasonable. Know when to quit. Remember, when you pay a vet, it's your money. I would have paid $500 to save that doe and not one red cent had it been one of my other goats. You have a right to know what the vet is doing and why. You have a right to know that you are getting what you pay for, and as much as you need. If you really think your animal needs an antibiotic, see that you get one; or get a satisfactory reason why you shouldn't. Vets are human too. They may very well intend to give you the antibiotic, but forget to do so.

Local pet shops may sell different medications, but they cost more.

Your local farm store (co-op) should be your second best friend, after the vet. It can not only sell you medicines in bulk, but the employees can put you in touch with other goat people who can help. They can tell you what other goat people are using for your particular problem and what products the other customers have said they didn't like.

Clean, clean, clean

Throughout this book and your association with goats, you will hear a lot about cleanliness. Just about every goat-related problem could be prevented if we would always start with clean barns, lots, milking equipment, your hands, you, your visitors' boots and the goats. Clean, as in good old-fashioned elbow grease and disinfectants!

Everyone has heard the bad comments concerning goats. "They're smelly, dirty creatures that can't be fenced, and get into everything, eat anything, and the milk tastes as bad as the animal smells!" Those of us who work with goats know this is untrue. So it's up to us to change the image.

Let's put the shoe on the other foot and see why people have these false impressions. Usually people get their first and most-long lasting impression about goats from an inexperienced attempt at raising goats or from someone else's inexperienced attempt. I've never encountered a person who has an educated reason to dislike goats.

Since nonowners don't go to goat shows, they seldom see a quality goat. They've generally come into contact with a scrub goat, tied behind a barn, after it got off its chain and into the garden. It's quite possible that the same goat was poorly fed and broke loose because it was hungry. Its bedding, if it had any, and the area around it was probably dirty and it did smell bad, though not as bad as the family dog would in the same circumstances. Chances are the owner of the goat didn't know much about the animal or its care.

A lot of people had a pet goat when they were children. Now, we know that children are not responsible pet owners, and when these children grow up, they don't remember their own childhood inabilities—just the goats' untrained faults.

When John Q. Public drives down the backroads and sees a goat operation, he also may see piles of junk, broken fences, overgrown weeds, garbage, and an altogether unkempt situation. When Mr. Public does meet a goat keeper, fate would have it that he meets someone still in chore clothes, not making a very good appearance. When he drinks the mishandled milk, from an unclean container, at the wrong temperature, it does taste bad. Fresh cows' milk won't taste good under the same circumstances. It doesn't matter that the public finds goat people to be very friendly, and usually very helpful. They usually find a situation that they would rather avoid, and they pass the bad news on to their friends.

If cows, horses, sheep, or dogs were handled the same way as some unfortunate goats, they, too, would be the brunt of some pretty nasty jokes. What is so sad is that it is not the goats' fault. It's entirely up to us to change the picture. The goats can't do it. The very fact that these hardy creatures have survived all these generations of mishandling, filth, and hardships only goes to show how much more valuable they would be under the ideal circumstances that is automatically given to other animals.

Show me a dirty, hard-to-handle goat that gets into everything and smells bad, and I'll show you one very sloppy, inept goat handler. No matter how nice and friendly goat keepers are, some — if not most of them — just don't know any better. And I am not really defending them because they have goats. Some people just don't know any better. They bought a goat; they fed a goat, they may have been lucky enough to breed the goat and have babies and raise them without a problem. They sincerely don't know that they had an "easy keeper" and that most goats do need worming, trimming, and cleanliness.

If you're one of those people who see a use for everything and can't seem to throw anything away, stack it. Build a roof over it. But don't leave all those priceless treasures lying about to draw mice, rats, snakes, mosquitoes, and disapproving stares of visitors. Did the wind manage to blow papers and trash all about your property? Gather it up and burn it. If Mother Nature continues to bless you with falling limbs and dead branches, make it a habit to try to keep up with the debris. If there's a garbage service in your area, use it. If there isn't, try to find a form of regular disposal. Hire someone, or trade a goat, but clean up your act. Keep your handyman tools put away. Turn over wheelbarrows and wagons, not only to protect them from rust, but to prevent one more place from collecting debris. Prop up, or store, hoes, rakes, pitchforks, shovels, and other implements, not just for their own preservation, but for you and the goats' safety. This also makes it easier to find them when you do need them, saving much time and energy looking for them.

When I became handicapped, this became a serious problem for me. I couldn't always carry the material that was needed, nor could I pick up the mess that was left. Things got pretty bad until my daughter volunteered one of the babies' little red wagons. This solved the problems with tools and buckets, but not bigger materials. I devised another plan that was cheap and easy. I took a small hood from a small car and attached it with a small chain to my car. I could pile materials on the hood, drag the hood with my car to the site and easily take care of repair work, without hurting myself. The hood works well for hauling trash and junk, too.

Goats' pens should be free of debris, not just for general appearances, but for the safety of your goats' feet, legs and udders. Broken glass and barbed wire can cause serious cuts. Standing water will draw bugs in summer and ice in winter. Now that we have the threat of West Nile virus carried by mosquitoes, draining or filling in pools of water is even more important.

Goats' housing doesn't ever need to be fancy but should be kept in good repair. Tack up flapping tarpaper and nail down loose tin and falling boards. Boards with loose nails can cause more hoof problems than you may ever be able to fix. If old bedding needs to be stacked somewhere, stack it away from living quarters and goat lots. There are plenty of uses in the garden, around young tree saplings, as compost for the garden, and as cover for bare ground. Right now, I'm using mine to level my back yard behind the retaining wall that goes around my patio. This will channel water to another area and add value to my property.

Once or more a month, stand at the front of your property and look at your place as a stranger would see it. Their first impression of you, your property, and your goats, will be a lasting one. Make it an impression that does not add to the misunderstanding about goats. Besides getting our own act cleaned up, we have to reach out and try to educate the public. Start with your friends. If they don't like your goat, that's fine. But make sure that they realize it is their opinion and not anything that is basically wrong with the goat.

Call the elementary school in your area and invite students and teachers to visit your goats. Daycare centers also love to educate their preschoolers. Call the local newspaper and ask that some extra space be occasionally dedicated to goats. Get in touch with the county extension service, and see if the staff can help with activities involving goats. Donate a goat to a 4-H youngster and help with 4-H projects. Contact the Scouts and other youth groups and let them know that you are available for visits. They may need to earn merit badges by spending time with the animals or working around animals. One of our local dens sends the Scouts out twice a year to earn merit badges in service to others and identifying different plants, animals, and birds.

If you have children and goats, put them in parades. If you have goats trained to pull carts, definitely show them off. One of the best floats I have ever seen was in a harvest festival and featured the grains of the harvest season. It featured the farmer and his wife, and following the float were several goats, a sheep, a cow, and a horse and rider. Several times during the parade one of the goats would manage to catch up to and jump on the float for a treat. Of course he would be shooed back off, but it was so typical of a goat keeper's life that it was my favorite float.

You may not be a neighborly person, but if you have goats you will need the good will of your neighbors. Be cooperative. Offer to let your goats help clear unwanted weeds. Keep the fence between you and your neighbors in really good shape, even if you have to double up on wire. Try to stay on cordial terms. If your goats get out, it will be easier on you if they know you.

The best time to invite people to see your goats is during kidding season. This has given you most of the winter to catch up on repairs while your doe was pregnant and if you're handicapped, you may be crawling to rake and clean up the mess that fall left behind. Your place should look better; fences should be ready for spring, and barns and lots cleaned and ready for newborn kids.

Strangers are most receptive to newborn kids. Let the babies help spread the good word. These are darling little creatures, not a curse to the public. I have even loaded up the kids and made eight or nine stops in a day to day-care centers and nursing homes (by appointment of course) to spread the cheer that only a baby goat can do. If the goats are on bottles, the children love to hold the bottle. Senior citizens will smile and recall the pet goat they had as kids 70 years ago. They may even remember its name.

During the rutting season (more in chapter 17, on bucks) try to limit visitors and keep your buck under control. Most of the bad impressions about goats started from a bad experience with a buck in rut. Don't try to lie about the bucks' atrocities. Be honest to your visitors. Explain to them the shape your buck is in, and why. Let them view him from a distance, if at all possible. Try not to invite visitors during breeding season. Don't think for a minute that he'll behave himself. He won't. In fact, he'll be worse because he will consider strangers a threat. He will throw a fit, try to keep the does away from you and your visitors and just generally be a brat. And please, stay away from those sick people who get a kick out of the blubbery, stumbling, extremely erotic buck in rut.

Remember, if your buck is running free with the does, they will stink as well and will pass the odor onto the unsuspecting visitor.

Later, you'll find more thorough information for clean milk, clean utensils and clean feeding habits. All of it is just as important as the appearance you alone can present.

Filth and clutter draws bacteria and causes disease, whether it is in the lots and barn, or right in your kitchen where you keep the milk container. Insects breed and thrive on a very small amount of standing water and create more problems for the goats, tools, and equipment.

Your goats won't produce as well, nor will the milk taste as good, under unsanitary conditions. The goats will contract disease, spend more down time with sickness, and show poor condition, bad health and smaller growth gains. You will be the unhappy loser under these conditions. In the long run, if you don't lose any goats, you'll lose the good quality of your milk, the respect of your friends and neighbors, and a very large portion of your investment.

You may think that the good will of others is not a goat-related problem, but unless you have a spot back in the mountains, miles away from the world, it is. Knowing that people in your area will not try to destroy your goats the first time you turn your back is a real big plus. And finding trustworthy help in an emergency may depend on that good will. If your goats manage to get out and nibble a few rose bushes, it's nice to know that a concerned neighbor will try to capture them (and will appreciate the pruning) before the goats cause damage to themselves and the area. My goats have gotten into the neighbor's cornfield and tore up more corn than what they ate. They will nibble at every flower, shrub, and sapling they come across, and they can scare ten years' life out of you when they get on a state highway. Drivers of 18-wheelers can't really tell the difference between a goat and a deer, or a dog, from a distance, and though they would just as soon not hit either one, they can't slow down a rig fast enough to keep from hitting the whole herd. I'm not sure why, but there is far more trucking industry in the South and East, than in the plains, and this is a major concern for goat owners. The trucking industry doesn't pay for a smacked goat in the highway, and unless the accident tore up one of his air or brake lines, the trucker doesn't stop and sometimes doesn't even know he hit something. These drivers aren't dumb; the rigs are too big for the bump to be noticed.

Visitors and visiting

Try to be polite and informative to visitors, and if they are rude, remember not to treat another person the same way when you go to visit his herd.

This is another time we have to worry about clean. Never wear your chore shoes to visit other goats, and never wear your visiting shoes in to your goats. Just as well, ask your visitor if he is wearing clothes or shoes that came out of another goat lot. This is another way that germs and disease can be inadvertently spread. Visitors will appreciate that you care enough about your goats, and when visiting, the owner will be glad to know that you're not bringing any microscopic visitors.

When visiting, ask questions politely and answer questions truthfully. If you don't know the answer, don't lie, offer to help find it.

Visiting other herds takes a lot more than just politeness. It takes a lot of tact. You're going to see situations that are pretty bad, but unless this goat owner asks your opinion, keep you mouth shut. This is no time to hurt someone's feelings. Also you'll see some really nice set-ups that can give you better ideas. Be sure to compliment these people and ask questions to gain more knowledge for your own operation

You have to be just as tactful when receiving visitors. If they want to be rude enough to tell you that you don't have to do things in a certain way, just tell them that this is the way you do it, or that you are still working on it.

Not only do you have to worry about their footwear and clothing, but if your goats are in the back of the pasture, don't let them drive through your gates. Chances are they have driven in their own pastures. If you can't call up your goats, or get them yourself, then make arrangements for the person to come back another time when you can have the goats corralled.

I once visited a herd that was knee-deep in loose mud. There's no way a goat would walk in these conditions if they didn't have to get to food and water. I bought every one of his goats, cleaned them up and sold them, just to get them out of that mess. I was so mad I was gritting my teeth, but I never once said a word to him about the conditions. I've also seen goats running in the woods, so wild they wouldn't be called up, and would only come to a truck; because that's how he fed them. They were in sorry shape, but I let that one pass, because they were at least free. You can't tell someone else how to raise their kids, so you sure can't be rude enough to tell someone how to raise their goats.

You will meet people who have no idea what kind of goat they have, so calling ahead on the phone can be a waste. You'll meet people who have had goats all their life and didn't know they didn't have upper front teeth, what the breed was, or when the last time they were wormed, let alone know that they needed their feet trimmed. Be prepared before you go. On the other side of the extremes, I've even seen goats that were kept in an air-conditioned trailer in the hot afternoons.

I've met people who didn't know how many goats they had and weren't even sure where they all were. They just feed or throw hay to the ones that come up and figure the others aren't hungry. They really don't even think the goats could be sick, in trouble, or gone.

Some of these people will call a polled goat a muley, a pygmy a brush goat, and a Nubian a hound dog goat. And the oldest female is really the mama to all the rest of the goats in the herd, but some people don't know that the young bucks can breed and would never believe that their entire herd was full of goats that were products of incest (line breeding/inbreeding). Bless their hearts, they will give you the shirt off their back and their last pork chop, but they just don't know their goats.

11

Equipment

The equipment necessary depends on the purpose for which you have the goat. Before investing, know what you will need and streamline your equipment according to that purpose. Milking equipment is useless to those not wanting to keep and process the milk.

The main necessities are adequate housing and sturdy fences. You need a good basic feed, hay, a sheltered box for salt and minerals (depending where you live), and an easy-to-clean water receptacle. With those basics, you have the foundation to shop for an active and healthy goat.

Call your vet or the county extension service to see what vaccinations are recommended. Some areas will require vaccinations, others will just recommend them. I suggest you go with the recommendations.

When problems do arise, make sure you can handle them immediately. Having tools of the trade on hand will save time, headaches, and sometimes a goat's life.

Keep the vet's phone number, location, and the telephone number for after hours beside the phone, in the phone memo pad, or on the computer. Since my handicap, I have found the best thing is the number of another reliable, experienced person to count on in case of an emergency.

Subscriptions to a reliable magazine can answer a lot of questions. The magazines will cater to the owners who breed for papers. The Internet is full of web sites, many helpful and some simply selling products, but all can add to your education. Keep all information in a place to which you have easy access. A drawer, filing cabinet, a box that's handy will do, as long as you can get to it. Most of my information goes into the computer, except for the notes I keep on clipboards in the barn.

There are some basic items that you should have on hand for any goat. Hoof trimmers or a sharp knife are important. I use a utility knife with a removable razor for trimming hooves. This device is handy, easy, and very dangerous. If you choose it, use it with great care until you are used to it. I do not want to stop my chores and go to the emergency room.

I believe that every goat should have a collar, and you will need a rope or chain to tie it. I have 8- to 10-inch chains with snaps already mounted in my barn for quick tying.

Worming products come in every size, shape, and color, and consistency. Since worming is done several times a year, this is a product to buy in bulk. If you live in a cooler climate, you can pretty well skip worming through the winter, until about three weeks before the kids come. If you live in the South, count on worming every month. You have to alternate wormers so the goat won't build up immunity, and natural wormers are becoming easier to get. Ten days after worming, check your herd. It has been my experience that 10 percent of the herd will not be affected, and will have to be rewormed. Never assume that since you worm regularly that it works. Goats are extremely susceptible to internal parasites, and to what degree depends on the goats, climate, and the product, the pasture, and their feed.

A seven percent tincture of iodine is the recommended product for dipping the naval cords of the newborns. I have used hydrogen peroxide successfully, and both products should be kept on hand for cleaning and disinfecting. The mother does a good job, if the bedding is clean. If worse comes to worse, you can use antibacterial soap and triple antibacterial ointment.

An udder ointment is handy for milking does and sometimes necessary. Bag Balm, Vaseline, Udder Balms and other salves for chapping are commonly used. Make sure the product will not cause irritation. These ointments are handy to keep around for other animals and humans and often work like a triple antibiotic. Vaseline applied to the udder and rump and back legs of a doe due to kid will eliminate most of the lochia that collects on the backside after birthing and draws flies and looks bad.

Many products are made to stop bleeding; one reliable product should be kept on hand. In emergencies, flour not only aids in helping the blood to clot, it also covers the wound to prevent flies and dirt from getting to the area. I try to keep a bag of flour around all the goats' sheds.

If you're administering your own medications, you'll need a supply of syringes and needles. Start with all sizes of both till you find the one or two that you use the most. Since I have other animals, I use all the sizes for something.

The California mastitis test is an inexpensive kit to check for mastitis. There is also a homemade check for mastitis in chapter 21.

A dehorning iron will be needed if you decide to do your own disbudding, unless you choose to use a caustic paste. In either case, plan to have them on hand well before the new horns arrive.

A tattoo kit is used for identification purposes. People who show goats and keep track of pedigrees need one. Breeders selling only the purebred with pedigrees will use these kits as well.

The elastrator and bands are for castration and some dehorning jobs.

Clippers and scissors for trimming the hair are necessary, especially for the udder of milk does, when you are showing goats or you are trimming the backsides just before kidding season.

It is a good idea to keep an antibiotic on hand for pneumonia and other infections. Some need to be refrigerated, and an extra refrigerator in the barn is handy.

Goats are just as prone to external parasites as other animals. You'll want to keep an insecticide for them and one for their area. Garden powders are safe on animals, take care of lice and mites, and are inexpensive.

Planting marigolds around the animals' area helps keep down the flying insects, including mosquitoes and wasps. Plant them where the goat can't get to them. They aren't poisonous— they just won't do any good if the goats eat them.

To keep fire ants at bay, mix ⅔ cup of antibiotic dishwashing liquid with ⅔ cup of Pine Sol and ⅔ cup of turpentine, add 2 gallons water, and pour liberally on hills. When using any product for fire ants, alternate every 30 days, or after every rain. Right now this seems to be a southern problem, but statistics show that the fire ants are moving north at a pretty good pace. So far, they do not have a natural predator.

Now I know I have given you a big list of items to be in barns, and the real problem is keeping it handy but away from the goats. Goats like to snoop. If they can reach it they'll get it. My father always said what a goat couldn't eat or tear up it would turn around and drop little berries on it. So true, so true.

If you don't have a building or area your goats cannot enter, hang an old cooler high up on the wall.

A milk stand is not a necessity but is handy for milking, hoof trimming, giving shots and general care. A stanchion is next best and equally convenient. Both can be homemade. Remember to adjust for any handicaps. Since I don't bend so well, and my goats still jump, my stand went higher. I can use a lower one by sitting on a stool or chair. The stool and chair must be hung up when you're finished, or next chore time, you'll be sitting in goat berries. I save all old blankets and lay on one on the ground if I have to tend to a goat and can't do it any other way.

Storage containers need to be large enough to hold feed, to prevent contamination moisture, seepage and waste. They also keep mice from getting into the food. Mice may not be your biggest problem, as opossums and skunks like the feed as well. Make sure your storage is set up so that you can handle it, clean it, and fill it. I built a shelf all the way around mine so that the feed bags can be shelved by my son-in law (or the first handy person who comes along), and when I need them I can pull or drag them to the edge, and drain them into a 30-gallon short container. The container can be rolled out for easy cleaning and rolled back in for easy filling.

Equipment for milking must be clean. Since many materials can cause an off taste, and sometimes bacterial growth, stainless steel is the best investment.

Seamless stainless or glass containers should be used for all milk and be small enough to clean and handle with ease. If you have a dairy, anything small and easy won't be enough for your operation. Paper filters for straining the milk can be bought in a variety of sizes and are easily disposed.

All materials need to be cleaned with the appropriate cleanser. I disinfect tools and scissors with alcohol, and I use an antibacterial soap for bowls, pens and concrete floors. Bleach isn't good unless you're going to keep the goats off of it for a while. Check with your feed store, or any local dairy outlet, for the recommended cleanser available.

By now you should have a better idea of which method of goat management you intend to pursue before investing in equipment. Plan your approach to each problem, and then get the necessary materials. Storage of the necessary materials is complicated enough without having to store something you may never use, not to speak of the unnecessary cash outlay.

Storage is almost as important as shelter. The last thing you need is a goat that has cut itself and you can't find what you need to stop the bleeding, or worse, the product you bought is caked and you made biscuits this morning and you're out of flour. An elastrator can cost more than $12 and the bands only 79 cents, but if one rusts and the other dry rots, neither are any good. This is a good time to note that bands and extra syringes should be stored in the refrigerator to keep the rubber from drying out. Syringes should only be used once and tossed.

Ropes and collars will rot, chains and wire cutters will rust, hay will mold, and the list goes on. If you can get the goats secure, the next job is to get your supplies secure. One-and three-pound coffee cans with secure lids are good to save for storage, metal cabinets under the carport, old freezers and refrigerators (remember to keep them secure and full enough children can't get in them) plastic tackle boxes, zipper lock plastic bags and anything else you can seal and keep dry. You are moving into a "save everything, recycling world."

Plastic buckets are not only good for storage, they make great stools and have the handy handle (bail) to hang them up away from the goats. Plastic buckets with lids can hold supplementary feed or be used as a step stool.

12

Housing

People can get carried away with housing for their goats, and so can a lot of goat-care manuals. And if you've got the money, then go for it. If you're building a dairy, you'll have to go the whole extra mile. I'm advising practicality to the small keeper, so I'll avoid the expensive and elaborate.

Cleanliness plays a major role in housing, so whatever plans you make, remember that housing will have to be cleaned.

One of my silliest mistakes was in this area. It was late fall, and we had to get ready for an Iowa winter. The house for my five doelings was too small to house them all winter. When building a new structure, we were careful to make the door large enough for them to get in and out as they grew. However, we did not make the door large enough for us. We had to crawl in with new bedding and when cleaning time came, we had to remove one whole side.

If you have the machinery, this type of shed can be picked up and moved. Or it can be built on skids and pulled off the old bedding pack. It is my goal to be able to move the sheds with my goats.

Build the shed on sled-type runners, with one end blunted so that you can tie onto it and pull it where you want it to go. Two huge eye hooks screwed into the 2-by-4s in the framework make it easy. If you make the sled without a bottom you will be pulling it off one dirty bedding pack and putting it in a clean spot to start over.

Another more unpleasant and disastrous situation was a hastily built three-sided shelter with a slanted roof. It was constructed in a light rain in the light of late evening, to shelter some newly purchased animals for the night. After a quick check to make sure it would be dry, we bedded the goats and left them for the night. During the night, the rain stopped, and some of the heavier animals jumped on the roof — which wasn't built to hold them — and a wether was crushed and killed. We should have bought those goats, gone home and built a decent house, and returned the next day to get the goats.

Never construct housing without planning. An oversize dog house may suffice for a shelter. There are many variations of a simple shelter. One is a short tepee type, for your kids. With this house, two doors, or boards 2½-feet wide, are placed together to form an upside down V (refer to sketch). A third door, or another piece of lumber, is nailed to the end. Cover the top crack with plastic, tarpaper, or caulking, throw in some bedding and watch to make sure your kids don't outgrow it. This can easily be moved to another pen when new kids arrive again or taken apart and stored till needed.

Goats have been housed in barrels and though I don't think it's a good idea, it does work as a temporary shelter and should be used only as a last resort. Barrels protect the animal from wet weather, not the cold. If you must use a barrel, make sure it is large enough and block it on both sides so your goat doesn't go rolling with every move. Don't be surprised if the goat gets bored, butts it and rolls it herself. It's difficult to put adequate bedding in a barrel and still have room for the goat. Tarps can be tied to poles or trees to make a temporary and movable roof for summer shelter and shade.

There are two types of housing. Both have disadvantages and good points, so decide which method is best for you.

Confinement housing is one larger house that usually holds several pens or stalls, and goats are kept in individual pens, much like a sale barn. This house is generally heated and ventilated by fans and is dependent on some form of electricity. The animals are fed and cared for from alleys adjoining the pens, and there is a separate area set aside for exercise. With confinement housing, goats are cared for individually and sickness is easier to catch, since you tend each goat individually. However, with separate pens come separate cleaning chores, and the animals have to be transported to the exercise area, causing more "hand to goat" work.

Confinement houses are usually larger and more of an investment than what you would want for the "home goats." If you must worry about canes, walkers or wheelchairs, make sure your aisles are wide enough to accommodate. I have found that an aisle or a railing down the middle of any barn is convenient for the handicapped to hold and be able to feed both sides or just take care of the animals.

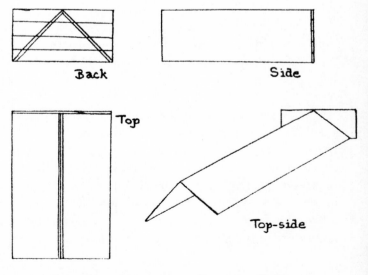

Loose housing is more

Boards in an upside-down V shape make a quick shelter.

common, with all goats of the same size in the same building and allowed to roam about. It is more practical and more natural and, although disease and infection will spread faster, cleaning is confined to the same area. Loose housing gives the goats a large enough area for exercising, providing they have access to an outside yard.

If either house is heated, the goats must have an exercise area on the inside. They can't go from a heated house to a cold yard without getting chilly and sick. In southern states, this is not even a worry, but in the North, I would bring my goats into the basement, complete with bedding, at night, and take them back out after morning chores.

Construction for goats' housing has several simple requirements. The house must be ventilated but not drafty. This means that air inside the shelter should be able to move around, up and out, but wind should not blow into the house.

This was tough for me to understand how a three-sided shelter could be made draft-free. Then I recalled some more of my third-grade science: "No two forms of matter can occupy the same space." Air is a form of matter and is already in the shelter along with the goats, therefore, no more can blow in unless holes or cracks are on the other side for air to escape. Then you have a draft. Ventilation can be obtained from windows and doors. I consider the spaces under the eaves as the most ideal ventilation.

Healthy goats can handle normal temperature changes quite well, though they will decrease milk production in cold or hot weather. Many dairies maintain a consistent temperature in confinement barns, to maintain consistent production.

If the goat has been allowed to roam in the pasture as temperatures drop, it will handle subzero temperatures quite well.

The shelter should never be more than 20 degrees warmer than outside temperatures in loose housing. If the mercury drops to minus 2 and the temperature in the shed is 18 or 20, the goats are okay.

The sizes of shelters vary with the size and amount of goats you keep. The typical rule is 15 square feet bedding area and 60 cubic feet of air space for each mature goat, with an extra 25 square feet for exercise per goat. To figure square feet you multiply length times width, and to figure cubic feet. you multiply length times width times height.

Do not put several sizes of goats in the same shelter, unless they are nursing or separated by a partition. An 8 × 10 foot shelter would have bedding space for five goats but air space for eight goats if it had an eight-foot ceiling. If you were to figure one square foot for every 10 pounds of goat for bedding, multiply by 4 for each goat for cubic feet of air space, and you have a viable formula for your goats' health and comfort.

Body heat will help keep the area warm, so the shed should not be any larger or ceilings any higher than necessary. If you have a larger barn to house the goats, it would be to their advantage if you provided them with a smaller stall for sleeping.

To ensure a dry building, the roofs and walls must shed water, not absorb it. Roofs can be of any type, but should always slant for drainage and in the South, for ice. In the North the snow will stack up and fall off, but in the South the weight of the ice will cave in a flatter top. When slanting the roof, make sure that the ground around the shelter slopes with the slant of the roof, so the water from the roof will not collect on the ground around the building. The roof should be high enough so that goats cannot jump on top or strong enough to hold them if they are allowed on it. If goats are to be allowed on their shelters, it's a good idea to keep that shelter far enough away from the fence to keep them from jumping out.

My most recent mistake was building a shed on the slope appropriately, but forgetting that the water coming down to the shed had to go somewhere, which was into my shed. I had to have it quickly trenched, as the water backed up behind it and soaked under it and up through the bedding pack.

Ceiling heights should not only be planned for air space and ventilation, but be high enough to let bedding stack up over winter. Since I am short and usually take most of the responsibility for the goats, my shelters are planned with a seven-foot ceiling. This allows enough room for bedding to stack 12 to 18 inches and me to stand (or crawl) comfortably when caring for the goats.

Floors are a big part of your shelter: They must hold bedding and be cleaned. Concrete floors are the only kind that can be cleaned and can really get clean. If concrete floors have drains to catch the urine, they can prove their value in compost. However, concrete is expensive and cold and needs extra bedding to protect the goats from the cold and protect the udders. Thus there is the extra cost and work for bedding.

Wood floors are useless. They hold dirt, moisture, disease and mildew and rot easily. Wooden floors must be treated and sealed seasonally, so it is too expensive for the small farmer.

Dirt floors are ideal if you don't plan to save the urine for compost. Remember, some of the urine soaks into the bedding, so all is not completely lost. Excess urine seeps into the dirt, and other bedding can be raked off the top. Dirt is easy to keep clean, as you only have to pick up the used bedding, let the area dry, and add new bedding. Some people will treat the floor with lime or move the shelter to new area to give the old area a rest. All in all, dirt is the ideal floor for goats.

Any floor that is off the ground provides an ideal breeding and hiding place for rats and mice and allows drafts to blow under the floor, lowering the wintertime temperature. If the floor is off the ground, be sure to safely apply poison and underpin around the building

Doors should be placed as a convenience for you to do your chores and for your convenience in moving the goats in and out easily. Windows should be placed high enough that the goats will not break the panes by jumping up to them. Windows work best on the south and west sides, to get the most light and heat. Burlap, blankets or sheets can be placed over doors and windows to cut drafts.

A simple three-side structure can be made from leftover lumber to house your goats. The open side should be to the south for lighting and warmth. Hay, feed, and water receptacles should be placed high enough so that the goats can't get them dirty. If the containers are below the goats' backsides, they will be constantly soiled, walked in, jumped in, and played on and will be impossible to keep clean. You can easily hang the receptacles or put them up on legs. When possible, try to feed goats outside, especially in cold weather. Goats can get spoiled easily and will avoid their necessary fresh air and exercise if everything is brought to them.

If you have access to someone who can cut and weld metal, old bins (feeders) from chicken houses work well as shelters. The bins have to be cut in half, and a door cut into each half, and the leftover metal from the doors welded in place on the tops. The smaller bins are easy to move by rolling them to a new location. Don't mess with the larger bins if you don't have help.

Bucks' housing requirements are about the same, as long as they are strong. In any goat house, walls should be constructed of a material that is nontoxic. Goats will chew or taste most materials in the walls, so chose carefully. In the south, a simple structure with corrugated tin for walls will do. Northern climates demand warmer walls of wood with insulation.

When constructing any shelter, there is an added touch that should be included just for you — a shelf or wall cabinet. These items are handy enough to justify the time used to build them. They should be five to six feet high and three or four feet long — big enough to hold the feed, pans, and tools that you carry to the barn at chore time. Never leave tools and medicine on that shelf when you are

Lonnie Northern built Mandy this inexpensive shelter with a chair inside for his wife, Tawny.

gone, because you're bound to need them in another lot for another goat, and the goats will find a way to tear the items up, if given enough time.

Woven wire hay bunks can be made simply, with a rainproof cover. Take a leftover piece of wire and stretch it across a corner, about 2½ feet from the ground. Fasten the bottom into the original fence, cover with a piece of tin or wood, and you have an instant hay bunk. More elaborate keyhole hay boxes can be made from plywood, with covers to protect the hay from the weather. Just make sure you always paint it with sealer to keep your work from rotting.

Large plastic garbage containers on rollers make wonderful hay bunks. They are big enough to hold a bale of hay, and once you chain or strap the lid down, the goats can't soil the hay. Cut a hole in the front, large enough for the goat to get its head in. You can roll the containers to the hay, slide the bale into them, cut the twine, and roll them back. Tie or strap the container to the fence.

Never leave the strings from the hay with the goats. They can get tangled in them and even hang themselves. Once again, save the strings or wire. In the goat world, something always needs to be tied, or the string can be saved for the craftier of us to make collars, hanging hay feeders, ropes and tethers or leads.

Salt and mineral blocks should be in boxes, off the floor, in the goats' house, or in protected boxes outside. I hang my salt from poles or rafters inside the sheds. The little rectangular rabbit salt blocks are easy to drill a hole into and can be nailed to the wall

Soda should be offered in separate containers freely. Don't put too much out at a time as soda collects dust and particles that float in the air. If the goats miss a day of soda, don't panic, but do keep it out regularly. Some goats won't touch it, and others seem to need it. It works as an antacid, and the goat will know when he or she needs it.

The manure from several goats can come in quite handy for your garden and other areas. All goats are different, and feeding methods vary, but the following is an average of the composites of manure.

One 100-pound goat per year:	83 pounds solid	0.7% nitrogen
	43 pounds liquid	0.3% phosphate
		0.9% potash

There are many kinds of bedding and each one will change the composition of the manure. Many types of bedding have to be cleaned each day, and others, like sawdust or hay, are so absorbent they only need to be raked or changed, or have more added as needed.

A deep bedding pack is the easiest and most practical way to bed goats. Start with a clean floor, preferably dirt covered with lime, and cover the top with clean bedding about two times per week, or as needed, depending on the size of the area, and how much time the goats have to stay on it. The goats will pack this down as you pile it up. Urine and manure sift to the bottom, ferment and make heat for winter warmth. The bottom continues to ferment and rot all winter, creating more heat as it composts, getting ready for the garden in spring.

Bedding materials vary, but I believe in using what you have. Grass clippings from the yard, leaves, hay and straw are all good. When using the hay bedding for the garden, some of the leftover seeds are going to take root in spring and sprout, but it also means more green growth for any sparse pastures that may need seeding. If you pick up leaves from someplace else, be sure they have not been sprayed with anything that will hurt your goats.

If you pick up pine straw from the woods, it may have poison ivy or poison oak in it. This will not hurt your goats, but if you or a family member have allergies, you'll be in trouble.

Old bedding should be stored in a cool place and protected from the sun and rain. I have found it much easier to rake when I need the bedding, throw out cheaper hay, or go pick up someone else's leaves. Storing new bedding really does take a lot of room and begs mice, rats and snake to come spend the winter with you.

Frequently, I have spread the goats regular hay, strewn loosely, and what they don't eat, they'll pack. It's highly unlikely goats will eat the contaminated hay if they are otherwise fed well.

In many areas, you can sell the manure. I've always had too much use for it myself, but I have been able to give away a few barrels now and then. When you need it, just pull back the top layer of bedding and dig up the nice peat below. To see if there is a market in your area, run a short ad in local newspaper, or talk to someone at your feed store. Garden centers can be good buyers if you can provide enough. I trade a local greenhouse a bucket of nice clean compost for spring plants.

Only goats of the same size should be housed together, the exception being goats that have been together long enough to be used to the little ones, or does with kids at their sides.

One year I had a bully doe and a yearling pregnant doe in the same barn. Though they weren't mother and daughter, they had been together all the young ones' lives. The bully managed to cause the younger one to miscarry. So now I don't mix the goats that know each other if there is a bully. In fact, I sold that bully before she ever had her kids because I was so upset with her.

If you can't afford the time and materials for two shelters, build a partition in the existing one or use a fence across the middle to keep the little ones safe from the big ones. For practical purposes, you really need a separate pen and house for the younger ones that aren't being milked. A special place needs to be set aside for sick or new goats and kidding pens. A kidding box can be as simple as a 3 ¥ 3 foot box that separates the kids from the older goats. My babies usually end up in the house anyway.

Each state has different regulations for selling milk. Rules usually require concrete floors, drains, screens, windows, cooling systems and stainless steel coolers. Check with your county extension service for the regulations in your state before starting such housing.

For home use the only real requirement is not to milk on, or in the bedding area, though many people do with no ill effects. Of course, this implies that you know the goat is healthy, does not have mastitis, and you know that your management practices are of the kind that will produce a clean product. The milking area should be separate from the bedding area and screened

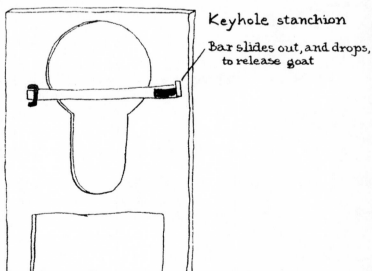

Keyhole stanchion

Bar slides out, and drops, to release goat

The keyhole stanchion is used for milking.

in from the flies, even if it's only on the other side of the same building. (I have only seen screens in two dairies, and never in a home operation.) My own are milked in an area separate from the bedding area, and sometimes the goats are left there with their kids to nurse at night.

The milking stand is ideal. It should be off the floor as much as you need for comfort and far enough for cleanliness. Another workable solution is the keyhole stanchion (see sketch).

If worse comes to worse, and no stanchion is available, you can use chains four to five feet apart, hooked 12 inches up from the floor, on a side of the building where the goats will not be bedded.

These last two methods result in the "squat and squirt" method, which puts me and my milk too close to the dirt for comfort. If a goat or a two-legged kid acts up, dirt can go everywhere. To escape some of these problems, get mosquito netting, cut it larger than your milk bowls, use clothespins to clip it onto your milk bowls and milk through it. This not only stops any unexpected debris from landing in the milk, but (lo and behold), it stops milk from splattering up on your glasses.

I have been visiting more goat farms and have noticed something that needs to be brought to the reader's attention. Far too many people are putting their goats far away. This may be fine if you are younger, or even if you do all your chores with a tractor or four-wheeler. If you do have access to this equipment it's nice. But your goats are too far away for you to see them and notice the early symptoms of disease. If you are handicapped, you can't make the trip. Consider your age and health when deciding where to put your sheds and lots. Mine are close, bordering my yard and drive, easy to access for a handicapped person, and in 20 years, not too far for me to get to easily. Unless you plan on losing a lot of goats or making a lot of trips to the fields, keep them close.

13

Cold Weather Care

Cold weather presents its own special problems. The colder your area, the bigger your problem, but there is a bright side: Winter helps to alleviate some problems, too.

When the temperature drops below 40 degrees and stays there, most of bacterial growth ceases. The parasite problem almost ends, and flies disappear. Both external and internal parasites cannot complete their cycles in cooler temperatures. Liver flukes are the exception; they will continue their cycles under 40 degrees. If you have standing water or a pond with snails, you will have liver flukes (another parasite covered in chapter 28).

Goats do not like the cold and they won't roam as much when temperatures drop below freezing. The goats stand close to their quarters, getting their needed exercise going from their shed to the hay bunk and water. Thus the goats won't tear up the fences like they do in the summer. With the disappearance of lush greenery, the capricious critters are less likely to try the fences and your patience. Less of your valuable time is spent on fence repair, and more is available for other neglected tasks.

With the fly season gone, many surgeries can be accomplished during the winter months. Most of the does will be pregnant during winter. Because of this and the cold, milk production will drop and lessen your chores. Those of us in the south have no such luck and pretty well live with summer problems all year around.

Goats adapt very well to cold weather as long as they are warm and dry and in a draft-free area. Since goats are susceptible to pneumonia, it is more important to worry about keeping them dry. This especially goes for bedding. If the top layer of bedding is dry, the heat from the lower area will keep the goats warm. This is of course, if you use the deep bedding pack, otherwise, other methods of keeping goats warm will need to be employed, such as heating built into the concrete, furnaces, or solar heating. Gas stoves and wood burning stoves are not recommended.

So much is being done with solar heating, that I would strongly encourage it for farmers in the north.

Bucks may need the backs of their front legs and their stomachs brushed frequently. Because of their strange and somewhat unsightly habits, ice crystal may form. My six-year-old granddaughter has been drying my bucks' legs for three years. She keeps telling him that he needs better potty training.

The goat house can be protected from drafts by using a layer of plastic around the outside. When using plastic, make sure all edges are covered. The goats will tear at any loose ends and rip the plastic off. The same goes for tarpaper. Tarpaper helps to draw the natural heat from the sun and is good for closing drafts, but does not hold up long. Feed sacks can also be used. Use them as insulation and as a draft-breaker. Extra care has to be taken with feed sacks, since the goats will try to eat the paper, so all rough edges must be stapled, covered, or trimmed

If you have the shelter too warm you may have condensation on inside walls, and this is moisture you do not need. The ideal temperature for goats' comfort and production is between 55 and 80 degrees, so cold weather is not an ideal situation.

Summer or winter, never have your shelters so airtight that ammonia has a chance to build up. Ammonia takes up a lot of oxygen space and causes the goats to breathe less oxygen deeply into their lungs, setting up prime conditions for the goats to catch pneumonia. Use lime or soda, or clean and ventilate to fix this problem.

Goats will drink more water in the winter, especially if the water is warm. This may mean carrying buckets twice a day if you don't have water lines to the lots. Electric waterers are extremely convenient and ideal for heating. However, because of the warmth, heated waterers are great places for bacteria to grow. Precautions need to be taken to keep them clean. Apple cider vinegar will help keep the bacteria down and is also believed to help does have more female offspring. Blue dicalcium phosphate crystals added to the water help the goats, and the crystals aid in keeping waterers clean. Check with your feed store to see what product is available in your area.

Water valves that fit on the side of your tubs or tanks are inexpensive, and if you can keep the lines from freezing, they are great for continuous water supply, summer and winter. Check with your feed store. Unless a water line breaks, my little red wagon is no longer used for carrying buckets of water.

Milk is 85 percent to 87 percent water, so the more water the goats drink, the more milk you can expect to receive. Snow is not a substitute for water, and though goats will eat it, it does not take the place of water. In the south the snow will melt quickly and leave puddles in every footstep. Goats will not drink this. But if the melted snow doesn't drain quickly, you must push it out, because nights still get cool, and goats must not go to bed on wet muddy feet.

Your goats will not want to go out to eat in subzero temperatures, especially if the wind is blowing. So on bitterly cold, windy and wet days, you'll have to make provisions inside the shelter. In the daytime, try to keep feeding outside to force the animals out for fresh air and exercise. This may mean shoveling a path for them to place their feet, but it is well worth the effort to get them out. If you live in a bitterly cold area and the goats will not stay out in the cold long enough to eat their rations of hay, try haying them inside but enticing them outside with the grain. Even if they only run out 25 feet for ten minutes and hurry back, it will do them good. Erecting a wind break around the hay bunk will help to keep them out longer.

Hoof trimming should not be neglected in winter months. The goats are not moving around as much, but their hooves are still growing. This can cause some real problems, especially on a warm bedding pack where bacteria can grow. Instead of playing outside all day, goats will be spending most of their time on a bedding pack. This is the biggest drawback to a bedding pack because it does not chip the hooves and will actually allow bacteria to grow faster because of the heat.

It's hard to put on gloves, trudge through the snow and trim hooves, but it has to be done. To make this chore easier, be sure to trim all hooves just before you expect the coldest weather. Then watch for the warmer days and trim. By taking advantage of what few warm afternoons you may have, you might be lucky enough to get through an entire winter without having to trim hooves with cold fingers.

Electricity to the barn is helpful because you can add light to help keep the goats warm and take a hair dryer with you to help keep you warm.

In drastic cases, bring your goats in for the important checking, trimming and other hand-to-goat chores. Most of your does are pregnant at this time, and this is no time to neglect their hooves, since they are putting more weight on their feet.

Most of the grass and summer browse will be gone in winter, so you will have to feed extra forage or hay. Fiber is the source of heat for a goat, so it should be available at all times.

There are two formulas on how much hay to feed. One: Feed as much as the goats can consume in one hour, twice a day. It is assumed that the normal goat only grazes or browses for two hours a day, spending the rest of their time playing, resting and chewing their cud. Since all goats are different, I don't always find that solution to be sufficient. Two: Feed 10 percent of the goats' total weight once a day or 5 percent of the total weight twice a day. This presumes that you know the weight of the goats and the weight of your hay. A normal 100 pound goat should have 10 pounds of hay per day. If you had 80 pound bales, you would feed one to eight goats. I try to total the weight of my goats and feed 10 percent, always stretching my numbers to the high side so that I won't short the goats.

To be on the safe side, check to see how much hay is left at evening chores time. The goats should have hay, free choice, all the time. They will not eat all night, so if they still have a little left at evening chores, you will know they are getting enough.

Rake up all leftover hay and use for bedding or feed to a cow, or put it on the garden.

In warmer climates, I have found it possible to feed 5 percent of the body weight of hay in the morning, and the goats will browse for an hour or so in the afternoon. All goats are different, so keep an eye on them. If they lose weight, feed more. They should not gain too much in the winter, but they should hold what they have. Pregnant does will gain and that aspect has to be taken into consideration.

Feeding grain is not necessary during winter, unless you do not have good quality hay. Grain is fed for reasons other than the cold, such as pregnancy, and for bucks used for breeding. Dry does, nonbreeding bucks and wethers do not need added grain if they have good forage.

This is one area where I do not save my money and take the advice I learned from all these years of research. My goats get daily grain, no matter what. I may not feed the best quality of grain, or as much, and I may miss a day, but I feed grain year-round. This keeps me and the goats closer, keeps them coming when I call, and frankly, I like them being dependent on me. It helps keep me on my toes.

Since my handicap, I have taught my goats, and all my critters, to come to the car horn, because half the time I cannot unload the feed and I feed out of the car.

Depending on your area, predators can be a problem. When ice and snow cover the ground it's harder for wolves and coyotes and cougars to find food. And they may come looking for your goats. Keeping a dog may be a solution to keeping predators from your goats, but then you may have to protect your goats from your dog. I keep electric fence on the outside of the areas where these wild hunters might want to enter your pens. However, many breeds of dogs can be raised with the goats and grow to protect the goats, even from people.

I walked into an unused shed one summer day and came face to face with a coyote. We both stopped dead in our tracks. I am not afraid of God's critters, but I knew I was blocking its only way out, so I slowly backed out of its way and whispered "Get out of here!" It shot past me in such a flash. I would not have known what he was, if I hadn't seen him standing still. Keep in mind predators may not be just a winter problem.

Unfortunately, another winter problem is man himself during hunting season. When deer hunters take to the hills with bow and arrow in the fall, I don't panic. With bows, they have to get close enough to my goats to see that they aren't deer. But in midwinter, when hunters head out with guns and, in some cases, dogs, I worry. I bring the goats closer to the house, especially the bigger, redder goats that look so much like a deer anyway. If you're not sure that your goats are in danger, find a spot 100 yards away and observe them as a deer hunter would. If they look like deer to you, they are going to be fair game for a hunter.

In areas where high-powered rifles are legal for deer hunting, it is possible for a hunter to mistake your animals and shoot them as far away as 400 to 600 hundred yards. Keep the hunting seasons in mind when grazing goats in the winter. Most hunters are considerate and will try to avoid populated areas.

Signs on the edges of your property stating that goats are on the premises will help, and advising would-be hunters of their presence will help, should they stop and ask your permission. I know a lot of deer hunters, and many are my friends.

Wintertime brings our holidays, and we travel more. Take precautions, in case you get snowed in, away from home, to have someone to check on your animals. Leave extra hay out for the goats, but not grain. Grain will be consumed immediately and is a waste. Extra water will freeze, so someone needs to help.

Your equipment will take a bigger beating, with the temperature changes. Condensation will cause many materials to rust, especially in the seams. If the equipment will not be in a heated area, take care that it is dried and placed so that it won't trap moisture.

You are your most valuable asset. You have to take care of the goats, so you, too, are important. You cannot do your goats justice if you are not warm enough to stay out and take care of them. Take the necessary precautions against catching cold. If you don't choose to wear your gloves, a least keep them with you in case you need them.

Take time to dress warmly so you don't get cold before your chores are finished. I have misjudged wind chill many times and gone out without enough clothes and had to make a second trip. When you get cold, you either have to make the extra trip back to the house to get warm, or you rush your chores and may neglect some to get out of the cold.

14

Collars and Fencing

Nylon rope makes ideal collars, looks good, and is durable. When using nylon rope, you may find it hard to keep it from unraveling. I tie the ends and burn them just enough to get them to melt together to stop the knots from pulling loose, and the ends from becoming frayed.

Chains, both plastic and metal, are most common. Plastic chains are light-weight, colorful, easily adjusted and wear well, though there're not as strong as may be needed for a harder-to-handle goat. For your goats to be where you want them, when you want them, you must be able to handle them at all times. The handling process starts when they are just born. Their mother will teach them within hours to run from you or to hide. Mine get collars immediately. Sometimes it's just yarn to mark the difference between twins or goats that look alike, but nevertheless, they get a collar. All goats need to be trained to lead and taught to stand tied. At one time or another, the goat will have to be restrained for worming, hoof trimming and other handling procedures. The goats are much less a nuisance if they can be caught when needed and led where you want them to be.

A goat will adjust to a collar as if it were adorned with fine jewels. Care should be taken when choosing a collar. It should be as strong as the goat pulling against it. Collars may be made of cloth, chains, nylon, elastic, plastic, and leather. If a collar is to be used for simple leading and showing, its purpose is lightweight and decorative. On the other hand, if the collar is to hold a large animal for trim-ming, shaving or medicine, its purpose is heavy duty. All collars should be secure. They need to be loose enough for a comfortable fit of two or three fingers between goat and collar and to allow room for the goat to grow, but not loose enough to slip over the animal's head.

Collars need to be safe with no broken loops or loose buckles to damage the throat. All collars need to be checked for wear and tear periodically and replaced if necessary. It is better to have an animal temporarily collarless than to have it seriously hurt by a poor-fitting one. Most collars will eventually leave some kind of mark on the animals, some not as noticeable as others, so if you plan on show-ing, you might not want to leave the collar on permanently. However, the collar does cover its own mark. The leather collar used for dogs will work, although leather wears off more hair and provides room for fleas and ticks to hide. It needs to be cared for periodically to prevent wear and cracking from the weather.

Metal chains also look good, can be adjusted and are strong. However, metal chains often have a loose loop that can get caught in fences and hold the goat cap-tive. Check all metal chain collars carefully.

Cloth collars are handy in a pinch and can be made from an old rag. How-ever, they hold moisture, rot easily, get dirty, and harbor fleas and ticks. Cloth is not durable and should only be used temporarily. I tie a pretty scarf for pictures and parades, and then take it off.

Collars can be braided, beaded, crocheted, or macraméed from string, jute, or twine with little trouble and expense, so there is no reason for any animal not hav-ing some kind of restraint, unless the owner plain doesn't want it.

Collars should be started at birth and used, not only for ease in handling, but for marking the new kids. I have gone to all-nylon collars. They come in all sizes, and colors, and are durable. I've only had one that actually fell apart; since it came with another goat, I have no idea how old it was when I got it and the goat. Nylon collars can be expensive, but I just started buying one at a time and now I have them all over the place.

People who let their goats roam timber and briars should pull collars off, as the goats can get caught and hurt themselves. If you're not there all the time, it's good not to leave permanent collars on the goats in case the get caught in a fence, or on each others' horns.

When training a youngster to lead, you have little troubles. The kid is small and soon learns to go with a tug. It is usually quite willing to go with you anyway. If you're like me and can't bend easily, a long handle with a snap that can be hooked to the collar can be used to train kids and in fact it can be used later to handle bigger goats that may be bullies. This long handle with a snap can also be used to move bucks around with out having them rub their scent all over you.

Never pick up or pull a goat by its horns or ears, unless you have a buck that is so dangerous that this is the only way to handle it. The ears have thin blood ves-sels and are easily broken, and the goats can feel you pulling their horns. It hurts, and they hate it.

Older animals will require more time, patience, and strength to train to a collar, but it should be done. A goat can be stubborn and refuse to be led. It will plant all four feet, brace its body, and not budge. It will fake death, throwing itself on its side and kicking its legs. It will fall over to keep from going where it doesn't want to be led, even when it doesn't know where you are taking it. The goat will calmly lie down and chew its cuds, waiting for you to give up. Goats are tricky and will pretend to go along until you are relaxed, and then bolt in another direction, either dragging you or the lead that they've managed to rip from your hands.

Often you will find it easy to entice the goat with a favorite branch or a bowl of grain until it has learned to lead.

No matter how well the animal has been taught, it has a mind of its own and will try to go its own way from time to time. Once you give it a tug, and remind it that you are still there, it will oblige if it has been handled properly.

All goats should be taught to lead with their collars, but they should also be taught to be restrained with a lead rope. The only requirement for a lead is that it be strong enough to fit your purpose.

Goats should not be tethered for a long time. Tethering is dangerous and restricts the goats' natural instinct to browse, forcing them to eat many things in their circle that might not be good for them. It is easy for goats to get their rope caught between their toes, twist it around their legs, and seriously injure themselves. Tethering prevents the goat from defending itself against any stray dogs and can result in injury or death. Goats are so active and agile that they can manage to get the rope around their necks and strangle themselves easily.

If you must tether, the lead should be long enough to provide the goat with plenty of area to choose to eat. Make sure there is nothing to tangle the rope. Tether the goat where it can get shelter from the rain and the summer sun. Provide water and tie or stake the bucket so that the goat can't knock it over, drag it over with the rope, or drop manure into it. Check the area carefully for poisonous weeds before putting the goat in it. Never leave the goat alone when tethered, and stay close enough to check on it often.

I don't sell a lot of goats, but when I do, I always ask why the prospective owner wants a goat. When someone informs me that he wants to tie it up to clear some weeds, I don't have anything to sell.

Fencing

Goats may be cute, but they are livestock. Unless you live in a remote area where they can be safe without control, there is one definite rule: Keep them behind the fences.

Fencing will pose one of the largest problems in goat keeping and one of the largest investments. Goats don't want to be fenced away from people. And they are even surer that they are supposed to be free. When they have found their freedom, they would prefer to keep it. They can lead a merry chase for hours, while only you suffer from the excitement, exercise, and good sport.

Do not put goats of different sizes together, and, without some improvising, don't put smaller goats where you have had the larger ones. The big goats will stick their heads through the fences and stretch the wire. Smaller goats just walk through the stretched spots.

This is the problem that sent me looking for an electric fence box and ultimately caused the handicap I've mentioned.

I had a lot across the state highway that was set aside specifically for dry does and does I didn't want to breed. For reasons I've since forgotten, I had to move some weaned goats to that lot, which hadn't been used for a while. They didn't like being away from us and continually would get out.

On a crisp day in December, my girls called me to come get goats. The three of us ran them up and down the fencerow, trying to prevent them from getting into the highway and trying to catch them at the same time. (I should have taken them to the house.) I got tired of it and when the last one ran by me for what seemed the twentieth time, I took a dive and caught it by the back foot. I knew something had happened in my back, but I had caught the goat, which was trying desperately to run back across the road. My girls said they had heard a thud and were hovering about me. I begged them to "Just take the goat!"

When I got up, I didn't feel much different. But by that evening I was hurting and within two months I was down. I had ruptured a disc, which at that time the doctors found I had inherited my father's degenerated disc disease. The doctors advised surgery, but I turned it down and spent three months in bed. Thankfully it was winter. When I could get up, I had to learn to crawl and then walk, all over again. The entire time, I was asked by doctors and therapists how old I was, and what a woman my age was doing chasing goats. I had not been, and am not yet, old. I honestly figured this was God's way of slowing me down.

Once I was up and slowly moving, the electric fences went up. Fences are supposed to keep goats in and dogs out. It's also nice if the fence discourages the stray hunter and uninvited children.

Chain link galvanized fences with custom gates are quite nice, but many of us can only dream about them.

Board fences work well, especially when erected between bucks and does, but wood rots. It needs some kind of preservative and, as the goats will taste the fence, any preservative has to be non-toxic.

Old bed springs and pallets make good fences for goats, so I use them inside sheds and on the backs of lots, where they aren't too unsightly. You can call trucking companies, grocers and recyclers to find used pallets. When using pallets, be sure you stand them on end, with the boards going up and down, because the goats can hook their toes in horizontal boards and climb out.

Fences for mature goats should be at least three and one half to four feet high and higher for bucks. Younger kids only need three-foot fences. The electric fence is a necessity but takes an initial cash outlay that you may not have. Frequently one strand of wire, 18 inches off the ground, will do. But most goats are smart enough to figure out how to jump, and kids will crawl under. Goats with horns will hook onto the wire and pull it out.

I have seen an antennae device for goats to be used with electric fences. A piece of wire is hooked to the collars, extending up for smaller goats and down for the larger ones. When the goats try to clear the fence, the wire connects with the electric fence and they back off quickly. The problem with this is that in the goats' normal activities, they bed down, mill around, and loosen the wires, so it never paid for me to do it.

The electric fence should be built with three wires. The bottom one should be 10 to 12 inches from the ground to prevent the goats from crawling under, the second 20 to 24 inches from the ground, and the third 34 to 36 inches from the ground. You may even want to space the third one on the top, to discourage jumping on the fence. When you run the wire, start at the top strand and go around the lot until you get back to the beginning. Without cutting the wire, run down to the bottom strand and then all the way back around. This gives you one complete circuit when the fence is hooked to the electric charger. Cut the wire and run the middle strand all the way around, not hooking it to top or bottom. It will act as a ground for any goat trying to go under it when it touches the bottom and any goat trying to go over it when it touches the top.

Electric chargers come in all sorts of voltages; I try to buy the one guaranteed for 10 miles. Electric, battery charged and solar varieties are available. When adding up your miles, do not count your middle wire as it is not technically hooked to the charger.

Wire also comes in several sizes, and some even looks like string. My best experience has been with a heavier gauge wire that won't break easily or blow out of place easily in a storm, and a charger that is guaranteed to shock through wet grass.

Goats and horses seem to be able to sense when the electricity is off and use it to their advantage. Once cows and pigs have been trained to stay away from an electric fence, you can leave a dead wire up.

For goats, all electric wire needs something behind it. If a goat sees just one strand of wire between it and the world, the goat will jump it or break it. For those of you who just can't stand the idea of your little darlings getting shocked, I need to tell you three things: (1) I've been shocked and though it's not pleasant, it isn't a permanent injury. (2) Goats are a little smarter than I am, they only get shocked once, and they don't forget where the fence is. (3) God protects the little babies. None of my four-legged babies, or my two legged babies that aren't old enough to understand, have been shocked.

Woven wire is highly recommended. The best is called range wire, which graduates from small holes at the bottom to larger at the top. It's a bit flimsy but easy to put up, take down and put up again. The 2 x 4 wire that you would think about using for kids won't hold up for adults, and so if you use it, keep it for the kids. A lot of people will use a strand or two of barbed wire at the top and/or bottom of the fence, but I am against it. Goats have a very high level of pain tolerance, and should they want to get on the other side, barbed wire will only cut them, it won't stop them. It is also dangerous to people.

If there's a loose spot, a goat will find it. If there is a little hole, a goat will stretch it. Foliage, trees, gardens, or your neighbors' roses on the other side will give the goat a good enough reason to go looking for a way to get through or over

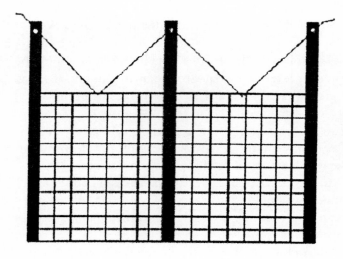

Rope or wire strung from post to wire to post to pull up a saggy fence.

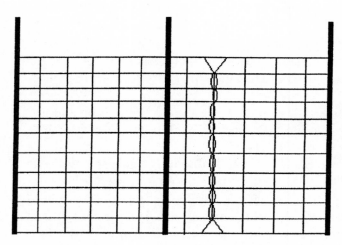

Using pliers or screwdriver, twist two rows together to tighten.

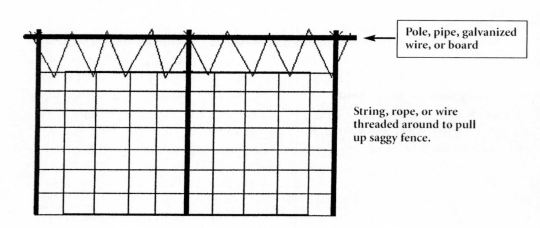

Pole, pipe, galvanized wire, or board

String, rope, or wire threaded around to pull up saggy fence.

the fence. Very young kids, left at their mothers' side, will walk right through ordinary woven wire, so it should be reinforced. Older kids will push till they have stretched the wire enough to go through; then the older goats will stretch it even farther.

That is one of the reasons I have stressed having different lots for different size goats.

Woven wire can be picked up at auctions and sales, and farmers will often give away used wire, if you'll take it out of the field. When at all possible, a second strand of woven wire should be hung above the bottom strand. For some reason, when the goat looks up and sees wire, it doesn't seem to want to check it out.

The woven wire that has larger squares at the top (commonly called "hog wire") should be turned upside-down for adult goats and sheep. This allows the goats to get down on their knees and eat the grass on the other side, helping you to keep the fencerows cleared on the outside.

Is the grass greener on the other side of the fence? No. The goats are smart. They have not defecated, played, laid or urinated on the other side. It's cleaner and maybe during certain times of the year, better for them.

Sixteen-foot cattle panels are easy to put up, easy to move and costly. I have been buying one or two a month for quite a while, for between $18 and $22 each. Eventually, I will not need electric, or fence repair, as these panels can last 30 or 40 years. They are made of a heavy gauge galvanized metal and will hold any of the goats, even the kids, because the bottoms have smaller holes. This is a goal that I would like to see everyone work toward. Predators can not come in, man cannot jump over, children will climb but not jump down and goats are contained. Counting the T posts, you're going to spend a little over $1 a foot. If I'd started this in the beginning, I would have it all done by now.

Keeping the opposite side of the fence trimmed of foliage will help to remove temptation. If you live in an area where the county or state sprays for weeds, call your highway department and ask the staff not to spray your property. Put up signs to remind workers, since many insecticides are poisonous to goats.

Fences should be tight because the weight of a large goat rubbing and scratching on them will easily drag them down, and the goat simply falls over it. Tightening existing fences can be done two ways. If a fence's condition isn't too bad, you can take a pair of pliers and bend the wire in several places down the row until you have taken up the slack. I prefer a short screwdriver. When the fence is really sagging, add a post. Another good resort is to tie the wire up with rope or wire. I've even gone to town after a storm and picked up the discarded power lines for this job.

Nail one end of your row to the top post, then thread the rope through the woven wire in the middle, and extend it on to the next post. Pull the rope tight to tighten the fence and pull up any tops that are bowed. Nail the rope securely, or in case of metal posts wrap it (check sketches).

I have strung rope, wire, twine and cable around entire lots to revive old

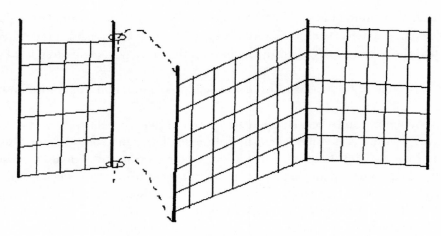

Loose pole sets in loops to close gate.

fences or strengthen poorly constructed ones. If you have access to lumber, old rebar or galvanized pipe, these things can be tied to your posts and your fence wired up to them.

A gate is a convenience to the goatkeeper and a challenge to the goat. Since you go through it the goats will think they should be able to go through it also. They are very clever and will figure out most simple latches. Use latches with safety catches, and install the latches on the outside of the gate, not on the goats' side. Old-fashioned bars that slide back and forth are the hardest for a goat to manage. However, the simple wire gate is easy and goat-proof (see sketch). A pole is wired or woven into the loose end of the fence and fits into wire loops at the top and bottom of the opposite, stationary end of the fence, when it is closed. To open it, you raise the top wire and pull the pole from the bottom wire. When using this gate make sure it is tightly connected, because smaller goats will squeeze through the gap. Clip loose pieces of wire on all fences and gates to prevent injuries to the goats and save wear and tear on your clothes. (Wire cutters go with me everywhere.) Pallets also make good gates and can be easily opened and closed by shifting them, and the goat can't.

Diagonal crossbars used in the corners to brace fences should be put on the outside. Goats use these corner braces as steps to go up and over the fence. If the braces are already there, cover them with a piece of wire to prevent the goats from using them to jump out.

Goats are easily trained, and once they realize they are contained, half the battle is over. However, their normal curiosity will accidentally lead them to weak spots, low spots, or holes. Check fences often for needed repairs. Again, electric fences keep this problem under control as well.

If you have a goat that keeps right on jumping the fences, try tying it to an object large enough to slow it down but light enough that it can drag it around. Make sure the rope you use is not long enough to allow the goat to jump and hang itself. I once hooked a large dishpan to the goat by a 2½-foot rope and stopped a consistent jumper.

When you consider fencing an area, make use of the natural fencing available. Creeks, cliffs, ponds, hedges, shrubbery, and brush piles often are situated in such a manner that if they don't provide a natural border, they will provide natural posts for your fence.

No matter how difficult it seems, the animal must be contained for its own safety, your nerves, your neighbors' good will, and a preventive to an injury like mine.

There are a couple of things you need to know about fences. If you are renting, you will need to use extra T posts, because they cannot be planted down past the T. Once that T is buried, it is considered permanent and belongs to your landlord. Keep the posts less deep, so you can grab them up and move them, if you have to move. If you own your land, you can completely bury the T, making it permanent. Keep in mind that when you own your property, the half of the fence to your right is your duty to take care of. The other stretch is your neighbor's responsibility.

There are a couple of setbacks to these laws of the land. If you or your neighbor put up a fence that is private, chain link, or otherwise expensive and raises the property value, it is the responsibility of the owner to repair.

Plus, you may have a neighbor like one of mine. The right hand side of his fence, (my left) is in poor repair, but he has no animals. When it was put to him that it was his responsibility to fix that portion of the fence, he was quite rude and said he would take it down, because he didn't need it anyway. Of course, I couldn't have that, so in this case, I have to take care of the entire fence row. When my animals do get onto his meadow, I really don't get in too big of a hurry to retrieve them. Nor does he complain.

Lots, pens and pastures

Exercise is a necessity for the goat's health and production. Every goatkeeper has a different way of providing exercise. Basically, there are three methods: The dry lot, the pasture, and the mixture of both.

Each mature goat needs a least 25 square feet for exercise, so figuring the size of your pens depends on how many goats you have.

"Dry lot" is a method by which your goats are penned in a small area with no vegetation, and hay and other forage are carried to them. Some of these lots are paved with concrete to aid in cleaning and to prevent worm infestation. Dry lots are convenient and use less fencing and have fewer worming problems, but cost more in feed and hay. Frequently goats that are kept in dry lot areas can be taken to a grazing area for a few hours a day, cutting down somewhat on the cost of feeding hay, but causing more work in transferring goats.

Pastures are more natural, more practical, and cut feed costs to about nothing over half the year. You can put six to eight goats on one well-seeded acre for forage. "Well seeded" for goats does not necessarily mean that prime legumes must be planted. Goats will thrive better on a variety of vegetation that includes weeds, brush, briars and several grasses and legumes. The left-over clippings from your garden, the neighbors' pruning (goatkeepers don't need to prune) and hay are just substitutes and/or treats for the browse goats really like. An acre is 43,560 square feet, so each goat would require 5,445 square feet for grazing. This is an area approximately 55 feet by 100 feet for a permanent pasture. Goats can pick up more worms in a pasture, so lots should be rotated every 10 to 14 days to help stop the worm cycle and allow for the vegetation to recover. This time can be extended, depending on the type of forage you have.

You can cut the lot in half, 22 feet by 50 feet per goat, providing you move the goats as needed. I don't measure lots or count the number of goats on them anymore. I watch the lots and move the goats as needed. If you supplement grain and hay, more goats can be put to the acre, but this tends to be more costly. At first this rotation may cause new goats some stress, but once they get used to it, they almost change lots by themselves.

Drainage should be provided to protect the goats' feet. I don't mean the babbling brook that runs through the pond you painstakingly made. I mean the puddles and mud holes we get from the wear and tear of weather.

When combining both methods of pasturing, most people feed the goats a good ration of hay in the morning and turn the goats out on pasture after the morning moisture has dried. The goats come back in the evening for chores and are kept on dry lot overnight. This method helps to alleviate the worm infestation on dewy pastures, provides the keeper with an extra chance to check them out, and in the hot, humid South, it is especially advisable for summer.

Wherever you put your goats out, all the trash should be removed. Lovely creatures that they are, their natural curiosity will lead them through, on, over, and even under most obstacles. Clear the area. If you have large rocks, the goats would love to jump on them, and they are good for keeping their hooves trim. Sturdy boxes and stumps are good fun when they run, jump, and play. Do keep the playthings at least six feet away from the fences.

Lots, pens, and pastures should be easily accessible to the goats' house, and to you, but out of the way of traffic, neighbors, and other fields. If you constantly go through the goat lot to attend other chores, you'll get tired of opening and closing gates, and the goats will outsmart you, getting out. A word of caution: When kids are small, we seem to think of any reason to pick them up. They should be led through the gates, not lifted over the fences. You don't want to teach them that fences are made to go over.

All lots should have sun protection. You can provide shade with a simple tarp to build a roof-type awning on poles. Planning the lots around trees is ideal, even if it means making an aisle to get them there.

Any pastures for the bucks should be down wind from the house and your neighbors, if at all possible. It wouldn't hurt to have one extra lot between the bucks and does. Should one or the other get out during breeding season, they would still have an extra fence to cross in order to mate. And, for the record, this has not worked for me. These animals can be pretty prolific and seem to find a way to one another.

When goats are restricted to dry lots, consider using your garden, or the neighbor's garden, for a winter goat pen. This gives the regular lots a chance to rest, and the goats will help clean up leftover vegetation in the garden. They will also fertilize the soil, and their hooves will help keep the ground soft and workable. I try to place my does main shed adjacent to the garden so they can be switched over during the winter when I have to feed more hay, with no change in the layout of fences. This also aids in mulching.

Another purpose gained in wintering the goats on the garden is that after they have spent a couple of months on that lot, they have eaten everything, soiled everything and lost interest in that spot. When they are taken off that spot and my vegetables are growing, they don't want back in that lot.

In the South we sometimes garden year-round and I found that goats can't stay on one spot from October to February because of worm infestation. I made two gardens and can rotate crops easier, as well.

One of my neighbors asked for my goats to clear her garden one fall, and I was a little concerned about the grapevines on the western border. She told me those grapes had never produced anything but leaves and she didn't care what happened.

She called me the next year and asked me to come see her new garden. Of course, it was beautiful, but the grapes were loaded with fruit. We could only guess that the vines needed a good pruning from time to time. She also told me that her broccoli had grown back, and the rest of her greens had thrived all through the winter.

In December I lock every one of my goats in the yard. They do a good job of pruning all the bushes and plants, and things grow better when spring arrives.

15

Feeding

I am well aware of the static I will receive from experienced goat breeders and qualified vets and breeders who read this chapter. This book is being written for the beginner and the small herd owner who is feeding a few goats for simple home production. I've not written it to make a social impression on fanciers or hobbyists. There has been a lot more improvement and knowledge in nutrients related to milk production, fertility and reproduction.

I am not deliberately ignoring that research, nor do I expect you to ignore it; instead, I am finding it impractical to use for home-based goats.

Goats can be fed extremely high quantities of high quality feed and attain the same fast gains that swine and cattle breeders strive to attain. A goat can reach 200 to 300 pounds in 18 months to two years if chemically reared. This is costly and impractical and I feel that it defeats the actual efficiency of the goats' purpose. I'm not sure about the flavor of these fast-grown goats, but since I try to avoid chemicals it was my decision not to try it.

There is no other area of goat care and maintenance that is as controversial as nutrition methods of feeding. During my research I have not found two authorities who agree with each other, let alone with me.

After much soul searching as to which method I should use I decided to listen to my goats. Were they contented? Were they gaining enough weight? Did my mature goats hold their weight? Were my newborn kids healthy? Did my goats' milk production suit my standards? When I could answer yes to all my own questions I had to ask why I was concerned. Worrying about something that is not a problem can cause too much trouble with the goatkeeper, not to speak of the goat.

If it's bred, carries babies and gives birth, the goat is going to give milk. By sticking to the basics you can maintain good health, even if you don't achieve top production. A good goat will produce, given the basics. Overfeeding will not achieve higher milk production if the doe doesn't have it in her to produce more. When working out your feed program, try to maintain good health and good weight gains, and milk production will come automatically, according to each doe's capabilities.

Another entire book has been written on the nutrients needed for a goat's good health and production. My purpose is not to analyze the food value of each grass and grain but more to show you that it doesn't have to be rocket science. And actually, someone else has done the rocket science. Just read your labels use your head, and watch your goats.

A goat's largest dietary need is roughage. If the goat is allowed to browse freely, there will be a large savings in hay and grain, and the goat will choose the plants for nutrition it needs if they are available. Goats browse as opposed to graze. Horses and cows graze along a path, eating as they go. Goats and deer browse, meaning that they nibble here and there, not staying with one grass or weeds too long. Goats like a variety in their diet, and for good cause. They need that variety for a balance in their vitamins, minerals, and proteins. If denied the activity of browsing, a goat will try to escape the pen to attain a balanced diet. Hay frequently can stop this, but we have to know what kind of hay we are buying.

When browsing, goats will pick the most tender leaves and shoots, leaving the more mature grasses and weeds to eat when they have no other choice. Goats should not be put on pasture until the grasses are three to four inches high, as they will eat too close to the ground and kill off many new plants, thus retarding the growth of the pasture.

For ideal growth, pastures should be a mixture of grasses and legumes. Without the variety, there will be a deficiency in the diet. The lists of what goats will and should eat are endless, but keep variety in mind.

With a small herd of goats for your own use, it's impractical to spend the money having the foliage on your pasture checked for nutrition value. However, if you feel it is necessary, you may contact your county extension agent to find out how to have your forage analyzed. I have not done this since I supplement hay and feed.

It is a good idea to provide good hay in a bunk in the barn or in a weather-proof rack outside while pasturing the goats. Don't be surprised if your goats turn their noses up at the hay and proceed on to the pasture. Many goats won't eat even the quality hay if they have freedom to browse, but hay should be there so they don't rush out too hungry.

Providing pasture for the goats can usually eliminate the added cost of extra hay and grain. Young kids, dry does, and nonbreeding bucks can do well on pasture alone. As long as they maintain good growth and health, feed is not necessary. I really go against my own advice here, but that's just me.

Extra minerals may be necessary, as the pastures may be deficient. Pastures may need to be limed, fertilized (with natural manure) or reseeded every few years to maintain healthy growth of the grasses and shrubs. Supplying a mineral block is not really a waste because goats won't use it if they don't need it.

A portable hay bunk may be used to reseed, without too much extra work or cost on your part. This bunk can be on wheels or skids and should have a protective top. Hay that is wasted by the goats still has some seeds in it that will grow again. By moving or towing the hay bunk to a new area every time the hay piles up, you can let the goats seed the area with their waste. Be sure not to leave the bunk in one place too long or the wasted hay will mulch, retarding new growth.

Protein is the goat's most needed nutrient and is in the variety of forages, such as alfalfa, lespedeza, brome grass, and timothy. These are all good sources of protein, as well as orchard grass, clover, Sudan grasses and millet. Soybeans and peanuts are also high in protein. One grass alone will not be a complete balance of nutrients. Southerners have it made in that department because the honeysuckle, blackberries and kudzu that grows freely are some of the greatest protein for goats. And the dreaded privet hedge will keep a goat happy and healthy for as long as it can eat it.

Goats have a natural instinct that tells them what they should and should not eat. Given free choice of pasture, they will ignore the poisonous plants and those that have little nutritional value. Only extremely hungry goats, or ones deprived of fresh forage, will eat enough of a poisonous plant to hurt themselves.

Although pasture grazing, tree trimming, and garden cuttings are good feed for a goat's diet, many people consider this fresh forage an extra or a treat in the goat's diet and still feed full amounts of hay and grain. Watch your goats to gauge for yourself how much extra hay and grain they need, and leave the experts to spend all their money on their own goats.

Cabbage, turnips, and other greens, may cause an off flavor in the milk and should only be fed after milking seasons.

For practical purposes, we can assume that a good pasture, with a variety of grasses, will supplement most of the hay and grain, thereby saving on the cost of feed. Buying hay can be a big investment and a real challenge as you have to try to get good quality hay for the amount of money you spend. Few of us are experts at recognizing quality hay.

The first rule is to ask someone else where he gets his hay. Someone who has horses is good. If it's good enough for them, it will be great for you. Then, check the hay. It should be a mixture of grasses and be leafy, and have some green color to it, even dried. Stemmed hay will be eaten, but the coarser stems will be wasted. Early hay cuttings are higher in protein and retain color better than later cutting, and also may be more expensive. Learn to watch the hay and how the goats eat it to be able to tell the difference between good and mediocre. This is important because the lack of green color in the hay may mean a lack of carotene, which can cause kids to be born weak or dead. Carotene is a source of vitamin A. Protein is the nutrient that is turned into energy and body heat. When you're not sure of the quality of the hay, I would advise feeding a higher protein grain.

No matter how good the grain, hay is still a necessity. Forage must be consumed to keep all four stomachs operating smoothly. (This is assuming that the goat is not getting enough forage from pasturing.)

A beautiful example of a Nubian doe, with a beautiful hay feeder.

Since hay is such a large investment, make sure none is wasted. Leftover hay can be retrieved and used for several purposes besides adding seeds to a few bare spots. The hay left by goats will be eaten by horses, cows, and chickens. It can be used for bedding for about any animal and put on the garden for mulch. You can apply it around fence rows to retard weed growth or add it to the compost pile.

Moldy hay is a waste of money. Goats deliberately won't eat it because it will make them sick. Don't use moldy hay for bedding for your goats as they clean themselves constantly and may accidentally ingest it.

Goats will eat silage, and corn silage is especially high in protein. Silage takes a great deal of storage space and does not keep well once removed from storage, therefore it is not practical for the small farm. If you know a farmer who is willing to sell or trade, silage is much cheaper than hay, and he may let you have access to the silo on a day-to-day basis. Of course, whether your health will allow you to get it, and if you have the time, would to be deciding factors. Silage is more common in the South, where it is not going to get frozen as easily as it does in the North. When feeding a good-quality high protein hay to healthy nonproducing animals, you shouldn't have to add grain to their diet. Once again, watch your goats. Let them tell you if they need something besides hay.

Depending on where you live, hay can cost anywhere from $1 a bale to $5 a bale, and I've seen some alfalfa more expensive. Figure the cost of your hay, the size of the goat, and the size of the bale, and you'll know what a daily cost is in hay. For instance a $3 bale of 90 pounds of hay will feed 100 pounds of goat nine days, which would be a little over 30 cents a goat. If that goat gives 1 gallon of milk a day, it is going to cost you a little over 30 cents for your milk, just in hay.

Formula: Pounds of hay divided by cost of hay times 10 plus
             Pounds of goat divided by 10, divide by pounds of goats
             Total equals cost of milk in hay.

Depending on your area, buying hay can be another chore. In agricultural areas of the Corn Belt, hay is easy to find, affordable, and generally of good quality. You can often pick up a winters' supply at once, without killing the paycheck.

In other areas, depending on drought, hay may not be so easy to get. Often, advertised hay will be nothing more than a straw. Don't be shy about examining the hay. Pick a bale of your choice and yank a handful out. Don't let the seller choose for you. He knows his business. He can pick the one bale in 300 that is good, green and leafy. You want to choose hay that is dry and still retaining some of its color. The stems should be small, and dried leaves should be visible among the grain and stems.

Don't be ashamed to tell a seller that your goats won't eat that stuff. If it is cheap, buy it for bedding. Stay on your toes and watch the market and the weather. You may be able to get hay cheaper if you have enough help to go to the fields and pick it up.

Many years ago I was given a barn full of two-year-old hay that was said not to be worth a dime. I hired help, got it home and planned to mulch the entire garden plot by about 8 inches. I no sooner started spreading it, when about 15 goats left their nice green pasture and started eating it. I don't know what was in that hay, but it fed my goats all winter and they stayed healthy, so sometimes you do get a good surprise.

If you doubt the quality of your hay, you can add alfalfa pellets to the grain. They aren't expensive and you can mix a 1 to 4 ratio to compliment the feed. (I do.)

All milking does, pregnant does in their last six weeks, and bucks during the breeding season need to be fed grain as well as forage. During this time you'll be looking for high-protein content at a low price and no chemicals. Read the tags, talk to the dealers, ask other dairy people for advice. If you feed the rest of the year, a simple 9 percent protein will do, but during crucial feeding times you're looking for a 16 percent to 18 percent dairy grain. If you can't find it, supplement with sweet oats, chopped corn, or soybean and/or peanut meal. Bucks may need a supplement of wheat germ for fertility. All additives are too rich to feed alone, so always add to the regular mix. I even add a handful of calf milk replacer to my milking does and weaning kids' grain. Dry grains come in coarse, rolled, textured, pellet and ground forms. Grains for goats should be coarse; even rolled or crimpled is better than ground. Ground grain will impact and cause digestive problems. (Keep the goats out of the chicken feed.) Pellets are neat and less wasteful than coarse grains, but many goats won't eat them, and pellets are just ground grains rolled into neat little balls. If you have a few yard chickens or even a pig, they will clean up wasted feed nicely.

Tetracycline is an additive in a lot of feeds sold for cattle and should not be fed in large quantities to goats. Read the content tag on the bag and talk to the feed dealer. One hundred grams per ton would not be too high of a dosage to upset the goats' digestive process.

When mixing your own grain, you'll have to experiment to come up with a mix that is acceptable in protein and vitamin content. Unless you can grow and store your own grain and have the extra time to spend with the project, it is more advisable to buy a prepared mix.

Over the years I have come up with three simple formulas that work for me.

For milking does and breeding bucks: I use a 16 percent dairy blend with one-fourth sweet crimped oats and one-fourth alfalfa pellets with a small percentage of dry milk replacer (two-50 pound bags of 16 percent dairy blend, one 50 pound bag of sweet crimped oats, one bag of alfalfa pellets and an 8-to-10 pound bag of dry milk replacer sifted through the bin.) With a decent hay, salt, mineral block, soda, and treats, this works well. It is said that corn will lower a goat's milk production and oats will raise it. I've not tested this theory, I just believe it, since corn is a fattening agent.

Winter: For dry does, weathers, and nonbreeding bucks, I feed a cheaper 12 percent range feed, two bags mixed with one bag chopped corn and one bag crimped oats. If the hay doesn't look good to me, I'll add one bag alfalfa pellets.

Summer: I feed a 12 percent range feed and add alfalfa pellets (two bags range to one alfalfa) if there are drought conditions.

Keep in mind that all of this is with the continued use of using salt, mineral block and soda, given free choice year around to all goats.

Any time you change a goats feed, do it slowly. Never change a goat's feed overnight because it could cause distress in digestion. If the feed store is out of your feed, ask the staff to give you the closet possible substitute, even if it costs more, and then remind them to keep yours in stock.

Milking does with good hay should receive one half pound of feed for every one pound of milk produced, up to three or four pounds. After that, excess feed is of little good.

Goats should never be fed enough to become fat. Obesity can cause abortion, sterility, and a sluggish digestive system. The animal should be fleshy, but not fat. When you compare a milking doe with a nonproducing animal, the milking doe will look less fatty than the one not producing, causing the nonproducing animal to look overweight.

Feed formula: cost of feed divided by pounds. fed to goat, equals cost of milk in feed, times 8 (pounds in a gallon of milk) gives you the price per gallon.

Now you can add the cost of hay, the cost of feed and have a good idea which goats are the ones to keep and which are the ones to let go. I keep the economical one that eats little and gives more regardless of breeding, over the "gas hog" every time.

Vitamins

A goat's system manages to build most of the vitamins, except A, D, and E, if it is fed the basic ration. Therefore, hay, forage, and grains must have a supply of these other vitamins, the best reason I can give for making sure there is a variety of forages.

This shouldn't be any cause for concern, providing the requirements for roughage and grains are met. Only a vet can tell you for sure if your goat has a vitamin deficiency.

The minerals necessary for the goat are usually in the feed and forage. However, mineral deficiencies are not uncommon. This is why I continually advise a mineral block.

A dicalcium phosphate and a monosodium phosphate should be kept in separate weatherproof boxes any time you have any doubts about the forage.

Water

Water should be fresh, clean, and available at all times. Water left in light colored containers will build microorganisms faster than water in darker containers. Water should be in a shaded area so the sunlight doesn't cause faster growth of bacteria. Water receptacles need to be kept clean as needed. Summertime water should be cold, and winter water should be warmer. Well water does this all by itself. Animals cannot be expected to thrive on snow. Studies have found that the fluorides in tap water can kill off many of the minerals a goat needs and that goats should be fed well water (the studies call it bore water) when at all possible. If you are on city water, be sure to add extra trace minerals, especially zinc and magnesium.

A mature goat will drink two or more gallons of water a day, depending on the weather and the moisture content of the forage that they eat. Some goats will drink less that one gallon if they are getting plenty of water from the forage.

Coccidia are microorganisms that thrive in the water and are internal parasites in most animals and poultry and even people. They are meant to keep bacteria under control. When they get out of hand, you have sick goats. The sickness is called coccidiosis and it may be fatal. The preventive (Coccidiostat) can be bought inexpensively and used in the water to correct this problem. Coccidiostats are also available in individual dosages for infected animals. Clean, noncontaminated water is a necessity in preventing coccidiosis.

Should a goat's water supply be a pond or lake, be sure that a dry approach is provided in the summer and a nonskid approach in the winter. Also, ice will have to be broken in freezing areas. Unlike cows and horses, a goat will not break the ice for a drink. Goats will, however, paw the snow off the grass to eat.

It is important that goat owners know that they do have choices. The feed store can be a fun place to hang out, listen, and learn, but your goats don't have to live there.

To summarize: Good quality hay, with a basic grain, minerals, salt, and water are the necessities in basic goat care. If the goats are allowed to pasture, the amount of hay and grain will be greatly reduced.

(Kid feeding is covered in the newborn chapter.)

Feed conversion is the formula we use to figure how much grain (by pounds) that it take to raise livestock. I have included the following chart to show how it works.

To figure your own feed conversion, total the weight of all the does, estimate the amount of kids they will have in a given period (the chart uses two years) and add the amount of feed that is fed to dams and babies. Figure the total weight of the kids and divide the total pounds of feed by the total weight of kids. The result is feed conversion. I used my own records from two years and not an estimate.

	One mother	*Produces*	*Feed consumed*	*Feed conversion*
Cow	100 pound cow 2 years from breeding	600 pound calf 2 years from breeding	8,800 pounds of feed for cow and calf	pounds of feed per pound of 13
Rabbit	100 10 pound does or 1,000 pounds of rabbit 2 years breeding	7,700 fryers 4 pounds each or 30,800 2years breeding	12,300 pounds Of feed for does and litters	4
Goat*	10 100 pound does or 1,000 pounds of goat 2 years breeding	3 kids or 3,000 pounds of of kids, 2 years breeding	9000 pounds of feed for doe (kids drink milk from dams and raised on grass	3

*These figures are from personal experience; use your own animals and your own rations to find your own feed conversion. If you were to leave the kids on the dams and pasture the herd without supplementing grain, feed conversion could drop to as low as one.

16

Breeding Methods

It would seem that for reproduction, all you would need is a buck and a doe, which is basically true. However, for good management and to maintain breeding improvement for your herd, it's not.

Unless you just have goats around to look at or to clear brush, you need to be a little more particular about breeding methods. How you breed, when you breed, and where your does are bred are all aspects with which the goatkeeper must be concerned.

Genetics play a part in breeding goats, as with any other animal, and research with goats in the genetic department is continual. The main thing that should concern the simple goat owner is that there is evidence that when mating two polled (hornless) animals together, the offspring stand a large chance of being infertile, or hermaphrodites. People who raise goats simply for butcher stock really don't care about the fertility of the offspring. Some breeders are trying, unsuccessfully, to mate only polled animals and cull out the horned and infertile. It is hoped that by continually saving only the polled and fertile, a pure strain will be achieved that is naturally hornless. So far, there is no luck in this area. A friend of mine is working within her herd to isolate the gene that produces polled goats, mixing those goats with others that have the isolated gene, and producing polled animals without the problem of sterility. This is too advanced for this book. The Arapawa (mentioned earlier) has been the only naturally hornless goat yet, and there are not enough of them to form herds.

I choose to keep a buck that was horned at birth but has been disbudded. In this manner, I don't have to worry about which doe is or is not naturally hornless. Selecting the right sire for your herd is covered more fully in the next chapter on male goats.

Another reason it's not as simple as just having a buck and a doe has to do with management and herd improvement. With goats, we have the right to practice genocide — not breeding two goats that will not produce an improved offspring.

Tinker is a La Mancha doe with a kid named Bella, from Rene Matthews' herd.

Domino is another La Mancha from Rene Matthews' herd.

There are four methods of breeding, although one is Impractical for small breeders.

1. Pasture breeding is probably the most simple. Just turn the buck in with the does and let nature take its course. The breeding season is usually from September to March, but August through April is possible. Saanens, Sables, Pygmies and Boers will breed at other times. Pygmies will breed twice a year, which is not good on their systems, and the others breed every eight months, or three times in two years. You'll start receiving kids approximately five months after the buck appears, or five months after the goats start mating.

Though pasture breeding is easy and natural, there are many reasons not to do it. The buck's odor will rub off on the entire herd and barns will smell like the buck. Any milk you will get tastes like the buck smells. Should you need to handle any of the goats (and you will), the buck will have to be separated because he will be protective and can be dangerous. The buck will keep the entire herd agitated during the rutting season. You, too, will smell like the buck. The odor clings to your clothes, your hair, and especially your hands.

The buck will not discriminate. If a doe is in heat, he'll mate. Milking does, undergrown does, defective does, sickly does, old does—all become pregnant. With pasture breeding, pregnancy is close to 100 percent. When the does do give birth, the buck will mistake this odor for heat and terrorize her, if he can. This results in her kids getting stomped to death while she is trying to fight him off, especially in close quarters.

The largest drawback is that you'll have absolutely no idea when to expect your newborns. They will arrive in zero temperatures, ice storms, and thunder storms. You may find them dead, frozen or sickly, or slaughtered by predators. Kids born in late summer have little chance to get healthy and grow before winter starts stressing them. Triplets, quadruplets, premature babies, undersized twins and undersized singles need help. The mother may have developed mastitis and you wouldn't know, or she could miscarry and you wouldn't know. The unknowns are endless.

If you do pasture breed, you must assess your does' faults as a herd and choose a buck for the whole herd preventing individual matings of does to different bucks. When you plan to keep the does for future reproduction, you have to change bucks every year to prevent undesirable breeding of families. Pasture breeding is not recommended because of all of the unknowns and because small herd owners need to make more responsible decisions concerning the offspring being born.

2. Hand breeding is the process of personally taking the doe to the buck. We don't take the buck to the doe unless she's alone because the herd does not appreciate a stranger on its domain. We don't like to mess with a buck in rut any more than necessary, but we don't want his smell everywhere either. By taking the doe to him, we avoid the whole ordeal. The only real drawback to hand breeding is the involvement in moving the doe back and forth. If she is in heat, that won't even be a problem, as you most likely won't have to lead her, she'll beat you to the buck. When hand breeding you have the opportunity to choose the time you want the doe bred, the buck you want her to breed with, and the luxury of knowing exactly when to expect the kids. You can hold back any young does you don't want to get pregnant or any does lactating that you want to milk longer. Hand breeding is simpler if the buck is on the same premises. With hand breeding, you know the does have mated, because you were there.

You also have the option to have two bucks, if necessary, so that you can breed the daughters of one to another buck or unrelated does to the buck that will complement their faults the best.

Stud service is an extension of hand breeding, but you must take your does to someone else and pay for it. Stud service can run from free, to over $100 but averages $25 to $500 for purebred bucks.

Stud service for all breeds in not available in most areas, but some kind of stud can usually be found. This takes extra time and expense. In many areas, your choices of bucks may be so slim that you may have to settle for buying one of lesser quality, or paying more for a fancy buck that you don't really need.

When choosing to use stud service, check around carefully. Try to find the buck that you want/need and an owner you can get along with during the proceedings. Often, breeders offering bucks for stud service have a strict regimen to follow. They may ask that you make an appointment, and to protect their herd, that your doe have health papers. Many require a minimum size, weight, or breed. I have seen breeders advertise "acceptable does" only, which means they will only allow their top-quality bucks to mate with top-quality does. These breeders won't help if you're upgrading, but they do let you know that they protect their herd.

Call ahead when looking at bucks to find out what arrangements the owner will make. Some herd owners will stable your doe until bred for a fee. Others want the doe brought to the buck for the first service and returned in ten or 12 days for a second stand, which doesn't make sense if the doe is only in heat for a day and won't be back in heat for 17 to 22 days. Never take your doe to a buck that doesn't look healthy and an owner that doesn't have the same concerns as you do.

There is a slim possibility of borrowing or renting a buck for the appropriate amount of time, although most of us are protective of our bucks and don't let them go.

3. Purchasing a buck for the period that you need it and then selling it when you no longer need it is risky and not really that good on the bucks. Plus, you stand a chance of bringing in disease faster.

4. Artificial insemination is becoming popular among goat breeders, but I still don't see this as a viable method for the small herdsman. I personally find this method unnatural, expensive, and complicated and advise that you search for more thorough information on the subject. There is a wide selection of bucks when using AI and breeders are reporting more than 80 percent conception rate. The breeders involved with AI are very dedicated to preserving the breed standards, and only the sperm from highly qualified bucks is saved. The initial cash output for the storage tanks and canisters can run well into $1,000 and that doesn't count to the cost of the sperm straws.

Type of breeding is different from methods.

1. Inbreeding is breeding closely related animals, such as father-daughter, mother-son and siblings. This should only be done after you are totally familiar with the genetics, heritability factors and conformation standards.

2. Line breeding is very similar to inbreeding, but it involves breeding animals no closer than 25 percent, such as grandparents, aunts, uncles, etc.

Line breeding and inbreeding are used by the very experienced breeder to continually mate family members to keep producing top quality traits in the offspring and is also done accidentally when the wrong does get to the wrong bucks. When this happened to me, I discovered a loss in the size of the kids. I would never do this deliberately without learning more about the genetics.

3. Outcrossing is breeding unrelated animals of the same breed and is most common among small breeders. The improvement in the herd is slow, but it is safe, and if matings are carefully chosen, effective. Animals are matched according to their best qualities within the same breed in hopes of diminishing poor traits.

4. Crossbreeding is mating two separate and different breeds. The offspring of these breedings may be larger, stronger, and more resistant to sickness and disease. Crossbreeding is not desirable if breeders wish to keep goats of one particular breed and stick with it. Breeders with several breeds will often "experiment" by mating two separate breeds. The ADGA recognizes those matings of two purebred or American animals from separate breeds, and the offspring are registered as "Experimental." Crossbreeding does not improve any one particular breed, but it may improve individual offspring of such matings, and eventually the whole herd.

After I spent years upgrading to American and Purebred, I found I had lost stamina and resistance to disease. Since I moved to an area where there was (at that time) no 4H for goats, and I don't show, I started a program of crossbreeding and have had much better luck.

5. Upbreeding (upgrading) is always breeding purebred sires to grade, or recorded grade does, eventually coming up with American registered stock. Upgrading is the best method for the small herd owner to inexpensively acquire "papered" stock. Buying a purebred buck or seeking stud service from a purebred buck is a minor investment, compared to the quality attained from these matings, providing that you're not happy with what you have. Make your breeding decision well in advance of the mating season. Know ahead what kind of buck you want and how you plan to use him.

The following table shows the heritability percentages handed down to offspring over six generations when always breeding to a purebred buck

GENERATION HERITABILITY PERCENTAGES

First generation	50.00 percent
Second generation	25.00 percent
Third generation	6.25 percent
Fourth generation	1.56 percent
Fifth generation	.39 percent
Sixth generation	.01 percent

From this table, we can assume that by consistently breeding grade does purebred to sires of the same breed, in the seventh generation, the offspring would be pure, but the ADGA doesn't. These same figures apply in people, and in some states are referred to as the Sixth Generation Rule. Throwbacks may be possible on the even numbered years, eighth, tenth, twelfth, generation, but are rare. However, this is where the Sable/Saanen debate arises.

If this is what you want to do, I would advise that you use an unrelated buck, totally out of your area, each year, to avoid accidental line breeding. I think this is a lot of the reasons that the breed resistance and stamina starts to fail. Frequently, animals are related somewhere down the line, and we are accidentally weakening the breed.

17

Males

A male goat capable of reproduction is a buck. The term "billy" is colloquial and generally used by nonprofessionals. Most goatkeepers who are serious about their animal consider the term offensive. Most of us will correct the unfortunate person who uses the term.

The buck is responsible for most of the bad publicity about goats. He is usually larger than the does, less easily handled, and can jump his fences. The buck is normally a proud animal, sporting a beard, and in many breeds will have a thicker growth about the neck, much like the mane of a lion. He is a masculine creature, and he does not always look as nice as a doe. Sometimes he can *look* downright mean.

Unfortunately, this proud, muscular, and graceful animal emits a very strong musky odor that can be offensive — except to the does. (Buck deer also have an odor, but not being in closed in areas, we don't often hear, or know, or smell it.) It will cling to everything, hang in the air during rutting season for a distance of a block or more, and be carried on breezes much farther. The odor gets stronger as the animal matures. A young buck may not have an odor until his second year, and Nubians the third year. Then it can be really hard just to stand next to one. The odor is present during the rutting season or when the buck is pastured with or close to the does.

The most pertinent words I've heard to describe a buck in rut were "The lust of a goat is the bounty of God," and this is so true. Not only will he be more dangerous during this time but he is also very amorous. His actions can be very disgusting to the inexperienced person and everyone should be aware of what to expect from the mating buck.

This very proud male goes out of his way to impress the doe with his advance. He stomps his feet, paws the ground, and moans. He urinates on his own beard, his front legs, the doe, and anyone else within distance. He grunts and makes low frog type sounds, and chases the doe in circles. He will try to bite her

Author's granddaughter, Jesi KayLyn Griffin, has control of Rocky, who has figured out that she means business.

and kick out at her, trying to capture her with a foot. He will be on guard and alert, to protect his right for his intended activities. The actual conception (mounting) is fast and generally effective. When finished he will stay beside her until his energy is revived and he repeats his routine. The buck will continue for as long as the doe is present and receptive. When she is removed, he will pace his fence line and cry out in lonely-sounding moans until he is presented with another doe, or until rutting season is over and the scent of does in heat is gone.

Since he can be obnoxious, many people will vividly remember his antics long after the memories of the clean, well mannered, docile does have faded. In reality, at any other time, he is also gentle and mild mannered. Few people are impressed enough by this creature to realize that Mother Nature is the cause of his actions. Experienced goatkeepers would get a little frantic if he *didn't* behave in this manner.

Owning a buck is strictly a personal decision, though you may find yourself buying one against your will. You may not have available stud service for your needs or breed. Often, buying your own buck is easier and cheaper than traveling back and forth to a stud and paying stud fees. Conventional wisdom is that if you have less than nine or ten does, it is too costly to keep your own buck. I find this untrue. Assume that stud service in your area is $25 and you have eight does. You'd be putting out $200 in stud fees. If you have to travel 20 miles to the buck and 20 miles back, with an average of 20 miles to a gallon of gas, you would use over two gallons of gas per doe. This could add more than $4 (depending on the cost of oil in your area) to the cost of stud service, making a total of $232 and up. This doesn't count any second trips to the buck, nor the inconvenience of loading up the does, when you can catch them in heat, and carting them off to the prospective buck. I know I can keep a buck for less than $232 a year. Though the initial investment might be more, I will get all of that back in resale value, if I choose to sell. I will also have the luxury of knowing he is healthy, well cared after, and gentle.

The added income, should I offer my own stud service, will pay any added cost the buck might incur. Should you decide to keep a buck he will require much the same care as the does: feed, hay salt, minerals and water. He will need a stronger pen with higher fences. He can use a smaller house, since he will most likely be by himself. He needs the same scrupulous cleaning, worming and hoof care. Since this animal will only need grain during the time of rut, he will cost less to feed than a milking doe. Again, I feed mine year–round but he will thrive from spring to fall on pasture and browse and the added hay if he stays in good health.

Bucks seem to be sturdier creatures, being less susceptible to colds, flu and pneumonia. Since there isn't any udder care, they can be less trouble than a milk-ing doe. His odor can be controlled, in some cases, permanently. The bucks' scent glands lie directly toward the center and behind the horn buds and can be burned to inefficiency when disbudding the horns. This is discussed more in chapter 23.

Other alternatives include bathing and constant cleanliness. Keeping the buck clipped free of extra hair on his stomach, front legs and his beard will help lessen the odor, although the does may not like him as much. Any good disinfectant that won't irritate the skin will help, as will regular baths. Adding tomato juice, lemon juice, soda or apple cider will also help control odor.

Choose a buck to suit the needs of your does, one whose traits you want to pass on to your new kids. Make sure that you can handle him. When looking for a buck, you must first look at your does. Find the largest fault that they all share and make sure the buck excels on that point. If they have some extremely good points, make sure he does, too.

When looking at the faults of your does, try not to get stuck on the little things, such as hockiness or rear udder attachments, in the beginning. Instead, be a little more general, and consider total appearance. If you mate two animals with the same defect, you will maximize that defect. On the other hand, mating two animals with the same good point will maximize them.

The buck is half the herd and therefore deserves twice the respect. For instance, if you have ten does and they all have twins, each set of twins will carry half of their mother's traits and half of their father's traits. All 20 kids will carry half the buck's traits. Therefore, the buck is responsible for half the new kids; each doe is only responsible for half of her own, or one-tenth (in that herd of 10 does).

Your buck should be good enough that your kids will show an improvement over their mothers, not only in milk production but also in body conformation.

Choosing a buck that can pass on the good traits that you need for your does can be tough. Buying a proven buck is next to impossible and can be ridiculously costly. By the time bucks' sons and daughters are old enough to prove themselves in the show ring or on milk test, the buck may very well be dead. Pedigrees can be useless, because they only show background, not whether that background produces animals capable of passing on desirable traits to their young. It is not always possible to find a buck that has producing daughters so you can check their merits, so there are several points to check.

His physical appearance, or conformation, needs to be as good, or better than your does, so their kids will be better than they are now.

His parents' appearance, if you have records, will let you know if that breeding held up in producing him and therefore would hold up in breeding him to another.

The appearance and records of his full sisters and his daughters should be viewed when possible. This isn't possible in young bucks of very young does. However, if the young buck's mother has other sons and daughters from previous years, check their records or appearance if possible.

His milking daughters' records, if any, will indicate if the buck has been able to pass down desirable milk producing traits in past matings.

The size of the testicles does contribute to fertility. When comparing two bucks, the one with the larger testicles will be the better choice.

In many areas, like mine, few people keep records on family. Get to know your goats. Study other peoples' goats. Carry the conformation picture with you. Right now I am using a grade buck with almost perfect conformation.

I generally prefer Nubians, but my buck is mixed with Alpine. He passes down the Nubian ears every time and strengthens the conformation and healthy vigor I like to see in a goat.

The following Heritability Chart will help you know what characteristics you expect from your buck. This chart shows an average, since each breed will be different.

As you can see, butterfat, protein and size are the largest qualities that the buck has to pass on to his offspring, which are two things we can't see.

Since these are seldom any concern to the small goat owner, it would seem that breeding for size and conformation would be a safe bet, providing the bucks' daughters' milk production was indeed better than that of the dams.

HERITABILITY

Butterfat/protein	50 percent
Size	30–50 percent
Teat placement	30 percent
Milk/butterfat	27 percent
Rump	27 percent
Top line and back	25 percent
Disposition	25 percent
Udder	22 percent
Hind legs/feet	15 percent
Front legs	14 percent
Udder quality and texture	0 percent

By going up the chart backwards you can see the qualities you need to find in a doe before you expect the buck to do much good.

Bucks can mature as early as two or three months and start mating, with Nubians being a little slower to mature than the other breeds. For that reason, even younger bucks should be kept separated from the does.

There are many advantages to buying an unproven, younger buck. This animal won't have any bad habits and he will grow with you. You will know the animal and be more likely to have a reason to trust him.

Your young buck should always be handled gently but firmly. He should be taught to lead and always wear a collar. The collar should be a nonporous material, so it won't hold the odor. The buck should never be teased. Children should be watched, as their normal behavior could be mistaken for teasing by the goats.

The whole idea here is that we don't want him to find out how strong he is. He should always be treated as though he were a full 250 pounds, as he very well may be when he matures. Most bucks, with good handling, can be gentle. I have never raised an aggressive buck. In fact, I wish mine were a little more standoffish, so they wouldn't be touching me so much during rut. I've been run out of a few pastures by other peoples' aggressive bucks, and I have been given, on two occasions, aggressive bucks that it did not take me long to take right to the sale barn.

The young buck needs attention. He especially likes his poll scratched. As he grows, he must be handled firmly. Frequent handling is the only key to keeping him gentle.

It's not wise to butt heads with any goat, and particularly bucks. This can prove hazardous when they mature. Many people only keep year-old bucks for breeding because they are easier to handle and the odor is less offensive, and the owners don't have to worry about breeding him to his daughters. I get too attached, so I keep two bucks.

Yearling bucks should not be allowed to breed more than ten does before they are 18 to 20 months old, to prevent wearing them out. An older buck should not be overworked with more than one doe a day, as he needs to rest, too. Although, when pasture breeding, he may breed as many as five or six in a day. I know this, as I have had five does have their babies within minutes of each other, and the sixth an hour or two later, so he doesn't rest when left to his own desires.

Never buy an older, strange buck if you don't know and trust the owner. Because I have made this mistake, I can attest to the danger. When you go to the sale barn, take an extra set of clothes and go into the pen with the buck you are considering. See how well he handles with you. Try to find anything you can about his personality. If you have any doubts, look for another buck.

The stupidest idea I had was to buy a good-looking buck, regardless of his attitude, turn him in with the does, use him for one season, and round him up and sell him, so his attitude meant little to me. Of course I had to get in to take care of the does and feed, water, and medicate, not to speak of trim hooves. I guess I thought that since he was wild, he would run from me and I could do my work and leave. Not so with this guy. After three days those were his does, and I wasn't allowed in with them. I had to lead the does onto the trailer, and then pull them out one by one, to get rid of him.

Don't ever put yourself between a mature buck and the doe he is wooing, as he will think nothing of removing any obstacle to get to the doe, or to get the doe away from you. Wilder bucks will literally jump over you to get to a doe, or to get away.

Lady goat owners need to be extra careful during their menstrual cycle, as a mature goat can sense the condition and become rowdy, whether it's the mating season or not. Explain this to young girls and female visitors before they visit or handle the buck.

A healthy buck will be capable of reproducing for nine to 12 years but should be retired as soon as his daughters stop showing improvement over their mothers, or when the does that normally have twins and triplets start having singles.

Only bucks that can pass desirable qualities down to their offspring should be kept for future breeding. If the buck can't achieve your desired goals, chances are he won't be of any use to anyone else for breeding, unless the keeper is just starting out and had the same desires you had at one time. Poor quality bucks should be castrated or slaughtered, regardless of papers or pedigree, as they will only keep passing on poor traits to their kids, lowering the quality of the breed.

Cattle breeders have, for years, maintained quality by not allowing poor quality stock to remain fertile. These breeders have been able to obtain high quality stock (and higher prices) by constantly culling out the lesser of the bulls. Conscientious goat keepers need to achieve this same goal.

A poor quality buck is not a waste. He can still be butchered and put into sausage or summer sausage. His meat will be a little strong to just grind into hamburger. It is best to wait 30 days after the rutting season before butchering. The best method is to feed him corn for 30 days after the mating season, then butcher him, have him made into summer sausage and you can't tell the difference in the meat. If your taste buds can't handle it, cook him down and make dog food.

When selling mature bucks for butchering, try to be sure the buyer will butcher. It is common practice for some unscrupulous buyers to knowingly sell innocent people your buck and say he's from genuine breeding stock. One buyer tried to sell me a poor grade La Mancha and told me he was a frost–bit Nubian! Once you read and study and know your goats, you won't get duped.

Castrating an older buck is a dangerous operation and can only be done by a vet. This procedure should be considered carefully because after three or four months of age, the shock of the surgery could be serious enough to kill the buck.

Your buck, as a stud, can bring in an added income to help pay his room and board. When offering your buck for stud service, don't be afraid to turn away unhealthy looking does. It is better to hurt a few feelings than to take a chance on losing the buck to disease. Protect your buck. As with all goats, cleanliness is a necessity, but with bucks you must add selective buying.

If you've never seen a top quality animal, you won't breed one, and you won't know a good buck if you don't see one. Make sure you see at least one blue ribbon buck so you'll know what you are doing.

The challenge is tremendous when it comes to upgrading and cross-breeding. You start out with a suitable grade doe and shop around for affordable good buck.

The first couple of years you can see the improvement in your kids, but you know they still aren't much to brag about. You exchange bucks, cull a few does, and keep only the nicest of the new doelings. Then, in a few years (It took me seven!) you go to the goat barn and find the prettiest little buck and doeling. At first you are skeptical. You check them for defects. You watch them grow and wait for a sign of hockiness, or a sloped chine. By the time they are six months old they look so good that you realize that you have finally met your goals in breeding a beautiful animal.

When that first doe proves herself on the milk charts, you'll be satisfied that your breeding procedures and the choice of bucks were the right decisions for your herd. Eventually, you will learn how to do this with grade goats and save the money. Nice surprises come in breeding good grade goats as well, if you know what to look for when choosing them.

I've really tried to give you all the bad points about owning a buck. I have not exaggerated one bit. But, somehow this obnoxious, smelly, blubbering fool will find his way into your heart and may very well be you favorite goat. There's just something about a buck that can't be explained until you own one.

Wethers

The wether is a castrated buck and is still called a "he," though he can no longer reproduce. The wether has many purposes for the goatkeeper.

The main purpose for a wether, of course, is slaughter. People who don't eat the meat themselves will sell the goats to those who do. In many areas there is a large market for butcher stock. To check out your area for a meat market, place a simple ad in the local newspaper, contact other breeders, or call one of the local meat processing plants. My feed store refers people to me. The prices will vary from one area to another, but wethers are usually easy to sell or trade. Frequently, you have to learn a bit of another language to bargain, because many buyers do not speak English. However, they usually bring a translator or know enough to talk money.

Depending on your area and the size of the goat, you can get from 50 cents to $1.50 per pound for your wethers. If you find that you are living in an area where the price for wethers is low, sell them early, before you have put much money into them, or keep them for your own freezer.

On the other hand, if you're in a good meat market area and the price goes up with the weight of the goat, you may find it more economical to wean the wethers and let them fatten on grass before selling them. Check the market and sell your wethers before you lose too much time and money on them.

Easter, June 19, the fourth of July, Labor Day, family reunions, and weddings and celebrations are good sales times for goat meat. People of some cultures will celebrate with goat meat and some will want a buck, because their culture requires the goat to be intact. If you are in one of those areas, set some goats back that you don't disbud or castrate. Make sure when breeding season arrives that they are sold, in a strong pen, or quickly taken to auction.

Wethers provide companionship for other animals and are worth their weight in feed if that is the only reason for keeping one. Your one milk doe will be far more contented, produce more and give better tasting milk if she has a friend.

He will eat just as much as any other goat of the same age. Often he may eat more, because a wether will usually grow larger than if it had been left to breed.

Wethers make great children's pets, because they don't multiply, they don't smell bad and they don't have udder problems. When giving a wether to a child, keep in mind that the goat will reach a mature weight of up to 300 pounds in three to four years. The pet may well outgrow a younger child. Wethers can also be trained as draft animals and help pay for themselves with the extra work they can do.

They are delightful in parades and great at amusing children by pulling them in a cart. They can also tow hay and grain in carts at chore time.

The wether is smaller than the donkey and the ox, and cannot be expected to take their place. He can't be asked to pull heavier loads. When training a wether to pull a cart, always start with a small load, adding to it as he matures.

The younger they are when you start working with them, the better results you'll have. Handling is the first step. Once the wether has been taught to lead and is willing to stand when commanded to stand, fit him with a small halter. A small calf or sheep halter can usually be fitted to goats. Often, a local goat club will sell halters for goats at sales, shows and fairs. Supply houses that sell products just for goats also carry halters, or you can design your own using twine, jute, or rope. Catalogs that specialize in livestock will often carry goat supplies at a reasonable rate.

Once fitted with the halter, the wether must learn the commands to stop and go. Be sure to use terms that are familiar to your vocabulary. It will do no good to teach the goat whoa and walk if you turn around and actually say "go" and "stop." Avoid the use of rhyming words, such as go and whoa, as the goat is likely to become confused and not learn at all. Train the goat with the words that you will actually be using, and teach anyone else working with the animal the proper words to use.

You might want to use a branch of his favorite leaves or some grain to entice him to go in the beginning, but once he has learned the commands, start withdrawing the enticement so that he will learn to obey the commands.

The next step is adding the reins. Reins should be lightweight, strong and long enough to go behind the goat. (For this step, you may need the help of a second person.) With someone walking beside the goat, you can teach him to turn by gently pulling on the reins as your helper leads him through the turn. As the goat be comes familiar with the command, your lead person can back away. This calls for patience and repetition. Teach one turn at a time. Don't teach left turns till right ones have been mastered. Once the wether has adjusted to the halter, reins, commands and turning, you can add the cart. The cart should be lightweight, with large narrow wheels, so that it rolls easily. Start with an empty cart and add the weight a little at a time, as the goat gets used to it, or as he matures enough to handle the added weight. Never overload the cart so much that the goat has to strain. A wether that has been pulling a cart will need a couple months of rest if you should decide to butcher him, so that the meat will have a chance to rest and tenderize.

Wethers that are going to be used for butcher should be handled frequently.

They need to be tame enough to be caught easily. The goat should never be allowed to get excited before butchering, as an overheated animal will cause the meat to be strong tasting. The animal should go quietly to slaughter, and die quietly, for the best flavored meat. All people butcher differently, so I'm not going into the details of which cut goes where. However, there are a few tips to butchering goats, besides keeping them calm.

1. Never do this alone, or if you are inexperienced. Nothing is safe.
2. If you do your own butchering, choose the season and place where flies will not contaminate the meat.
3. Butcher in a well-lit area that is clean, and have access to water, or plenty of filled water buckets handy.
4. Knives should be clean, and sharp, and sheathed for safety.
5. Skin quickly and avoid getting any hair on the flesh.
6. The meat should be rinsed and completely cleaned before storage.
7. The meat can be cut and frozen immediately, or cooled for two or three days at a temperature between 38 and 44 degrees before freezing or canning.
8. Save the bones, because they can be cooked down into broths and stews.
9. If something happens that a goat has to be butchered during the wrong season, please take it to the slaughterhouse and let the staff do it right.

You've heard me say many times that I have done most of this alone. My late husband was an experienced deer-hunter and experienced farmer, and experienced in skinning just about any animal. He was an extremely patient man, took his time and did things right. But to the best, there may need to be only one thing go wrong.

On July 4, 1986, he died when the knife handle he was using broke and the knife stabbed him in the femoral vein, in the upper leg, while butchering a goat. He bled to death, alone, in seconds. The coroner said there wouldn't have been anything anyone could have done, even if we had been there.

The police came out, because it really was all pretty suspicious, but they said that perhaps a bee, a fly, a snake or something distracted him, because he was renown for his patience, intelligence, and the great care he gave everything to do it right. I said it had to be the hand of God, that God must have needed a man like him more that we did. But I could never forget that it was the wrong time of the year.

Friends thought that I would have got rid of the goats, but I felt that he would then have died in vain. I finished raising my girls and fell apart, which is the time that I mentioned earlier that my animals did not get the best of care. It wasn't until my oldest daughter was pregnant, in '98 and made me see a doctor and get medicine, that I pulled myself back together and put my goatherd back together.

But knowing that the goats needed some sort of care and supervision kept me going home every day, and made me go home when I didn't want to be alone, so they saved that little string of sanity that helped me come back.

Sure enough, that granddaughter from that pregnancy is the light of my life, loves the goats, handles them, could milk at age 2, and loves the milk she drinks for her allergies.

If you have any doubts about butchering, pay someone else. It took me a couple of years, but I learned to butcher and went back to selling dressed meat. I do not ever see a certain hunting knife that I don't shiver.

But I know, though I faltered, I have not failed his memory, and staying with the goats was just as right after he died as it was before I married him.

18

The Female Reproductive System and Cycle

Getting a female goat does not mean that you will automatically have milk. The doe must be bred and have the kids before you get the milk. (She may miscarry, and you might still have milk.) She should have milk for approximately ten months. This is called lactation, and could slow down during the heat of the South or the cold of the North or the stress of moving to a new home. Disease, infection, and worm infestation can slow down or stop lactation. Some people are fortunate enough to stick it out and continue milking for two years by not allowing the doe to have kids except for every other year.

The doe must be healthy, wormed, and the right age and size before she is bred. Many does will be old enough to breed at four months but are certainly not large enough. Some breeders prefer waiting to breed does when they are ten to 18 months old, but waiting until they reach 80 pounds is the generally accepted idea, although the doe may not agree. Before your doe reaches breeding time, you should have decided on your breeding method and your choice of buck.

Keep in mind: In the wild they breed when they please, and to whom they please, but the mortality rate is low.

The breeding season is generally from August through April, depending on the area where you live, and the breed. Pygmies are more likely to mate two times a year and have singles or twins. Boers will breed two times in three years. Most does will have twins, but a single baby or triplets are common. quadruplets (four) are frequent, quintuplets (five) arrive rarely and sextuplets (six) are very uncommon.

There is an old saying that a goat will breed during any month with an "R" in it. This is basically true, as none of the summer months happen to have the letter, and goats do generally mate in the fall and early winter. Some goats, mainly Pygmy, Saanen, and Sable, will mate in the summer.

Before breeding, the doe must come into heat, which is called estrus. The healthy goat will go through her normal cycles without ever seeing a buck.

There is a great deal of evidence that the decreasing daylight has something to do with the goats' estrus cycles, with the decreasing light affecting the pituitary gland thus inducing estrus. When the days get longer in the spring, the cycles cease. This would account for the difference in breeding seasons in different parts of the country. This would also explain why a few goats will come into heat and mate during the summer; as the pituitary gland in goats would be as individual in its operation as it is in people and not always function the same. In many cases, heat cycles can be artificially induced by keeping the doe in total darkness for 16 or 17 hours each day.

I do this in January, February, March, and April if I have a doe that did not breed in the fall. It's not easy, and may not be considered natural, but simply means that I do the chores a little earlier, shut her up with a friend, and not allow her back out until after morning chores with the others. This will usually get me a later lactation and ensure that I have milk all year.

This isn't convenient, and it's certainly not natural, but it works over 80 percent of the time. Nubians, Saanens/Sable and Pygmies are more likely to carry their heat cycles over longer in the spring than the other breeds. Normally speaking, if they aren't bred by Christmas, they most likely won't get bred.

Detecting the does' estrus cycle can be tricky, or extremely obvious, depending on your goat. Some does will jump the fence and when you get up, they will be standing at the bucks' gate wanting to be with him. Others aren't so easy. Knowing your goat, watching your goats, and recognizing behavior changes is the key to any good management program, especially during estrus cycles.

The common signs of heat are anxiety, tail wagging, frequent urination, swelling of the vulva, and repeated bleating, especially the Nubians. Since Nubians are so vocal anyway, sometimes it's hard to tell if they're noisy from heat, or just "talking" to you. Nubians are usually quiet if no one is around. So if you hear them when they can't see you, and nothing is going on, that's a good sign that something is going on with their cycles.

The doe will show an active interest in the buck and will stand for mounting. If not in heat, she will fight him off, run from him, and in many cases, chase him away until she is ready. Often other does will mount the one that is in heat. The doe may show all of these signs, or she may not show a single one of them. It takes time, experience and knowing your goats to detect heat in some of the more demure does. Unlike the buck, the doe does discriminate. You may want her bred to one buck, and she will do her darnedest to fight him and get to another. I'm not proud to admit this, but the doe usually wins in these matters, especially if you don't have the fencing to stop her from carrying out her own ideas.

Having the buck close by is an advantage, because the doe will hug the fence and try to get to him, or at least show an interest in him, when she's ready. The disadvantage would be that they can also get together through a weak spot and breed either to the wrong buck or at a time you didn't want them to breed.

It used to be common to detect estrus with the use of a buck rag. The rag comes in handy when you don't have a buck on hand. This is a very absorbent piece of cloth (a diaper does nicely) that has been rubbed on the buck and then stored in an airtight container to retain the odor. When you suspect the doe is in heat, allow her to sniff the jar, and if she shows a great amount of interest, pack her up and take her to the buck. Since the rag is new, the doe may show some interest anyway, so this is not foolproof.

The heat cycle can last from six to 72 hours depending on the goat. Cycles can be light to heavy, with the does less likely to mate on the lighter cycle. If not bred, the doe will come back into heat every 17 to 22 days throughout the breeding season. Breeding the doe during the heaviest part of her heat is recommended, should you recognize the difference. During the heavy cycle, ovulation begins just hours after the cycle starts, and breeding for female offspring is more easily accomplished. Several breedings during the heavy heat can also stand a bigger chance of obtaining multiple births. The number of babies born depends on the number of successfully fertilized eggs the doe manages to produce and the number of fetuses that actually survive through gestation.

If you have a younger doe or smaller one that shouldn't be carrying multiples, it is advised to pull her from the buck early.

It is a common practice to plan for over 50 percent does by putting apple cider vinegar in the water a month before and during estrus. The acidity in the doe's system is supposed to weaken the male sperm, thereby producing more does. Without interference, you should get a 50–50 chance of does and bucks, but in my experience, without the vinegar, I've found a 60–40 ratio in favor of bucks.

Before deliberately trying to plan for multiple births, there is more to consider than the size of the doe. There has been some speculation that three or four fetuses in the womb may somehow rob one or more of the females of their fertility if there are also males born. The research on this subject is sparse. In my own research I find absolutely no difference. I had one doe that consistently kidded with two bucks and a doe for over eight years, and her daughters also kidded with twins and triplets for more years to come. It's a good idea to check the does that are born with brothers in groups of three or more for extra teats, enlarged vulvas, a pea-shaped pod at the base of the vulva, and especially, very tiny teats.

Naturally, these things need to be checked with all new does, but extra caution should be used during multiple births until someone actually can come up with enough research to dispute the theory. It may be a genetic thing, as many of us haven't had any problems. Even if there isn't any sign of any defects, watch these does as they grow for masculine behavior or a lack of femininity. Should they not come into heat normally, keep this in mind and consider them for slaughter. My herd commonly has multiple births of both sexes, and I have not encountered this problem, nor do I know anyone who has.

Records kept on heat cycles, the time of breeding, and the sex of the kids indicate that a doe is more likely to have females, if bred early in their estrus, and males when bred late in the cycle. Again, I don't see that in my breeding.

Once you have detected the heat cycle, the earliest breeding could result in more does, but I have left the buck with the herd and still had a ration of 60–40 to the bucks' favor, so I cannot advocate messing with nature on this discussion.

Once heat has been accurately detected, the doe should be taken to the buck for mating. If you don't want to overwork the buck, you can repeat in 12 to 24 hours. I leave mine with the buck three days. This helps keep him busy and may protect her daughters, as they will come in heat at about the same time. It will also keep his mind off any other doe that I may not want to have bred yet.

When breeding a younger doe that you don't want to carry multiples, don't allow her to stay with the buck too long. A larger, more experienced doe that can handle three or four kids can be left with the buck or returned several times for added breedings, without worrying that too many kids will harm her.

Watch the mating procedure. Make sure there is an actual insertion, and as the buck ejaculates, both he and the doe should hump their backs, slightly, and very quickly. This process does not take more than a minute so you must be pay attention if you want a clear due date. It is recommended to return the doe to the buck in 17 to 22 days to see if she will refuse him. If so, she has "settled" and should be pregnant. Watch the doe for future heat cycles in case of a miscarriage.

There are some sophisticated methods for diagnosing pregnancy, but they can be expensive and time consuming, and the small goat keeper is not likely to find them feasible.

With some goats, it is hard to detect the does' heat cycle. There is one last resort. If your doe is not bred by the latter part of the breeding season (you may have a little longer with Nubians), you can put her in with the buck and watch daily for activity. You may not catch any activity, and not have a due date, but she will likely breed. It is not unusual for does to miss their first year, though it can be expensive to hold them over a year. A young doe can go to the buck late in the season and breed, and continue to grow during her pregnancy, not resulting in a growth stunt. Should your doe never come in heat, there are many tests that your vet can run to find the cause. Unless you have high hopes for the doe, I would recommend she be used for butcher, rather than take the chances on her being infertile and wasting more time and money on tests.

Obesity could prevent a doe from undergoing normal estrus and can cause infertility, promote abortions and force a doe into premature or fatal delivery. Also, a worm infestation will stop a does' estrus or a buck from being interested.

After she is bred, it takes approximately five months for a does to have a normal gestation. Those of us who want to have a say about when the kids are born plan the matings accordingly. Many people breed early to achieve January or February kids so they are growing well and are strong enough to face summer problems. Also, kids sold for the Easter and Fourth of July markets will be heavier and bring better prices.

You may not want kids born early if you have frigid winters. To plan your kids conveniently, refer to the following chart of gestation due dates. To use the gestation table, take the month and the day the doe was bred and follow the column to the right to find the month she will be due to kid. Then subtract the indicated number to find the exact day the kids will be born. Actual gestation is 145 to 155 days (less, by two weeks, with La Manchas) so it would not hurt to watch your doe for five days before the date and be prepared for them to come as much as five days later. With my experience, nine out of ten does deliver on the exact day indicated by this chart, and the others are within 12 to 24 hours. I've only had one goat carry past the date. She was a first freshener and was eight days late. Given that I leave them with the buck three days and I figure their due date from the first mounting, she may have not bred till the last day; so she would have been five days late, which in actuality, was not late at all.

GESTATION TABLE

Month bred	Month due	Minus days
July	December	-3
August	January	-3
September	February	-3
October	March	-1
November	April	-1
December	May	-1
January	June	-1
February	July	0
March	August	-3
April	September	-3
May	October	-3
June	November	-3

Your doe is going to be pregnant for five months. For strong healthy kids and quality milk production, there are two stages of pregnancy care.

The first three months is the first stage, though you will notice little difference in your doe. Most of the fetal growth is carried on one side. As you stand behind her, you will notice a filling-out on the right side, as early as two months. (I have a Saanen that will look four months pregnant in two weeks and stay that way.) Once pregnant, a heavy producing doe may show a drastic drop in milk production. Some of mine will go from 1 gallon a day to two squirts within two weeks. Some does will stagger the decreasing quantity over the entire pregnancy. Some will dry up in a few weeks or months, and there is the occasional doe that won't slow down at all.

During the first three months, continue with the regular management of hoof trimming, worming and cleanliness. During this first stage the doe can be milked as usual, even though production drops. If you don't decrease grain, they can be taught to stay in their lactation longer. I add oats during this time, because an old-timer told me oats would help keep them in milk. I haven't been doing it long enough to put my stamp on it, but will continue until I can disprove the theory.

The milking doe needs a six-to-eight week drying off period before she should be expected to produce again. This begins the second stage of pregnancy care. If you have a particularly hard-to-handle doe, you may want to discontinue hoof trimming. She shouldn't get rambunctious enough trying to avoid the trimming to cause damage to the unborn babies.

To dry off the doe, simply stop milking and cut her feed intake. Never cut down on the hay. In persistent milkers you may have to stop all feed and use just hay. If the udder becomes too full and tight, release just enough pressure to ease the udder. Technically speaking, the udder should fill to the same pressure as the other body pressures, then the fluid should be reabsorbed into the body and the udder will begin to shrink. The doe will not give as much if she is not allowed this time to rest, and the udder will break down prematurely if not allowed time to rebuild necessary tissues.

I trusted a vet once and did not release the pressure on a special doe, and her udder split. She lost one side. Always release enough pressure for comfort.

Now is the time that the nonmilking pregnant does need to be included in all the plans for the last two months. About 70 percent of the fetal growth takes place during the last six weeks of pregnancy. Therefore, good eating habits need to be maintained. Make sure the pregnant does get free choice of the hay, and start them on a grain ration necessary for a milking doe. This is when I start at least a cup of 16 percent to 19 percent protein, sweet dairy blend, still mixing with sweet crimped oats, once a day.

If you have does of different sizes you may need to house them separately. The housing should be large enough for the does to move about freely, with doors and gates wide enough to prevent stomachs from bumping. Older, more aggressive does may spend time butting against the younger ones, causing damage or death to the unborn kids, so separation may be the only safety measure. As always, don't let the animal get fat. Continue to check for extra fat at the withers.

Strange as it may sound, a dairy goat often looks her best when she is pregnant and may appear overweight when she really is not. Frequent checking of the meat on the withers will avoid this problem. Additional grain is necessary if the doe is to maintain her weight and care for the kids, and withdrawing grain may be necessary for the doe that gains too much.

At the beginning of the last month, you will want to get first fresheners and any new goats accustomed to the routine of twice-a-day chores. This is the time to worm, give the prescribed vaccinations for your area, and begin them on their new schedules. This includes tying them for milking, using the stanchion or milk stand, and giving grain twice a day. As they are tied for their grain, run your hands over their bodies and udder to get them used to the idea. Once they freshen, they will pay back your efforts with increased production and easier handling. I call this my rehearsal time, not only to prepare the does, but me. People with arthritis or carpal tunnel syndrome need to start workouts with their tennis balls. Other handicaps may call for a stool, so practice squatting and sitting to get in shape.

A week to ten days before they are due, the does need to be clipped and mani-cured. The flow that follows kidding is called lochia and comes from the womb. This discharge is sticky, dries quickly, and clings to the does' back legs and udder. Left alone, it will remain for several days and be messy. By clipping or shaving the back legs, the vulva and the rear and applying Vaseline, you can greatly alleviate one of the largest problems of the first-time milkings.

The milk will be cleaner if the udder is shaved or clipped, and the doe will suffer less discomfort if you aren't pulling her hair as you milk. If she's apprehen-sive about the electric trimmers, set them to the side while they are running, and go on about something for a minute, until she realizes this is not going to hurt. I have used scissors, but this could be dangerous, as the goat has wool under the hair, and you're not really sure where the skin lies. I do not advise using a razor.

Two to five days before kidding time, the udder will begin to fill with milk and harden. Don't panic if it doesn't; some does wait until after the kids to drop the milk. If the udder becomes too large, or too tight, it may be necessary to milk only enough to relieve the pressure. (Save and freeze this milk.) Should the udder be hot or inflamed, there may be a touch of mastitis, which must be treated. You will have to take samples of the milk to the vet for an accurate diagnosis and proper antibiotics, because several bacteria cause mastitis. (I have more on this in chapter 28.)

During the last couple weeks of pregnancy, there will be a looseness of the vulva, a much larger rear barrel, and the tail will start to rise due to the gradual loosening of the tail muscles.

As pregnancy proceeds, the muscles beneath the tail continue to loosen and at the end are almost nonexistent. If you run your thumb and forefinger down and under each side of the tail, you will notice this as it proceeds. Just before delivery, these muscles are completely relaxed. I make it a habit to check these muscles throughout the pregnancy, as a matter of habit, like checking the withers. This is a good way to find out ahead of time if the doe did not mate, or if you had your date wrong and she may be earlier or later.

A few days before the kids are due, the experts advise removing the doe from the herd and putting her in her own private "kidding" pen. This is to provide her with all the peace, quiet and privacy she requires for the event. The kidding pen should be large enough for her to move comfortably and freely, and water should not be left at a level in which the kid could accidentally be born into and drown. Provide plenty of clean fresh bedding. Many people advise pulling the doe off full grain and feeding a laxative or bran feed the last few days.

When I tried to separate my does to kid, they had fits and they bleated constantly for their companions. I felt they were doing themselves more damage by being separated and I returned them to the herd. I don't change their feeding habits, either. The normal healthy doe on adequate grain will make the proper changes in her system without flushing with extra feed, or laxatives. These are decisions you will have to make in your own management. If you choose not to separate the doe for kidding, make sure she has access to a private, clean area and watch her closely, because she probably won't use it unless you lead her in. As far as clean bedding, she is going to scratch (or paw) it all away.

Many does will continue eating and have their kids in the midst of the herd. Some will go off feed for the event, but others will not. It is best to leave these choices up to the doe. Kidding is too important to interfere too much. This is an area that should be left up to the does, but you should be there to watch her choice of maternity beds because she may not be too choosy about cleanliness. I have always been there with a clean sheet or blanket to drop under the kid before it lands where she planned. Your job is to help, not to interfere.

No bucks are to be around the does during the last two months, and definitely leave the bucks out of the kidding area.

Preparing for kids

No matter how much trouble your animals give you throughout the rest of the year, it vanishes with the birth of the kids. Temporarily, for a couple of days, the joy of the newborn overcomes all the blood, sweat and tears of the last year. Suddenly, you forget all about hoof trimming, mucking out manure, vet bills, and fixing fences. The curious little critter, wobbling on four tiny legs, with the tiny little voice that sounds so much like "ma ma," absolutely steals away your heart.

I was lucky enough one year to stagger my kids from January to June, and the delight was never-ending as one chore after another was rewarded with a baby or three.

On the other hand, I really messed up my sleep schedule one year when I had a night job and just let the does breed. I had another couple living in a trailer beside me, and they helped with the chores. I would no sooner doze off when they would call me about another baby. Four does had 10 babies in one day, and I hardly got a nap. The next day, it was two more does with three kids. On the third day, when a first freshener was due, I stayed up but she waited another week.

Not many animals can compare with the newborn kid for keeping your interest and adding pleasure to your otherwise humdrum routine. I had a friend who despised goats, but newborns found their way onto his lap, and he would be caught cuddling them behind our backs! One landlord threatened to send us packing should one of the goats ever get in his way, but when kidding season came, he was the first visitor, begging to feed the baby.

The new one will stand on his feet within minutes after birth, take the nipple almost immediately, and within hours will be trying to jump. The baby goat is born with hair and teeth and very soft hooves. If it doesn't get up and try to nurse, the doe will think there is something wrong with it and leave it behind, especially if it is born outside. She's not so bad if they are born in the barn. She will stay close by and keep checking, and when the little one gets up, she'll be there for him. Since I pull my kids and bottle feed, this is not a problem. If your goats have some of the diseases mentioned later in this book, you will need to take the babies from their mother anyway.

In a few weeks the kid will simply be a goat, running, jumping, and checking out new domains. Then you once again become the caretaker of goats, with all the work that goes along with it. Don't be too busy to take the little time you have and enjoy the new ones. Goat owners don't get much of a chance to really stop and enjoy their work. Your life will be happier for it, and the kid will be much easier to handle for all the extra love and attention it gets.

By the time the kids are due, you should have the doe ready and think about getting ready for the kids. You should have already made up your mind what you are going to do with the kids. If they are does, will they be kept for future breeding, sold to control the size of the herd, or will the doe be sold? You need to know what you will do with the bucks before they are born, because they will steal your heart, if you don't steel your emotions the little guy could become a pet you don't want or need. I have held over a buck for a year to see how he would look, but it was definitely with the aspect in mind that if he doesn't live up to my expectations, he goes. Prepare your family ahead for unwanted animals so they handle it better. Children are very adaptable and can easily love even the ones they know will not stay.

Know what must be done for deformed and defective kids, and prepare for the situation. Be prepared for multiple births, but don't allow single birth to be a big disappointment. Kids born singly are generally larger and healthier, though they might be lonelier until playmates arrive.

Make plans for raising the kids. Even if you plan to leave the kids with their mothers, or just the mothers' milk, it would not hurt to have an extra bottle and nipple around, just in case it's needed. The same goes for some kind of milk replacer. Store-bought milk can be expensive.

Have your kid pens and boxes clean and ready before you need them. Gather plenty of absorbent towels, rags, and/or burlap to aid in cleaning the kids and other messes you may make. A disinfectant for the cords and hooves should be at your fingertips.

Extreme weather conditions may call for extreme solutions when it comes to caring for the new kids. If your doe is due to deliver in a frigid winter, you'll need to take precautions against the cold. Generally speaking, the new kids need clean, dry bedding in a draft-free area. Bedding should be absorbent, but not coarse. If the temperature is below freezing, the kids may need the extra shelter of your house, basement, garage or porch. If at all possible, try not to bring the kids into the house, as you will have to keep them there until outside temperatures equal those inside. A very small box with a top, sheltered in the barn, will often hold enough body heat to keep the kids warm and comfortable. Heat lamps work wonders, but they have to be hung high enough that the kids, or any other goats, can't jump up and tangle in them. If the lamps are real high, drape sheets or blankets around them in a fire proof manner, to hold the heat in the smaller area. This can be done by nailing or stapling sheets or blankets to the rafters, or hanging the material from hooks in the ceiling. Clothesline can be strung up around these areas to hold the sheets or blankets up.

Should you have a way to raise the box, putting a heat lamp under it is the safest method. However, make sure that no urine can leak through to the lamp and short it out.

When it is cold, wet, or windy, or if you're a worrywart like me, you may want a temporary "goat coat." Children's' T-shirts work well, or an old blanket, cut into 8-by-12 inch squares, can easily be tied or pinned to the new kid. Kids should be completely dry before covering. A hair dryer set on low or medium can be used. Should you have to bring a new kid in out of the cold, chances are that it will have gotten chilled. It will need to be dried and should be put under a vaporizer. Keep your vaporizer ready. Should you reach the newborn in subzero temperatures and retrieve a half-frozen kid barely alive, don't panic. Wrap the kid well and get it to the house. Dry it immediately, and stimulate circulation by gently massaging. Don't try to feed the kid until it is warm, because milk can easily be taken into the lungs. Severely frozen kids may be submerged into warm water to thaw, and then dried and massaged.

Newborns that arrive in cold weather stand a greater chance of catching pneumonia. Consider the fact that a newborn arrives, wet, at a body temperature between 101 and 103 degrees. Breathing extremely cold air, under 20 degrees, into the warm lungs, causes condensation; which causes moisture in the lung. It's a good idea to treat these kids for pneumonia before it becomes acute. A healthy dam, with all her immunities, is the first precaution.

Should you need to keep the kids inside the house or basement, or any other area that was not intended for animals, there are several tips to ease the inconvenience.

The area needs to be dry and ventilated, with access to light, but away from the heater. The cooler the temperature, the sooner they can be returned outside. To aid in cleanliness and odor control inside the boxes, it may be helpful to use a bedding of several layers.

I put a leak-proof piece of plastic on the floor and up the sides of the box at least four inches, to prevent leakage. Put two to three inches of sawdust in that and cover with a layer of deodorized kitty litter or soda to aid in odor control. Put the normal bedding of hay or straw on top. This top layer can be changed as needed and a deodorizer used as needed, and the bottom layer goes to the garden when the goat goes back out.

If the kid is kept in the house long enough, take the opportunity to band, burn horns, and worm, vaccinate, and trim waddles if you don't want them while you have it in the warm area.

Don't let the sick ones cause you to forget to take care of the others in the barn. They need the same care. They can be brought in for the short time it takes for maintenance.

Whether you let the dam raise the kids, or you decide to take them, is a management decision you'll have to make. I have noticed that it is more common to leave them with their mothers in the South than it is in the North. There doesn't seem to be a reason.

Bottle raised babies will always be your pets, as long as they are with you. You will not want these bucks going to an auction and take the chance of being bought and sold every other year and passed around all their lives, so it is best to castrate (wether) them and sell them for pets, or for butcher goats.

19

Parturition Is the Actual Kidding

When the due date nears, you are going to worry as much as any expectant mother, or rather, like the father in the waiting room. The doe won't. While she is sedately continuing her daily routine, you'll be dashing out to check her many times too early.

You can't sit by her side day and night, nor can you ignore the situation, although I can say that my girls have taken their sleeping bags to the barn for the night, and I have been known to fall asleep when I sat down for a few minutes.

Many goat owners have gone to the expense of installing closed–circuit TVs in the barn. Baby monitors work well and are cheaper, if your barn is close enough to the house. The doe should be watched, but not interrupted. This is a good time to do some of those chores around the barn that you've been neglecting as you keep an eye on her. Overly anxious goatkeepers try to avoid working near the doe because they are afraid of upsetting her. None of my does have ever minded my presence.

If your doe was hand-bred and you kept track of the due date, you've eliminated most of the guesswork. You've got the time narrowed to a ten-day period, with the due date being closer to the middle. You will be relieved to know that over 85 percent of the kids are born in the daytime. My experience has been that the same percentage will start the labor process in the morning.

There are many signs to watch for approaching birth. The doe should start filling the udder, but this is not foolproof. The belly will deepen at the bottom, rather than at the sides, as the kids are dropping in preparation for the birth canal. The vulva should begin a drainage of yellowish liquid and become loose and flabby, swelling two to six times its normal size. The udder may become large and swollen, with the secretion turning to yellow.

The tail muscles should so relaxed that is seems they are nonexistent. This is

137

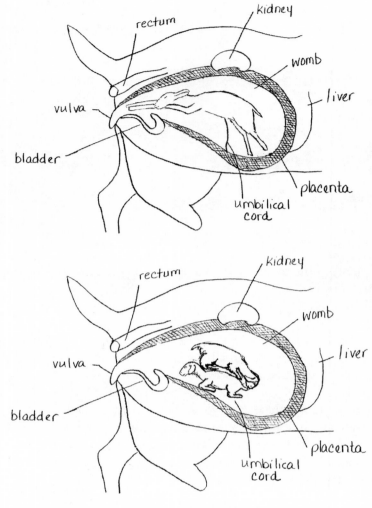

Womb positioning for kids.

your first solid clue that the first stage of labor has begun. You have a good reason to check those tail muscles frequently throughout the last month, so you will be familiar with them and know what completely loose really feels like. The doe is supposed to segregate herself from the others, but she will not always. She is likely to be restless and may stop eating. During this first stage, you're not likely to notice much. Most of the activity is internal, as the uterus is working the kid into the birth position.

If the doe seems to be nervous with you there, move far enough away to lessen her anxiety but close enough to be within earshot. She may change her mind. You should try to make it a point to be there during delivery, even if you're not needed. Frequently, you will be needed, if for nothing but comfort and moral support. If you plan to let the doe raise the babies, (dam raised) this is all not so important. But if you plan to bottle feed or separate the doe and kids for some time, then you need to be there. If your doe has CAE (chapter 27) the kids can't nurse until the milk has been pasteurized.

As the first stage of labor progresses, the doe may become more restless, pawing at the ground and looking back at her sides, sometimes licking or biting her sides as the contractions continue. You should notice the tail rising with the contractions. She may moan and groan (especially the Nubian) and want to be with you. First-timers may want to be in your lap. The doe will get up and down, and turn, and maybe even change bedding places.

Generally, the contractions will be 15 minutes apart and 16 to 30 seconds long. As labor progresses, they will increase to three minutes apart. This stage of labor can last from 12 minutes to 12 hours.

Watching for all these signs of approaching parturition helps to take the element of surprise out of the birth but is not always effective. If there is a possibility your doe will birth when you can't be there, tape her teats so the kids can't nurse unless you will dam raise and CAE is not an issue.

At the beginning of the second stage of labor (the actual birth), you will notice a string of clear mucus hanging from the vulva. This is a signal that birth should occur within the hour. Don't let anyone, or the weather, or your nerves talk you out of doing something after that hour. During this stage, the kid is pushed from the uterus, through the cervix and vagina, and finally out.

After arming myself with all this information, I was able to successfully detect the signs of labor beginning in five out of six does in a row one spring. Very proud of myself, with a pen full of new kids, I was not too concerned about the sixth doe. However, after careful observations and hourly checks, No. 6 did surprise me. At 8 the morning after her due date, she showed no symptoms of starting labor, making my sleepless night a waste of trips to the barn to check on her. At 8:20, I glanced out to see her sniffing at the ground, nowhere near the other goats. I went to investigate and found triplets at her feet. I still have no idea how all that happened so quickly, as the experts advise that multiple births are generally 20 minutes apart. Never assume that you know it all, because it is possible for a goat to deliver triplets in 20 minutes. If anything is possible, I assume that at one time or another, a goat will do it!

As the kid is arriving, the doe will usually lie down, sticking her legs out straight, and push with the contractions. She is likely to accompany this with grunts and repeat the process many times, getting up and down. She may cry out but don't let this scare you (women have been doing this for years). Some does will deliver while standing. If this goes on for more than an hour, without progress, get to a vet, or a person whom you can trust with your goat, or be prepared to take over yourself.

The first thing you should see is two little hooves. The first time, you will not recognize them as hooves, because they are really soft tissue and look more like white or cream colored clumps. One of my friends actually panicked and thought the hooves were parts of the goat's "innards falling out." Within a couple of inches, or at the same time, the nose is appearing. It should still be covered with a membrane, which you do not remove. Trying to clear the nostrils before the kid is out will cause it to take in air prematurely, the chest will swell and delivery will be more difficult. Shortly after the arrival of the nose and feet, the doe will push the kid out. (If feet come out, up to the knees, with no nose, the delivery is in trouble.) Often the delivery is so fast that you will see the whole kid before you notice the nose and feet. Sometimes the doe will start to deliver the kid, and withdraw it after the contraction. This may happen many times and is another sign that she may be in trouble. Try to keep the doe calm and give her extra time to deliver on her own. If after two or three attempts, the kid keeps appearing and disappearing, or only legs are showing, try laying the doe down and raising her rump up to six or eight inches from the ground. A bag of feed, an old tire, and blankets rolled up, anything that will raise her. With the rump raised, the kid should fall back in the uterus, reposition itself, and have a better chance for the next attempt.

If the doe is still having trouble, you need to be in a position to try to get hold of the kid on its next appearance. This is tricky, because the newcomer is pretty slippery and hard to grip. Once you have it, don't pull. Just hold it, to prevent its disappearing again, and tug gently with the next contraction. Before you know it, you'll have the new one. Now you can clear the nostrils.

If you are just getting legs, and you've tried raising the goat, and you still get just legs, call for help, find a vet, or should worse come to worse, you may have to go in yourself. Don't delay this for more than an hour, as not only is the life of the kid in danger, but the life of the doe.

It is very seldom that a doe needs help. In 20 years I've seen it happens twice, and when I was a kid, I recall my dad helping only once.

For those of you a bit skeptical about helping a doe, let me assure you that there is almost no blood involved. There may be a spot of blood with the cord and the placenta (afterbirth), but the kid is relatively free of it. This is not to say that there is not a mess. The kid is wrapped with a mucous membrane that ranges from a clear color to a dark yellow. This membrane is slimy and sticky but wipes off easily when wet. Observers usually have more trouble with their stomachs when the doe tries to clean up than with the actual birthing process. (If you are taking the kids, don't let the doe clean them, but let her clean you.)

When you have to help the doe, start with scrupulously clean hands and gloves. A lubricant such as KY Jelly, Vaseline, baby oil, or udder balm, is a necessity. Clip all fingernails, and gently insert your hands in the goat. If only the legs are present, very carefully push them back, following them with your hand, slowly and gently. Any barrier should mean a slow reposition of your fingers to prevent tearing. Once the legs have been pushed back into the womb, carefully feel for the neckline, following it to the head, and try to get the head turned into position. Once this is done, relax with the goat, hope she has another contraction, and slowly start the kid back out with the legs and head properly lined. Second and third kids should come normally.

This really is a job for a vet, but when you have goats you will find that getting a vet on the weekend or a holiday to give a darn about a goat is pretty tough. Practice this procedure in your mind over and over until you feel completely satisfied that you can do it. Talk to your vet, and other experienced people till you feel as though it will be second nature, and not second guessing.

The second stage of labor can take from 12 minutes to two hours, depending on how many kids are being born. The cord should break by itself as the kid arrives. If not, cut the cord and dip in disinfectant, inside and outside the cord and all around the naval. Germs will crawl inside the cord, so it's helpful to clip or tie it.

The kid should breathe immediately. If not, turn it upside down and gently massage the chest area to free the passages for air. Sometimes it might be necessary to sling or shake the kid to start breathing, but all action should be done gently, because the small bones are fragile. Ask the vet's assistant to show you the method used to sling new born puppies (after a C-section). A newborn kid averages between five to seven pounds. Three and a half pounds isn't unusual, and neither is 12 pounds. Check the kid for defects and help clean up. If you find this chore distasteful the mother will do it, but if you plan to take the kids, it's best not to let her clean them. That is one of the bonding processes. It is the opinion of many breeders that the doe should not clean the rest of the mess, but all my new moms always have. It seems like its second nature to them and I don't have a chance to get it done before they do it. It seems to help them to settle down, and they deliver the next kids faster.

If more kids are coming, they should follow in five to 20 minutes. Frequently, the second kid will be born breech (rump first), and just as frequently, the doe will need help delivering the breech kids. This is a good time to raise the rump and hope the new one will reposition itself to arrive properly.

The tail is the first thing to arrive with a breech birth, and there is nothing to hang on to and tug. In this case, very gently try to insert two fingers and try to extract one leg, then the other leg. The doe should be able to handle the rest with the next contraction. (When you assist, I must repeat, be clean.) You can check the doe for more kids by lifting or pushing up on the stomach, right in front of the udder. If there is another kid, you can usually feel it. If the birth is over, you will most likely get a gush of water from the doe, so don't do this from the rear of the goat.

The last stage of labor is the expulsion of the placenta. This may take several hours, maybe up to three days, but is usually immediately. Massaging the udder, milking the udder, and massaging the abdomen will help stimulate the hormone that helps the uterus begin contracting and pushing the placenta out. Don't try to pull this out yourself, as it is connected to the uterine wall, and any premature pulling could tear the fragile tissue. Leave this to the doe or the doctor. The doe will clean up the placenta herself if you let her, but a few breeders will advice your to retrieve it and bury it. I let Mother Nature have her own way and leave it to the doe.

When to call a vet? Naturally, it varies with the animal, and common sense is the key factor. Here are a few basic time tables to follow, but even this should be used with common sense.

1. If your doe has not delivered within three days after her final due date, giving her 158-day gestation, recheck your calendar and your figures. If your dates are correct, consult a vet.
2. Once contractions have become regular, this stage should not continue for more than 12 hours without some sign of the kid. If the mucus membrane has dropped, wait no more than one hour.

3. The doe should not have to work more than one hour (hard labor) to deliver the first kid.
4. If it takes more than 30 minutes for signs of the next kid and you've tried raising the doe's rump, call for help.
5. The placenta should take no longer than three days. Unless you really watch closely, you will probably miss it. After the placenta is discharged, the doe may have a bloody drainage for up to three weeks, but normal is three days.

Once delivery is over, don't forget mama. She would love a drink of warm water, and if she has missed a feeding, she will be hungry. Watch her carefully for the next three or four days and check her temperature each day, in case of infection. It is all too easy to be so excited about the kids that you tend to neglect the real star of the show.

I failed at the common sense factor myself on Valentine's Day, 2004. Arkansas had a freak ice and snow storm and my best doe went into labor. I knew she was having trouble and called every vet in town to find out they were all away at a convention. I did not trust myself to do it alone.

The next morning she was no longer in labor, and when my daughter and I went to pull the kid, his neck was turned backward in the uterus. She had three extremely large kids, all dead, and she immediately died.

I now have found a vet that lives next to his office, and I can drive in bad weather, but should this ever happen to me again, I doubt I will take the time to call anyone. I will simply do what I know I should have done. That's why I advise you to memorize everything you have to do until it seems like second nature so you won't second-guess yourself. The fear factor will cost you your goat and kids.

20

Newborns and General Kid Care

When the kids arrive, you'll have plenty to do. If you have a busy schedule and wouldn't have time for a new baby, then it would be best to leave the kids on the dam. It's hard to tell which task comes first. You'll avoid a lot of tension and confusion if you are prepared and know which management practice you want. The babies need to be fed, checked for defects, weighed, marked and settled in

Sue Karber's kids stay in the house for safety.

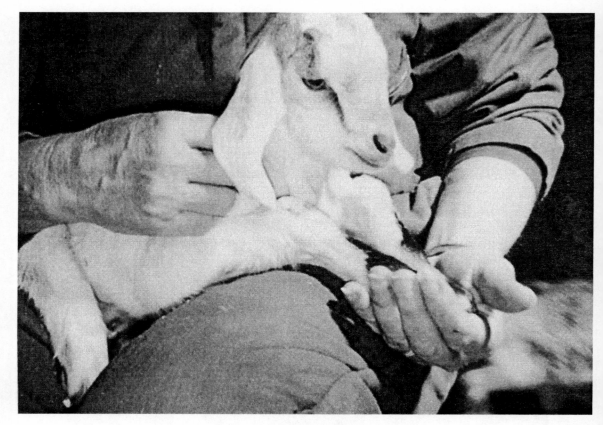

Sue Karber holds a Nubian kid.

comfortably. All vaccinations recommended by your vet need to be taken care of promptly. If you have a CAE positive dam, milk has to be pasteurized.

Take one step at a time. Though the kids need to be fed soon, there are other considerations. If there are any sexual defects in the little does, they may be more obvious at birth and disappear shortly after birth.

I have known people to check the sex of the kids first, even before cleaning, though I do find it a little easier to do a quick cleanup first, then check and record the sex. This is the time to check the doelings for an enlarged vulva, with a pea shaped pod at the base. This may mean an intersexed animal and need to be marked for culling. This pod could disappear in a few hours, or a day, so check early.

Attend to the cord and hooves, and finish the cleanup, trying to get the animal as dry as possible. Cord and navels need to be completely dipped in a seven percent tincture of iodine or equal disinfectant. Hooves should be rinsed with disinfectant to prevent bacteria from attacking the tender growth. Sometimes I disinfect before I finish the cleanup and check the sex.

Settle the kids into a comfortable, warm, dry, clean area and wait for his/her siblings to arrive. When they have all been born, and delivery is over, mama needs to be taken care of properly. Then it's time to think of feeding them. In cases of an emergency, you do have up to 12 hours. If something happens so that the doe doesn't make it, or doesn't have milk, or the kids were dumped on you by someone else, it's nice to know they will live a while. There are several methods of feeding kids, but all newborns need the mother's first milk, colostrum. Although this is not actually "standard" milk, it is wholesome food, and though it is not generally recommended, colostrum can be used for human consumption. Colostrum contains vast amounts of vitamin A, is high in protein, and acts as a laxative to get the kids' system started. Immunities from disease are passed from the mother through the milk, along with antibiotics, antibodies, and anything you've given the doe in the past week.

In case the mother cannot be milked, or for some reason, colostrum is not available, you can make a substitute. It does not contain the antibodies or immunities or the mothers' milk, but it is a last resort if you can't get the first milk from the doe. This is the biggest reason to freeze whatever leftover colostrum that we do get.

COLOSTRUM REPLACEMENT MIX

3 cups milk
1 beaten egg
1 tablespoon sugar
1 teaspoon cod liver oil

The next time you go to the store, buy some cod liver oil. Since it does have other goat uses, it should become a staple. The newborn needs the mother's milk for at least three days, and then if you change it, change it slowly, just as you would a baby, so you don't shake up the digestive system.

I weigh and mark my kids just before I feed them so I can tell which one eats and how much it eats. I used to do this with each feeding, but I've found that daily for the first week, and weekly for the first month, is good.

When the kids have been fed and settled, take a break and rest your back. You'll need it.

Once refreshed, return to the kids and check for more birth defects. Many people don't like the looks of the harmless waddles hanging from the chin and clip them at birth. If you choose to do so, simply cut with a sharp knife and disinfect.

Kids, especially Nubians, will often be born with a folded ear. Flatten the ear and gently massage to increase circulation. In most instances this defect will correct itself. If in three days it doesn't, then cut a piece of cardboard the same size as the ear and gently tape the ear to it. Don't bind the ear tightly enough to cut off circulation. Check the ear, and change the tape every couple of days until

Rene Matthews' La Mancha kids.

it is corrected. The goat should not be allowed to keep a folded ear; it could increase the chance of ear infection, ear mites, and chaffing.

Other problems include weak or misshaped legs, which are most common in multiple births. If the goat has a crooked or weak leg, don't give it up for lost right away. Crooked legs will often straighten themselves with the help of a homemade splint. For a splint, use a Popsicle stick, or something similar, and lightly but firmly wrap it to the leg, straightening the leg. I use old strips of elastic bandages, the kind used for sprained knees and ankles, and cut them into two-inch strips. Change the splint as the leg straightens, or as the kids the kid grows. Often a crooked leg will straighten in two or three days, and the kid will grow up as healthy and as strong as the others. If the legs are weak, the kid will have trouble standing, and it will either drag the weak leg or walk on the first joint. You can fashion a brace with the same principle as the splint, wrapping it to the weak leg or joint, forcing the leg straight and holding the kid up. Check the legs every two or three days and discontinue the brace when the kid walks well without it.

I once saw a newborn with his front legs so badly bent back that he could not stand. The knees were stiff and the legs could not be straightened by hand. I advised the owner to massage and wrap the legs with elastic and pray for the best. Two weeks later, the kid was romping with the rest of the goats. The owner said he

Judy Erhlich, who lives in Alaska, keeps the kid warm by dressing it in a T shirt.

practiced physical therapy on the kid five times a day, rewrapping the leg straighter each time.

You can check for blindness by simply moving from one side of the kid to the other to see if it shows any reaction. Check for deafness in the same way, but clap or "baa" at them. Blind and deaf kids can grow, but it takes more care to maintain them. They should be butchered early.

Undershot and overshot jaws are defects which, in severe cases, can hamper a goat's eating habits. The overshot jaw will be the upper jaw extending too far out from the lower. As a result the goats' gums do not meet and will prevent it from eating properly. The undershot jaw is just opposite, with the lower jaw extending too far away from the upper. Make a note of all defects on your records for culling, as most defects are hereditary.

Kids will not eat much at first. They should be fed within one to 12 hours, and then every three or four hours until three or four ounces is being taken. This means you have to decide which method of kid feeding you'll be using. Each goat-keeper has a different idea on feeding, and each one is sure his way is best. I will try to cover the different methods, so you can choose.

If you don't plan to keep the milk, the obvious solution would seem to be to leave the kids with their dams to nurse. Since this is the most natural, it is best for the kid. Kids left with their mothers show the greater weight gains at weaning and are the healthiest. On the other hand, kids left by their mothers' sides tend to be a little more skittish and harder to handle. The doe may also be harder to handle in her effort to protect her young.

Many breeders with show stock believe that allowing the kids to nurse causes extra wear and tear on the udder and they immediately remove the kids. Frequently, nursing kids will favor one side of the udder, causing a lop-sided effect. Both sides of the udder need to be drained.

When kids nurse, you have no idea how much milk they are consuming or how high the doe's production is, so you can't keep complete milking records. If the kid is not getting enough milk, you may not realize it until his weight suffers. There is a theory that does will produce more if the kids are allowed to nurse, however, with the kid getting all the milk, it is hard to prove this theory.

My theory is that one kid will not need as much milk and therefore won't drink as much and the doe's system will adjust accordingly. On the other hand, if she has three very large healthy kids all fighting for a nipple, there's no way her udder can keep up.

Kids allowed to run at the mother's side will more than likely speed up the worm cycle and cause faster infestation for the does.

One way to solve some of these problems and still let the kids nurse is to separate the kids from the does and return them to the does at feeding times. The kids will be easier to handle, the does won't be so protective, and you can supervise the feeding so make sure all the kids are allowed to eat. In this manner, you can keep an eye on the udder to prevent the kids from favoring sides. By milking the doe when the kids are finished, you are not only getting the milk, but you know that the udder has been emptied and that the kids did have a chance to get enough. You are also encouraging the udder to produce more, because experts say the udder will produce as much as is removed.

When I do this, I put the kids in a clean pen, adjoining the does. At nighttime chores, I turn them in with their mothers. They have all night to feed, and the doe doesn't have to sleep on an uncomfortable udder. At morning chores, I take the kids out, give the does their grain, and milk out each udder before the day starts. This clears the udder, stops the does from rushing out to green grass too early, keeps the kids off the green grass too early, and the kids bond with me. They have free choice of hay when they are ready to nibble, and after a week, I leave a pan of grain so they have free choice. Water, salt, and minerals are handy, but the young ones seldom use them. It has been suggested that the babies learn to eat from their mother, and being at her side will teach them better and earlier. But goats' natural curiosity causes them to be quite snoopy, so they are going to taste everything.

Weaning can be difficult when kids are left with their mothers. These youngsters will try to get back to their mothers and their mothers will let them. This can try your patience to the limit.

Since the milk is not used for people the first three days, you can allow the kids to nurse for that time, and then take them from the doe. This can be traumatic for the doe and kids, though it does save work and cleaning during those first days.

Pan feeding is much harder to teach, and shouldn't be taught for three to four weeks, but is easier to maintain once the kid learns. You still have the disadvantage of not knowing how much each kid is getting. To teach the kid to drink from a pan, allow it to suck from your fingers as you dip the fingers in the milk. Eventually, the kid will catch on. Since this procedure could take two or three days, early pan feeding is frowned upon. There are biological reasons against early pan feeding. Pan feeding represses the natural or instinctual tendencies of the sucking and can cause a temporary loss of weight. The kid normally nurses with its head up and neck stretched out, so the opening from the throat to the stomach has a special way of handling the situation. When the kid stretches the neck upward to nurse, the opening automatically funnels the milk to the right place. When the neck and head drop, the opening becomes smaller and prevents unwanted particles from getting into the stomach. Because of this system, it is harder for the kid to drink with its head down. In a few weeks when the kid starts to nibble, the opening ceases to close and pan feeding is easier to accomplish.

Several kids may be pan-fed at once, leaving only one container to clean. Larger kids, or kids with an overzealous appetite, may get more than their fair share, leaving less milk for the smaller, weaker ones. It may help to feed the slower kids in separate pans until they catch up. Kids are every bit as noisy, fast, and messy as hogs and though they aren't vicious, they are just as selfish when it comes to dipping their noses clear up to their eyeballs. Nubians and Boars will get their ears in the milk and when they are finished, they will shake milk everywhere.

Another disadvantage is that you have to dry to goats after pan feeding. There is an acid in the milk that will cause the skin on the nose and ears to dry and get scaly. Though this will pass, it can get infected, so towel drying is easier.

Bottle feeding is easy, effective, and most popular. Any soft drink bottle with a nipple is sufficient. Nipples for lambs are sold in feed stores, vets' offices, dairy supply houses, and pet supply stores. Ordinary baby bottles will work, but the nipples are not durable for goats.

Buckets are available with several nipples for feeding several kids at a time, which means that you won't know how much they get to drink. Racks for bottles are easily built to hold more than one bottle to speed feeding time. When teaching new kids to nurse, simply put the nipple in their mouth and wait for the natural sucking instinct. Every once in awhile, you will run across a kid that will stick its head out, hold that nipple and not do another thing. You have to be patient and squeeze its jaws together to try to simulate nursing and wait. For the first few days, you may have to help the kid find and hold the nipple. Always hold or place the bottle at an angle so the kid doesn't take in air. You can stick a hypodermic needle in the nipple right above where the nipple and bottle meet, to allow air to leave the bottle and aid in the kid feeding. Always get the needle back in the same hole, or

you will have a leaky, worn-out nipple before its time. Scratching the poll or rubbing the backside like the doe would, will help.

Continuous feeding is a system by which the milk is automatically piped
to the kids and lands in containers with nipples. The milk is automatically kept
at the right temperature, and the entire set up is expensive. It can also be done
with bottles, in temperature-controlled containers, but takes a staff to keep
changing bottles.

With this method, you don't know how much milk each goat gets, and sickness or disease is easier to spread and harder to detect. When using this method,
the milk is gradually allowed to get colder to the point the goats are not drinking
warm milk at all. This situation causes more scours and bloat.

Generally, milk should be heated to 100 degrees for feeding newborn kids.
The goats' body temperature is 101 to 103, so this is close to what the kid gets from
the mother. As the kid grows and holds its own, the temperature of the milk can
be dropped a little at a time. If scouring occurs, raise the temperature and wait a
few days before lowering it again. Some people never feed cold milk. They just
lower the temperature to lukewarm and keep it there till weaning. This system
helps to put something warm into the kids stomach twice a day and keeps them
warm on chilly days and nights. I do not lower the temperature until I see them
drinking water.

Naturally, goats' milk is best for goats, but cows' milk, powdered milk, and
milk replacers may be used with success. If you use powdered milk or milk replacer
meant for cows, cut the manufacturers directions by at least ¼ of the quantity. In
other words, if the manufacturer calls for a cup of powder to 1 gallon, use ¾ cup.
This product has an ingredient that irritates the kid's stomach and could cause
scours. (This is a good reason to breed one of your heavy milkers first, so that her
milk can help get you through the others with as little milk replacer as possible.)

Milk replacers need to be thoroughly stirred, no lumps, and continually
shaken, because it will settle quickly as you carry it to the pen. Powdered milk
replacers are not advisable in continuous feeding programs because of settling.

With any feeding method, all utensils should be thoroughly washed, rinsed
and drained. The kids' stomach will not digest foreign particles, and dirty utensils
will cause digestive upsets.

When pan or bottle feeding, you will replace the doe in the eyes of the kid.
Some people feel this is a disadvantage, because the kids may become overly
attached to you. I consider it an advantage. Because they think you are the mother,
they will follow you anywhere. Handling is easier, clipping and hoof-trimming are
not so tedious, and you have a one-to-one relationship with the animal. Within a
day or less the kid won't know its mother, and the doe will not recognize her own,
so there isn't a problem with the kid getting loose and stealing the milk from
mama. The doe may be anxious for a couple hours, maybe longer for yearlings,
looking for her young. This passes shortly, and they all settle down. The sooner the
kids are taken, the easier the work gets.

One of Rene Matthews' La Mancha kids.

Once the kid has learned to nurse from a bottle, it is hard to put it back to nurse the doe. It is easier to suck the nipple because the sucking muscles aren't strong enough to pull milk from the udder.

Many goatkeepers find bottle or pan feeding unnatural and refer to it as artificial rearing, many others (myself included) prefer it. I have many reasons.

1. I know exactly how much the kid is getting.
2. I can administer liquid medicine, crushed vitamins, and crushed Coccidiostats, etc., easier.
3. The doe's teats may be too large, the kid too small, or the kid too weak, to hang onto and nurse.
4. The doe may reject the kid.
5. Local nurseries love to bring the preschoolers out to bottlefeed.
6. I have more hand-to-goat time to get to know each animal's personality and weird behavior, and can detect poor behavior in a matter of hours, rather than a day or two.

Weaning is when the goat is taken off milk, and it can be difficult. Frequently, kids are weaned as soon as they are eating hay and grain well, or at about three to four months. Depending on the goat, the feed supplements, and the grazing available, there is no way to tell exactly when to wean. Standard weaning time, and the most popular, is about four months. Kids allowed to nurse naturally will continue through six or seven months, or till the doe dries up.

Taking the kid away from its mother after several months can be traumatic for all. The kid must be separated for the length of time needed to break the nursing habit, or until the doe refuses to allow nursing. Separating the kid takes a kid-tight pen and strong nerves. Kids and does will adjust and settle down in three or four days, but you will need another week to recuperate.

When you wean from the pan or bottle, you simply decrease the amount of milk at each feeding and add water in its place. This way the liquid consumption is the same. Before the kid realizes it, it is dependent on hay and grain and water. Kids are more likely to miss seeing you at feeding time than to miss the milk. This way you are not making any drastic changes to the diet or the kids' schedules.

Kids will start to nibble at the hay between one and three weeks and will test the grain at the same time. Hay should be made available, but only in small quantities, to prevent waste. I delete the grain after a couple of months if the kids are on good pasture and eating well. This is purely a management issue. Always keep hay out, free choice all the time, so if you don't trust the pasture to be varied enough, or if the weather is bad and they can't get out, they can still eat. Be sure to watch how your kids are doing, and adjust the hay accordingly. No weight gain means more forage, not more feed. Feed is for protein, nutrients, and vitamins. It does not take the place of forage in a goats' diet.

FEED CHART, FROM BIRTH

Age	Method	Amount	Feeding per day
Milk:			
Birth–24 hours	nursing/bottle	Free choice	4–6
24 hours–48 hours	nursing/bottle	4–6 ounce	3–4
48 hours–3 days	nursing/bottle	4–6 ounce	3
3 days–3 weeks	nursing/bottle	6 ounce–3 pints	3
3–5 weeks	nursing/bottle	3 pints–3 quarts	2
5 weeks–3 or 4 months	pail	up to 2 quarts	1–2
3–4 months	pail	decrease milk for water	1
4–6 months	pail	decrease milk for water	1
Water:			
3 days	bottle/pan	free choice	3
3–5 weeks	pail	free choice	free-choice
5 weeks–adult	pail	free choice	free choice
Hay:			
10 days—adult	hay bunk	free choice	10 percent body weight

Milking does and producing bucks:

One-half pound for 1 pound milk, or 4 pounds grain per 1 gallon milk per milking. Bucks need a quart of grain per 100 pounds, daily.

For kids, grain should only be fed in small quantities, because the kid could eat too much, causing some digestive problems. I don't give any of the kids grain if they are doing well on their browse and milk.

Milk replacers can cost more than regular milk. Figure out the cost and compare. I prefer the powdered milk replacer for cows. It is expensive but it is fortified and full of all the vitamins and protein that the animals need. Since it is made for cows, we usually use less than the directions so it is cheaper in the long run.

I usually disbud my kids at three or four weeks of age (see chapter 23), so having them on the bottle at that time eases the procedure and helps me cradle them.

Most people castrate at three or four weeks, but I like to wait till eight to ten weeks (this is a management decision, not a feeding instruction) when I have transferred the kids to a pan to make castration easier. At this age, they don't have to be handled as much anyway, so I don't have to worry with them while they are adjusting.

Hoof trimming may have to begin as early as two months.

Kids will pick up worms early, so they should be wormed at two weeks and one month, then monthly for six months if you're in a hot humid climate, less if you're in the desert or colder climates. Again, this is a management issue. Some people who have their goats on full pasture in moderate climates don't have to worm.

Moving the kids every two to three weeks and keeping the ground around feeders and bunks raked and limed will help.

Getting kids on green grass too soon may cause bloat, and they will die if not treated. An oral product quickly stops the problem, but you have to treat it immediately.

Check with your vet to find out what vaccinations are needed, not just by law but for the goats' health. Frequently there are minerals missing in the soil or the foliage in a particular area, and these would need to be added to the diet.

Vitamin B and calcium are usually big additives for goats, and you need to be armed with that information.

If your vet does not want to discuss this situation with you, call the state livestock commission for information you need.

You can also take samples of your hay and samples of your ground to the county extension service and have them analyzed, at a moderate cost, and the staff will let you know what your goats are missing.

21

Udders and Milk

Udder care can turn out to be easy or a daily chore. For some reason, most does will mature and freshen many times and die of old age without an udder problem. Other does will have frequent problems, or only have troubles once, while still others will have problems only at freshening. An udder problem threatens not only the goats' health and future milk production, but also the quality of your milk.

The first rule in udder care is cleanliness, not only during milking, but in the bedding, too. When the doe lies down, her udder lies on the bedding. Damp and dirty bedding is not only an irritant, it is full of bacteria. Keep the bedding area clean and dry, and you will prevent most of the distress.

Udders may become chapped and tender when exposed to cold weather. Make sure the doe has adequate dry shelter from the wind. If chapping still occurs, a variety of salves are available for the udders. Vaseline can be also used for simple chaffing.

Briars present a large and severe source of scratches and cuts to the udder. The best cure is removing the cause. In many areas, removing the briars can be a neverending job, and not always a successful one. In pastures where briars are a problem, I turn the bucks, wethers, kids, or dry does out onto the lots ahead to clear it. This process may take a year of grazing. Then, in the spring, the milking does can be turned onto the briars early, to keep them under control. After a few seasons with the goats, the briars will be gone.

Barbed wire, broken glass, and assorted junk take their toll on an udder. Again, the cure is removing the cause.

After a rather rambunctious doe of mine found hidden obstacles and received 11 stitches on two occasions on both sides of the udder, I decided this stitching was a trick I needed to learn. Unfortunately, I did learn. The next time the same doe ran into another sharp object was during an Iowa blizzard. No traffic was moving. I could not have taken the goat to the vet even if I had found one to come out in the storm.

Having just learned the procedure, I was caught offguard and without the proper equipment and had to improvise. I used hydrogen peroxide to clean the wound and the udder. (I now keep betadine on hand to clean the wound.) I searched my medicine cabinet and came up with a product that is used to numb baby's gums during teething. If the product was safe for babies, it had to be safe on the goat, so I used it. I found out later that there are many similar but stronger products sold that are used to numb peoples' tissues. These products have a brief effectiveness, so you have to hurry and reapply frequently. After cleaning the wound and numbing the area, check the wound for serious lacerations of main vessels or milk veins. If the wounds are too deep, or veins have been damaged, it's best to get help. Stitches may close the wound and stop the bleeding, but will not repair other internal damage unless they are done by an experienced vet.

Once you are sure you can repair the damage, give the doe an ample supply of grain to keep her busy. You may have to throw her and tie her down if she gets rowdy. A curved needle and surgical thread are ideal, but since I was not prepared, I had to use a regular needle and fine fishing line. Both were soaked in rubbing alcohol to sterilize. I discovered later that I could have used regular household thread. A pair of freshly cleaned pliers came in handy.

By closing the wound with my fingers, I calculated where the middle of the wound would be and took my first stitch. Getting the needle into the tissue at the edge of the wound is not a problem. Pulling it through the tough hide is hard, which is why I needed the pliers. Once the thread is through one side and out the other side, you gently pull the wound together so that it is shut, tie a snug, firm knot and clip the thread. Continue this process until the wound is shut and not open in any spot between the stitches. Your stitches should be ¼ to ½ inch apart, depending on the consistency of the flesh and length of the wound.

You can also start at one end of the wound and suture in and out with one continuous thread until you get to the end, and then tie it off.

When finished, cleanse the area again with peroxide or an equivalent disinfectant. Apply a light coat of salve, or the spray sold to keep flies off the wound. It's usually blue. Let the goat rest, watch the wound and administer an all-purpose antibiotic.

Watch for swelling or heat until healing begins and the wound scabs over. The healing should take two to three days. Only apply more salve if it looks as if the stitches are drying and trying to pull. If you are milking this goat, it is best to cover the hand that will be milking that side with salve, and milk with the wound in your palm to prevent pulling.

If you use fishing line and some surgical threads, you will have to clip the stitches and pull them out in eight to ten days. Household thread will rot on its own, as will catgut. Again, when removing stitches, I use the numbing product and give the doe grain. If you've had stitches, you know there is a slight tingle when they are removed, and the doe would not be used to that feeling. When

Above and right: Bea, a Nubian, in the author's homemade milk stanchion.

manually pulling stitches, recover the wound with antibiotic salve to keep the stitch holes from getting infected.

I have done many does now (not all were mine), and when it heals, the scar is better than, or at least as good as, the one left by the vets.

Use caution. Don't do any stitching that is exceptionally deep, terribly jagged, or will puncture internal organs. If it's anywhere else than the udder, shave the area first. The udder should have already been shaved.

Ask a vet to show you the procedure, even if it's on another animal. Most vets are more than willing to turn the little stuff over to you so they can devote their time to more severe problems.

Mastitis is an infection of the udder. It can affect one side alone, both sides together, or first one and then the other.

When mastitis occurs, the udder becomes swollen, hot to the touch and lumpy. I thought mastitis would be easy to detect, but it wasn't. Lumpy doesn't mean little bumps. It means a knot on the inside where the milk is. It can be as small as your thumb or as large as the udder. It frequently occurs before, during, or shortly after birth, when the udder is large and swollen, or during times of stress. The fastest form of detection is experience. I check my does' temperature

frequently during the last few days, and for a week to ten days after delivery, because I have found a rise in temperature a good cause to suspect infection (more in chapter 28).

When massaging or milking, we are told to be gentle. Newborns and nursing kids are not gentle. They butt the udder and pull the teats with gusto. However, they are not cruel or rough. With udder care, gentle must go with firm and determined.

By placing the hands on both sides of the udder, and rubbing the palms and fingers around the udder, you'll soon learn the "feel" of massaging and how much pressure the doe will stand. Any hardness in the udder area is suspicious, except for up high in the rear of the udder and toward the center of the back. Mastitis will cause the lumps to be large and toward the inside of the infected udder.

Many breeders do not use the infected milk for the baby, which is the biggest reason to freeze extra colostrum, and I agree with that theory. However, babies have gotten back in with the doe and nursed without any adverse affects.

When milking an infected udder, expect to get anything from cottage cheese-type clots to long strings of the infected milk. This needs to be done five to six times a day to get the infection out. It may cause the doe some pain, as the clots and junk coming out are bigger than the hole, which is why so much massaging is necessary. It helps to break it all down so the infected milk can be ejected from the

Good udder   Unbalanced, lacks capacity   Teats too large   Pendulous

udder. You may get some blood, which is part of the infection. Milk with blood in it is a sign of an infected udder.

At each milking, keep each goats' milk separate, and as you strain it, watch for blood at the bottom of the bowl. If it's there, you need to treat the doe and keep her milk separate.

New udders, especially in first fresheners, can be tender and uncomfortable during milking. Very gentle massaging and milking three or four times a day, for the first three days, usually helps get these udders in shape. Talking to the doe and taking your time with her is a must and helps both of you get through the chore easier. However, due to the milk letdown, speed in the actual milking is necessary. Milk letdown is an internal process for the goat. Washing and massaging the udder stimulates the nerves in the udder. This triggers a release of a hormone that helps force the milk from the udder. Most goats get this stimulation automatically when they are going to the barn, getting on the milk stand or just hearing you call them for chore time.

The hormone only works for five to seven minutes after stimulation. After that, the milk letdown is incomplete and can cause shorter lactation if it occurs regularly. You should learn to milk in eight to ten minutes or less, to get the most from your goats.

How do you milk?

It's safe to say that a milking goat is only half as hard as a milking cow, or that milking a goat is twice as easy as milking a cow. There are some pretty ridiculous directions trying to teach (or show) how to milk a goat. Each individual has his own touch, technique, and ideas. Though none of us may milk the same way, if we get the milk, most of us do it right, so there is nothing to panic about when it comes to hand milking.

You must keep in mind that the newborn grasps the teat and sucks the milk out, and that is the same theory with a milking machine. If a 4½-pound kid has the strength to draw the milk out by suction, it can't be held up there too tight!

Hand milking is forcing the milk out by grasping a teat in each hand and squeezing the milk out in squirts. Imagine each teat as a liquid-filled balloon with a hole in the top. If the top of the balloon were not tied or sealed when you tried to the squeeze the liquid from the other end, it would reverse and spurt out the top. If you try to squeeze milk out of the teat without closing off the top, it'll flow back into the udder. You and the doe will get tired of this nonsense rather quickly.

Find your own technique to stop the flow from going up as you squirt the milk down. Milking is great therapy for the hands, wrists, fingers and forearms. If you notice a mild discomfort in the muscles, don't panic. Once you've used the muscles for a while, the soreness disappears, and you'll find yourself with a firmer handshake, stronger fingers, and a good grip.

Milking is also good therapy for those who suffer from carpal tunnel syndrome and arthritis, since it is a gentle and relaxing exercise.

If I've had a dry spell in the winter, (not milking the goats), I start preparing myself about a week or two ahead. I squeeze a tennis ball for eight to ten minutes twice a day to prepare the unused muscles.

You're not going to hurt the goat as long as you don't grasp too tightly. Keep your nails trimmed, the udder trimmed, and don't yank as you pull. When first learning to milk, don't worry about hitting the bucket until you've figured out how to get the squirt in the first place. Once you've got the flow going, then you practice hitting the bucket.

My 6-year-old granddaughter was milking at age 2. She had to do everything Mama Mary did. Granted, they were little bitty squirts, and some missed the bowl, but by golly if she could do it, I can't figure out why adults are so afraid to try. It wouldn't bother me a bit to let her go out and milk now.

Always wash the udders with a rag dipped in mild detergent, and dry the udders thoroughly. I have found that it is much easier to take of bucket of warm water to the barn, and dip the udders, washing them by hand, and drying with a clean towel, than to have to mess with two towels. If you don't want to wash that udder, just watch where she puts it when she plops down.

When you're finished milking, be sure to strip the udder till it has the consistency of an empty leather glove. Stripping has two purposes: It empties the udder, thereby telling the hormones they can make more milk, and it gets the last drop of butterfat, as butterfat comes in higher content at the end of the milking process.

Raw milk

The laws on selling raw goat milk (or any raw milk) vary by state, but it is safe to assume that you can't sell raw milk legally without a license. Qualifications for a license also vary by state, but generally require that the seller make expensive modifications to his operation.

All state laws differ so I'll just explain the basic aspects. Usually, the milking room (parlor) has to have concrete floors, be equipped with drains, running water, electricity, screens, windows and whitewashed walls. It must be a specified distance from the general bedding and exercise area. There are specific requirements for temperature control and size and material used in equipment controls. Many states require coolers and a sterilization process for the jars, or a bulk tank. Because the previous specifications demand much larger investment, it's safe to assume you would be starting a business with a large number of goats. Check with your county extension service and your state agricultural department for accurate and complete details before entering the business venture.

What if you have a couple of gallons of raw milk left over each week that you'd like to sell to a neighbor? Technically, it's illegal to sell it without a license. Some states don't enforce the law too strictly, while others adhere to the books and will prosecute. I know of two cases where the state has jailed people for the sale of raw goats' milk. The state wants make sure that the quality of the milk is good, thereby protecting the consumer and preventing disease.

Ignore the fact that the consumer trusts you and your goats and wants or desperately needs the milk. To legally have the right to drink raw milk, the consumer most own his own goat or find a licensed dairy. In many states there are no licensed dairies or they are too far away.

I don't advise disobeying the law and selling the milk Eventually you would pay the price, whether it would be in fines, or the wear and tear on your nerves from the fear of getting caught. You can, however, trade the milk to the consumer for other goods.

At one point, I met a couple who had a baby who needed the milk. Refusing to sell the milk (as I also refuse to go through the bureaucratic red tape and never-ending expense of getting a license), I gave it to them for a while. They didn't have the time or the space to own a goat, but they did not want to take advantage of me, so I sold them a goat. They paid me to keep the goat and milk her for them. It was similar to room and board. Strangely enough, the cost of the goat and her room and board was cheaper than the money they would have paid me for the milk. When they received extra milk from the goat, they gave it back to me. This practice is legal, as long as it doesn't approach a kennel situation, in which case there would be more bureaucratic red tape.

The container that you put the milk in can be marked "not for human consumption." I sell milk to a lady who breeds poodles and has a mama that never has enough milk for her litter. However, when she feeds the mama the goat milk, she produces more milk for her own. I believe these people, but to protect myself, I mark the jars because I don't have firsthand proof of what they do with the milk.

When one if my neighbors had AIDS, I gave him the milk with no markings for free. His doctors said he lived a year longer than he should have.

It also seems highly unlikely that a state could expect that it would receive a large amount of revenue from the income taxes of a small dairy goat owner. Thus, it's only reasonable that the purpose behind the prohibition of raw milk sales has to be consumer protection. It is tragic that the ordinary person must change his lifestyle, buy goats, and become a goatkeeper if he wants to enjoy the good, clean, pure, unprocessed nutritious goat's milk.

As for the amount of milk production you can expect, each breed has a different average, and each goat is different. Most of these figures on averages are from herds that are "on test." More details on DHIR test recordings are found in chapter 30. Many goats are producing huge quantities of milk, and the owners are not going through the headache (sometimes heartache) of having the production recorded.

The law of averages tells us that only top-notch breeders are going to be on test, as this venture can run into some dollars, too. These averages might just be higher than the average that you are going to receive from your beginning goats.

However, this could work to opposite effect. When a herd owner goes on test, every milking animal in the herd must be included. So these herds may be well above average, but if the herd has an individual goat that isn't, it will bring that average down.

Individual goats across the country that are not on test may just beat the averages and few people would know it. Some of these average figures come from show goats in a one-day test. People only show their best goats. My old grade doe had one floppy ear, was unrecorded, had no tattoo, and was unable to be shown anywhere, had a very pendulous udder but she found a loving home with me and never failed to top the scales at 12 to 14 pounds per day. This isn't a record but easily competes with the averages. She is just one example of many goats that are not included in test averages.

The averages on the following chart are based on a ten-month lactation period. Lactation is the time the goat is milking, which is usually ten months, or 305 days. Many factors, such as worm infestation, hot weather, cold weather, pregnancy, sickness, and hereditary factors will shorten lactation. Also, a doe may start lactation with a small amount of milk, peak with a huge quantity, and dwindle off toward the end. Some will start out way above the averages and dwindle as they go. The averages are based on the total 10 months.

AVERAGE MILK PRODUCTION

Breed	Pounds per Day
Alpine	16 to 18
Toggenburg	12 to 14
La Mancha	9 to 11
Oberhasli	9 to 11
Nubian	13 to 15
Saanen/Sable	18 to 20

All the above breeds have individual goats that hold higher records, with some going to 20 pounds.

Milk is measured in pounds and ounces for accuracy. A gallon of milk weighs approximately eight pounds. Depending on butterfat content, one gallon of milk from one goat may weigh more or less than a gallon of milk from another, so there is no real way to get an exact weight of each and every gallon of milk. Also, because goats are fed differently, cared for differently, and suffer through different climatic changes all over the world, the averages on their production records will change from one area to another.

Don't let these records throw you. If you've got a grade doe that gives under a gallon of milk and improves her offspring, don't dispose of her just because she's not up to par on averages. Your needs are more important than what the averages say, anyway.

I have known people who have kept very small does that barely give a pint at each milking because that's all the people need.

Milking three times a day will increase production 15 percent to 20 percent, but feeding three times a day may not be worth the extra percentage in milk when you would be feeding 33 percent more and putting out the extra hours.

Proper milking practices help to ensure a healthy, good-tasting product. The goat should be up off the ground, but when that is not possible, at least take her away from the bedding area.

Keeping the udder and surrounding area clipped helps to eliminate the problems of dirt. By keeping your hands, your shirt sleeves, and the udder free of clinging dirt you should be safe in carefully brushing the udder, provided that adequate clean, dry bedding is provided. I don't recommend this if you or your baby goats will be drinking the milk.

Be sure you milk quickly into clean containers. Seamless, stainless steel containers are recommended and expensive. Glass containers are okay but breakable. Plastic will retain bacteria, and the milk may taste bad, or taste like whatever was in the plastic before you milked. If you use plastic, make sure it is smooth and clean and not used for anything else. Rinse all containers with cold water first, and then wash with hot water. This is because there is something about the lactose in the milk that will not rinse off in hot water.

Immediately after milking, the container should be covered so no dirt from the air will float into the milk. Cover does not mean sealed. The milk should then be cooled to 40 degrees as quickly as possible to prevent the growth of bacteria and preserve the flavor. If you have several goats to milk, it's wise to have a cooling container in the milk room. If I am milking more than five goats, or if it's hot, I carry a bucket of ice to the barn with me to hasten the chilling process.

Once you get back to the house with your fresh milk, strain it into cold, clean jars. Filters for milk are available. Immediately after straining, refrigerate the milk. You can cover the containers, if you like, but goats' milk should not be sealed.

Goats' milk should last from eight to 14 days in the refrigerator. I don't keep goat milk more than four days unless I freeze it. Milk that is more than 12 hours apart in age should never be mixed, and warm milk should never be added to cold milk.

When serving this delicious food, serve it cold in clean containers. Don't pour the milk until the meal is served. If the family wants seconds, let them get milk from the fridge. An air-pot or a large thermos can be used to keep the milk cold at the table, but that just adds more cleanup.

Now, what is this stuff that you're drinking? A nutritional breakdown follows: Protein (trytophan, leucine, lysine, methionine, phenylalanine, isoleucine, valine, threonine), carbohydrate, fat, thiamine, riboflavin, niacin, vitamin A, sodium, calcium, phosphorus, potassium, and magnesium.

If you have a goat producing an average of five pounds of milk a day, with about 3 percent butterfat, she is packing a wallop of nutrition for you and your family. This is enough protein for an adult for a year, and about 80 pounds of lactose (milk sugar) and six pounds of butterfat, which is more than one pound of butter every week for that year. There are over 11 pounds of ash in that year's milk and enough calcium, phosphorus, and riboflavin for an adult for about two years. The energy in that milk is enough for an adult, with no other food, for six months.

Over 80 percent of what the goat eats is not generally consumed by people. The goats' milk comes to us already homogenized, easily digestible and, in most cases, clean. If it's not clean, it's not the goats' fault.

How do the goats make milk, since it doesn't taste or look like grass, brush and tree tops? A high-producing doe will change up to three-quarters of her feed and roughage into milk. This is a complicated process, as the feed and nutrients pass along to the true stomach and the nutrients are absorbed into the blood where they can be used by the liver and udder to be converted into milk. Vitamins and minerals leave the bloodstream and enter the milk through the udder. During this time, the liver is continuously working to make glucose, which is carried in the blood to the udder. The udder and the liver are working continuously to produce milk.

Most small dairy goat operators are not too interested in butterfat content. However, that content does have quite a bit to do with just plain handling the milk. At one time, my daughters were ready to pitch out some milk because it was darker in color, thicker, and did not strain easily. They feared that the goat was sick or had eaten something bad. Upon some research, I learned that when a goat is nearing the end of her lactation, the milk is higher in butterfat content. This is nature's way of giving the young an extra boost before weaning. The milk is fine. Fattening, but fine.

Butterfat is important if you want cheese, butter, buttermilk and other by products of the goat. Many variables will affect butterfat content, color and texture of the milk. Length of time between milking will affect butterfat content, with the time after the shortest period having the highest contest. Butterfat can be higher in colder weather, though production may be lower. Since a high percentage of butterfat comes at the last of the milking procedure, failure to completely strip the udder will lower butterfat content. Stress, poor weather, discomfort, too much exercise all will lower butterfat content. Irregular feedings and sickness can either raise or lower butterfat content, but underfeeding a normally well fed animal can temporarily raise the content. Don't do this deliberately. It is not only temporary; it really isn't good to mess with the goats' schedule for your own benefit.

Quality and taste

The quality of milk will vary from goat to goat and milking to milking and will be affected by the care you give the goat, the milk, the equipment and the goats' general mood. Discounting the fact that you cannot taste many forms of bacteria, the flavor of your milk is a test of its quality. Since few odd and off-flavors can be detected in really cold milk, the best way to detect any potential problem is to taste milk that is 60 or 70 degrees. Having an actual bacteria count run on your milk is expensive, unless you own your own microscope and know what to look for.

Since each milking would be different, a bacteria count run on the milk would not be reliable. Milk that is 99 percent clean is still 1 percent dirty. The clean part of the milk does not grow, the dirty part does. So if you begin with a product that is relatively clean and care for it improperly the bacteria is going to continue growing, especially at a temperature over 40 degrees, and that 1 percent could easily grow to 99 percent!

If the goat is healthy, the milk is almost perfect in the udder, so therefore, we are the causes of any bacteria forming in the milk. The udder and teats, especially the orifices, have to be as clean on the outside as they are on the inside. Any dirt and hair from the goats' sides, udder, legs and your hands will affect the taste of the milk. The surrounding air should be as sanitary as possible. The biggest offender is the odor of the buck. If the buck's odor is anywhere around the doe, that odor will contaminate your fresh milk. Small goat owners cannot always afford a totally antiseptic area for their goats, but cleanliness is vital. Start with scrupulously clean containers and carry them, covered, directly to the milking area. I use pieces of clean sheets to cover things on the way to the barn and back.

Many weeds and scraps such as onions or cabbage can give the milk a bad taste. Sometimes a doe will simply give bad tasting milk. If your milk tastes bad, check milking and cleaning practices first, then check the feed and pasture. A doe may give poor tasting milk after an unusually long lactation or if she has been ill, upset or lonely. If all areas have been checked carefully and you can't find the cause of the poor taste, you may have to blame the goat.

I did have a doe that gave very poor tasting milk. I put her up for sale and told each potential buyer about the milk and suggested that she be used for breeding or weed eating. After the sale, I kept up with her progress and when she came fresh the next year, the owner went ahead and milked her. His kids drank the milk and they loved it. Being skeptical, I went and tasted for myself. There was nothing wrong with the milk.

Since this doe had grazed with my does and her milk had been cared for right along with my other milk, I know that the problem with her milk could not have been with my management. I can only guess that she simply had a bad lactation that year.

La Manchas have a tendency to have smoother tasting milk. I have a friend that will drive twenty miles one way if I have a La Mancha in lactation, and otherwise, I might not see them until milking season again.

The equipment deserves as much attention as the health of the goat. All used equipment needs to be prerinsed with cold water, then hot water, and then brushed clean with an alkaline cleanser. Everything should be rinsed with a hot water and disinfectant rinse and put aside to air dry. Before using, re-rinse with disinfectant again.

I rinse all milking equipment as soon as it is empty and then wash all milking equipment as I do my regular dishes, with an antibiotic soap. I do all the milk things before I do the rest of the dishes. Not so much as a water glass goes into my wash water before my milking equipment. I rinse in hot water and don't disinfect until I'm ready to milk again. I have not had a bacteria count done on my milk, but I have never had a bad batch, and none has ever soured prematurely in the refrigerator.

Any cleaning supplies should be bought from a supply house that sells equipment especially for dairy.

Since I advocate a natural product, I don't pasteurize. However, many people feel safer if they do, and it can be easily done. Pasteurization causes some breakdowns in the milk and gives it a different flavor.

To pasteurize, simply raise the temperature of the milk to 138 degrees. Some directions call for 143 degrees, so find the medium you can reach best with your particular method. Hold this temperature for 30 minutes. Cool quickly to 40 degrees. Pasteurized, condensed, and powdered goats' milk can be purchased, but it does not have the same rich healthy quality and the price can exceed $16 a gallon.

Pasteurization prevents tuberculosis and Bang's disease from being transferred to humans. If your goats have tested positive for CAE (chapter 28), milk will need to be pasteurized to prevent passing it to the kids.

Goat's milk can be canned successfully. Start with fresh milk, properly cooled. Pour into clean jars, within a half inch from the top. Cap jars according to manufacturer's directions. Process the jars in the pressure cooker for 10 minutes at 10 pounds, or for 60 minutes in a water bath canner. Canned milk will taste like canned milk, but is absolutely delicious in puddings, soups, baking, blended drinks, and ice cream, and will keep indefinitely on the shelf.

A tip at this point: When storing canned milk, turn the jars upside down. The milk has a way of settling and sticking to the bottom of the jar, making it really hard to clean. When you reverse the jars, it's easier to clean the lid and top of the jar.

Goat's milk freezes much better than cow's milk, and though it tastes a little different (my girls think it tastes watered down) after freezing, this is a satisfactory way to save the milk and excess colostrum.

Butter can be made easily from goats' milk, and it is white. For large amounts, you would need a separator. To make butter in small quantities without the separator, use ½ gallon milk and add one cup buttermilk and let stand at room temp for 12 to 24 hours till it thickens. Chill and churn approximately one hour. The yield is five or six ounces of white butter and a gallon of lowfat butter milk. The butter must be washed thoroughly before use, in cold water.

If you have a separator, you can refrigerate one quart of heavy goat cream and for 24 hours, then let it sit out for four to six hours. Rechill and beat with electric mixer at high speed until the butter separates from the milk. Pour off water and repeat. Add salt to taste, and work out all the water by pressing butter against the side of the bowl.

ICE CREAM

5 eggs
2 cups sugar
1½ tablespoons vanilla
Enough goat milk to make one gallon.
Your favorite additives: fruit, chocolate chips, etc.
Mix together and freeze.

22

Tattooing

Many people don't tattoo their goats, but they should. When you own one or two inexpensive goats, tattooing seems an extravagance. The equipment necessary to tattoo can be expensive, so it's easy to neglect the job. Not knowing how to do the job will stop others from trying.

Tattooing an animal identifies it as yours and protects your ownership. Your tattoo is the only mark that makes an animal an individual. If it were placed in another herd of goats with similar colors and markings for a few days, you would have a hard time identifying exactly which goat was yours. Should your goat be stolen, the authorities would need positive identification to retrieve the animal. If you take your goat out for stud service or attend a show or a sale, you stand a great chance of your goat getting mixed up with another, and your ID number might be the only solution. Frequently, in one herd of goats, several are alike, and multiple births may be identical. I had a doe give birth to four identical purebred kids, three bucks and one doe. During the same period another doe gave birth to a grade buck that was identical to the purebred bucks. I marked the kids with colored collars and tattooed early. When they were six weeks old, all the kids got into a briar patch and two identical bucks lost their collars. Collars were replaced immediately by matching colors to the tattoo. This mixup could have been serious, as one of the missing collars belonged to the grade buck. I might have had a difficult time deciding which was the grade and which was the purebred had it not been for the tattoo.

So, tattoo. Protect yourself, protect your goat, and prevent a mix-up.

If tattooing equipment is beyond your budget, check your area for other breeders who would be willing to lend or rent you the equipment. Sometimes experienced breeders will perform the tattooing for a small fee.

Tattooing can be done at any time, but the younger the goats, the easier they are to handle. Keep in mind that it's easier to handle seven pounds of young excitement than 120 pounds of pure and practiced stubbornness. The youngster

Sure, this goat looks special, but would you know the difference if there was an identical one? Be sure to tattoo.

can be pacified with a bottle, but the veteran caprine is not so quickly quieted. Should you decide not to tattoo, find some way to mark your animals. Collars can be placed on adult animals permanently, only if they are in a pasture where they cannot catch on something and kill themselves. And bolt cutters can cut off the best of collars should your goat be stolen.

Old-timers still notch the ears. This is not only defacing, but it has been so widely used that it's not a personal identification anymore.

Horns can be notched and tags can be applied, or rings imbedded in the horn, though these methods aren't practical, considering we really don't want to keep the horns in the first place.

The equipment generally comes as a complete kit and looks like an exaggerated pair of pliers with pads. The symbols are inserted according to your logo. Tattooing is done mostly in the ears, but on the La Mancha, tattoos are often placed in the tail web area.

Study the procedure well before you start. The animal should be held still. Tying or placing the goat on the milk stand in the stanchion is a must. The area to be tattooed needs to be cleaned completely. Rubbing alcohol works well, though other products can be used. Insert the symbols correctly into the pliers, making sure they are clean, and place the pads firmly over the needles. The pads will help to get the needles back out of the skin. Stamp a piece of paper or cardboard, to make sure the numbers are in the correct order. Wipe ink on the area to be tattooed. Green ink is most effective on darker goats and can be seen easier. The area to be tattooed needs to be as free of freckles, warts, and scar tissue as possible. Put symbols parallel to, and between the veins and cartilage of the ear or tail web.

Stamp the tattoo quickly and firmly, and immediately apply more ink, rubbing it continuously for at least 15 seconds to make sure it completely soaks into all the holes. A soft toothbrush or a fingernail brush helps to work the ink into the tattoo.

It can take one to four weeks for the area to heal. During that time, leave it alone, since the ink must not be disturbed before the healing process is over.

Those of us with pierced ears know this is a relatively painless process, but the goat may jerk as the stamp is made. Most goats don't like their ears messed with in the first place, and they are more likely to be upset about that than the actual discomfort of tattooing.

Tattooing equipment should be cleaned immediately after use, and all numbers recorded. Both ears may require a tattoo, and it is easy to forget what symbols went into which ear. Take a pad and pencil with you and record the numbers as they are inked. To make tattoos easier to read, shine a flashlight on the ear or tail area, and they will show up easier.

One of my Internet friends bought a goat that was supposed to be purebred, but had no papers. When she looked, she found the tattoo and was able to get the papers for her goat. So that is one more reason for tattooing. The next buyer may not keep track of papers and the third buyer will want to know.

23

Getting Rid of Horns

Goats may be horned. It is a myth that all goats are horned. It is also a myth that a true Nubian does not have horns. Regardless of breed or sex, they may have horns.

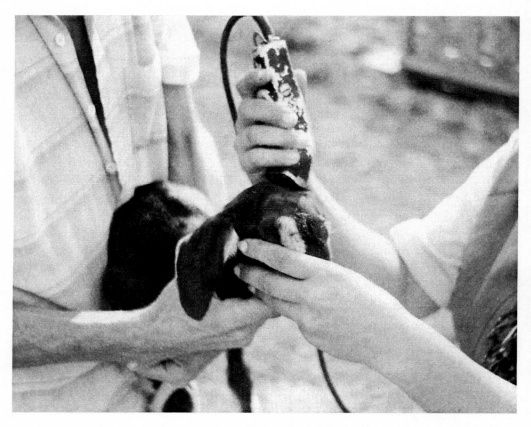

Shaving the head makes the disbudding cleaner and easier. In Southern or warm climates, disbudding can be started as early as three days, especially Nubians. I suggest waiting until later in colder climates.

After the head is shaved, it is easy to see the horn buds.

My best research brought up only the Arapawa, now not even recognized because of its rarity and being bred to anything else, the only goat in America without horns.

To most goat owners' distress, more goats seem to be born with horns. There aren't figures on how many goats have horns, since this is a genetic factor and would vary from bloodline to bloodline.

I've kept records for more than 23 years, totaling over 200 kids, and found that even my own figures were sporadic. It is safe to say that over 75 percent are born with horns.

When breeding polled (naturally hornless) does to polled bucks, I received 100 percent horned kids, however, both the buck and the doe had siblings that were horned. When breeding polled does to horned bucks, the horn percentage was 66 percent. When breeding horned does with a horned buck, my percentage was 82 percent horns. My total was 75 percent horns.

It's a pretty safe figure to assume that you can expect over three-quarters of your kids to be born with horns unless you take some special measure with your breeding practices.

Because of the theory that breeding polled to poll can result in hermaphrodite offspring I always breed with at least one horned parent. I depend on seven out of ten kids to have horns. Frequently, both parents may be horned. Strangely, I have

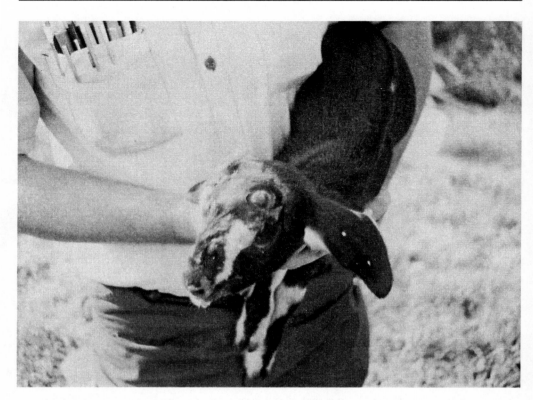

The finished horn buds have a circle all the way around. Very young kids hardly realize the disbudding is happening, and are easier to hold. In colder climates, where you have to wait for a warm afternoon, the kid will be harder to hold, and you may need help.

had polled does that have never delivered kids with horns, although they had been mated with a horned buck on several occasions.

Other people are still working on the genetics of breeding polled goats without the side affects.

Goats also use their horns to scratch themselves, dig through hay and leaves, and ward off unwanted goats, dogs, and perhaps people.

Normally, there are two horns, and they generally grow up, back, and out, although each breed may differ on the manner of growth. The horns are permanent unless removed and carry major blood vessels almost to the top of the solid shell.

Many people consider the horns pretty and a natural artifice and prefer to let the goat proudly carry them through life. However picturesque the horns may be, they can create more trouble to the owner that they are worth to the goat.

The goat knows exactly how to use the horns, and since they are solid, they can be dangerous. It's interesting to watch the new kid as it adjusts to each new horn length. The first couple of inches don't seem to have much effect. Then suddenly, you will notice the horns being used for scratching and gentle play with the other kids.

When the horns reach four to six inches, the kid weighs about 40 to 60 pounds or more (depending on breed and management) and he's using the horns a little less gently on his playmates and learning to butt them against your restraining hand. This is about the time he may decide to rip down parts of his house or hay bunk with his natural weapons.

By the time they're a year old, the horns can reach a length of eight to ten inches (again, depending on individual goats, breeds, etc.) and the goat is able to use them well. Goats show a special enjoyment in scratching their heads and horns and spend a good deal of time rubbing against solid surfaces. If they haven't eaten the young saplings on the property, they will surely strip the bark from most of the trees with their horns. Actually, goats damage more trees by scratching them than they do by eating them. Horns will continue to grow through the goat's life, and the goat never stops practicing with them, learning new advantages that the horns can provide with each new growth. Young kids will drive a goat owner crazy by putting their heads through the woven wire and getting their horns caught. You will waste a lot of time releasing animals from the fences and paying for fence repair.

One of my youngsters got his horns caught in the fence when I was gone for the day. He ended up getting stranded in a series of early winter showers. By the time I rescued him, he was nearly dead from the cold, wet and stress. He recovered after a week in the house. That was the last year I allowed the horns to remain.

Goats' horns can cause serious injuries. Children have had eyes injured and adults have been badly bruised. Younger goats have been forced to miscarry because of being bullied by a bigger goat with horns. I recently had my lip cut and my upper dentures cracked when a kid that was given to me jerked its head back. These turned out to be pretty expensive horns.

Horned animals are practically impossible to put into a stanchion or milk stand and cannot be fed through common key-hole hay racks and feeders. Therefore, natural or not, the horns present problems for the domesticated goat and should be removed.

There are several ways to remove the horns, though none of them are 100 percent effective and safe. There are three methods of removing horns from older goats. The first is surgery. Since cells for the horn growth lie beneath the surface, major surgery is required with the goat sedated, and goats don't sedate easily. There can be a large loss of blood and this may result in death. Make sure the vet you choose has performed this surgery successfully.

The sinus gland and cavities lie right below the horn roots, and once that is cut there is a lot of blood and a hole straight through to the sinus cavity. This is, of course packed immediately, and the bleeding stops immediately.

Another cruel method is to saw off the horn with a hacksaw and pack the stub left. To me, this is also dangerous because a lot of blood is lost. This does not stop the horn growth, it simply removes the horn growth.

Bands are 50 percent effective, and with persistence can be 100 percent in stopping horn growth, but they do safely remove and retard future horn growth. This is the same elastrator bands used on sheep and goats for castration (chapter 24). Start by clipping or shaving the hair away from the base of the horn. Then with a small file (a small round chain saw file works great), file a groove around the horn as low and as deep as the goat will allow and as close to the head as possible. You may get a spot of blood in the groove which, at this point, is not serious. Roll the band from the top of the horn down to the groove. The band will stop any spot bleeding and slowly shut off the circulation to the horn. In 50 to 70 days the horn will rot off a younger kid. This process may take longer in older goats, with larger horns, and bands may have to be added as the old one may start to rot before the horn does. New bands should be placed as soon as you notice the old band rotting. If you wait too long the horn could get tender and you could cause the goat discomfort getting the newer band on the horn.

When the horn does fall off there may be some bleeding, though it's not usually serious. Protection should be taken against flies and tetanus. When using bands to remove the horns, watch the horns daily and take care not to grab the horns or cause premature breaking. The best time to start banding the horns is in fall, so the horns will fall of during winter, after fly season. This also gives you time for a second attempt if the first band starts to rot or fall off.

The safest disbudding is done with a hot disbudding iron — much like branding — as shown in the pictures. The kids feel pain only for that time. You may feel better if you add a burn salve to the circles, but is is not necessary.

24

Castration

Castration is the process by which bucks are made sterile by rendering the testicles useless; the final result of this procedure is a wether.

Any buck not having the desirable qualities necessary for breeding should be castrated regardless of his pedigree. Castration is to prevent the reproduction of undesirable animals. This is a necessary culling practice.

Castration is easier to accomplish when bucks are young. Younger than four months is the best time. After four months, castration can result in shock or even death, and should be done with an anesthetic.

Castrating older animals should be done 60 days before the butcher date to allow time for fattening and to give the meat a chance to lose the strong flavor the bucks have. People of many ethnic groups butcher bucks without castration and wait 60 days after breeding season.

Generally, wethers will show a better weight gain than their buck brothers, and the meat will be pinker, juicier, and more flavorful, another advantage of castration.

Castration can be performed as soon as the testicles drop into the scrotum, the pouch that contains the testicles. This may be from one day to three weeks in age. I like to wait until the kids are weaned from the bottle and onto a pan (six to eight weeks) before I castrate. Once we begin pan feeding, we handle the kids less, and thereby disturb the tender area as little as possible. Also when pan feeding, it is easier to stand behind the goat as he eats, and check for post-castration swelling. Castration should be performed on a warm, sunny day to prevent excess chilling and/or shock.

There are several methods of castration, some of which are minor surgery. In these cases, I recommend the use of a steroid injection, the same as with dehorning, to lessen stress and prevent shock. I also use an antibiotic. You will want to consult with a vet concerning the use of a tetanus vaccine.

One method not requiring surgery is with elastrator bands. The band is small and very firm and is fitted onto an instrument (similar to pliers) that expands the band. Once the band is stretched, it is slipped up over the scrotum, with the testicles pulled gently to the lower part of the scrotum. When the band is released, it closes tightly and cuts off the blood supply to the testicles.

It takes about two weeks for the lower part of the scrotum, complete with testicles, to rot and fall off. The bands are safe, effective and easy. The kid has some minor discomfort and pain for a few hours. Sometimes they will go off and lie down for a while, but as soon as they see feed, they are up and going again.

Bands are inexpensive, and you usually get more than you need to a package, even if you use them for dehorning. To keep them from one year to the next without drying out, put them in a moisture-proof container and store them in your freezer.

Emasculatome is an instrument like pincers, used for castrations. The instrument has blunt edges that crush the cords to the testicles. It is applied to the scrotum between the testicles and the body. Once crushed, the cords can no longer carry blood. If the cord is not completely crushed, the organs remain functional, and unwanted breedings may result. This method is so seldom used without surgery that few people even know how to use it any more. It is not advisable because without surgery, there isn't any way the owner knows if the cords were indeed damaged.

The testicles can be removed with a knife. This is quick, simple, and effective, but it does leave an open wound, can be bloody, or even fatal if bleeding is not stopped immediately. This is against everything I believe in, and definitely not advised.

Another surgical method is quick, clean, and effective. The scrotum is slit at the bottom with a sterilized scalpel or razor blade. There is very little blood. The scrotum is then pushed back to display the testicles. The testicles are pulled (cord and all) gently, and firmly, and quickly till the cord breaks up inside the body. Wrapping the cord around the fingers helps prevent slippage. Once the testicles and cord are pulled free, disinfect the scrotum, and pull it down. The kid has only a slight amount of discomfort, and frequently doesn't realize anything has happened. The flesh of the scrotum heals in a few days, and simply hangs there empty. It should be watched for swelling and infection.

The scrotum can be cut and sterilized thread tightly around each cord above the testicle. Once tied, the testicle can be cut off. The thread will stop all the bleeding. If it should slip off, it could result in a fatal loss of blood.

Most of the materials for the castration are usually around your home. Bands and emasculators are available wherever sheep supplies are sold. Keep plenty of rubbing alcohol around for disinfecting you and your tools, and a disinfectant for the goat.

Post-castration care simply consists of watching for infection. By keeping the area clean and free of flies, the problems should be minimal.

Although the previous methods of castration may seem distasteful, even cruel, the end result without a castration is worse. A buck that is not worth much is seldom treated well. The animal is usually in poor condition, has a nasty temperament, and continues to produce more bucks that will be treated the same way.

Whether you butcher for your own meat or not, do the goat a favor and castrate.

25

Hooves and Foot Care

When left in the wild to run, jump and play on the rocks, goats manage to keep their hooves broken down and trimmed. However, our goats are kept in flat pens and on soft pastures. We give them soft bedding and keep the rocks and boulders away from the pens. Their hooves grow too long, and we must cut them back. Part of the hoof may grow outward, causing the goat to have trouble walking, while the other side will fold under the foot and cause a hole for bacteria, resulting in foot rot.

A goat's feet are important. Goats can have everything else going for them, but if their feet won't hold them up, they can't eat, drink and exercise properly. Milk production may be lowered and lameness may occur.

Many buyers won't consider an animal if it has hoof problems, as overgrown hooves can be permanent. The foot is very complex. It is split, and each half is called a toe. The soft part inside the hoof acts as a shock absorber. The outside is hard and similar to our fingernails, though much stronger. Frequently called horns, the outside of each toe will grow longer and faster than the rest of the horn.

The foot is the sole support of the legs. Any problems in the foot will affect the legs. The hoof grows at a different rate for each animal, and trimming is needed from every three to six weeks. A hoof trimming schedule is a must.

When the hooves are not properly maintained, the pastern is not well supported and the goat will walk back on the heel and eventually back on the pastern. This breakdown in the pastern also leads to lameness, which is sometimes permanent.

When the hooves become out of shape, it may take several trimmings over several months to correct them. Some of the damage in the pastern will heal, but it may never be completely normal.

Trimming hooves also prevents foot rot, an infection spread by a virus. Keeping the hooves trimmed makes it harder for foot rot to get started. If you trim hooves regularly, you'll detect foot rot if it does occur.

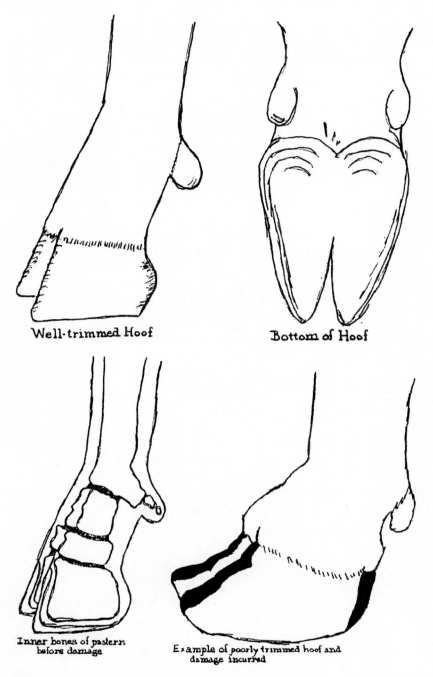

Well-trimmed Hoof

Bottom of Hoof

Inner bones of pastern
before damage

Example of poorly trimmed hoof and
damage incurred

Regular hoof trimming by an experienced person can be done in a few minutes. Trimming should be started early, when the kid is three or four weeks old. Hoof trimming is then continued throughout the goat's lifetime. By checking the hooves of a newborn, you will know exactly what the perfect hoof should look like when you're through trimming.

Early trimming ensures proper bone growth and allows the kid to be familiar with the routine. When it grows to be 150 or 200 pounds, you won't need a block and tackle to keep him quiet. I do my goats' hooves out in the pasture, with no grain, ropes, or stanchions to hold them. When I pick up a foot, the goat stands still.

Until you and your goats are used to the routine, you'll need a stanchion or milk stand to keep them quiet and a little grain for distraction. Tying them in a corner, with one side to the wall, will also help to minimize problems.

If you do get your hands on an older goat and you're not sure of its temperament, get help. Don't trim the hooves of a pregnant doe after the third month of gestation unless she is very docile because her struggles may harm her and the unborn kids.

Trimming is best done after the goat has been on wet grass. This softens the hoof and helps to clean the debris beneath it. In dry weather, I have soaked the foot in warm water, although that takes more time and trouble than trimming them dry. It's easier to wait for rain or morning dew to moisten hooves.

You need hoof trimming shears or a sharp knife. I prefer a razor blade cutter, commonly called a utility knife. I wouldn't recommend this instrument for a beginner. The blade is dangerous and best used with gloves to prevent nicking of the knuckles. Care also needs to be used to prevent nicking the legs and knees. Hoof trimming tools are available at any place that sells sheep supplies. Knives need to be sharp, small enough to handle easily and easily cleaned. All hoof trimming tools should be cleaned after each use and stored in a moisture-free place. I suggest you keep your hoof trimming tools in the main area where you will be doing most of your work with the goats so they will be handy when you need them. If you have to walk back to the house (or tool shed) to get the tools, you're not as apt to do the job when it's necessary. I carry my utility knife in the pocket of my chore clothes or purse and trim the hooves when they need it.

It helps to have iodine and bandages on hand just in case.

The first time you trim, pick a time when you're relaxed and not pressed for time. Later you'll be able to work the task into your other routines without extra planning.

Once you have a goat under control, turn your back to the head, run your hands down a front leg, and gently pick up the foot backward. If you feel like a blacksmith that's fine, because that's also how a blacksmith handles the horse he is shoeing.

With the end of your knife (or shears), carefully clean away the dirt, manure, and grasses. This can be a smelly chore. The cleaning will expose the soft pad of the foot and show just how badly the hoof is overgrown. The hoof needs to be trimmed down to the pad. In some cases, some of the pad may need trimmed to obtain a flat surface. When trimming, cut from heel to toe, one thin slice at a time, until you get the desired effect. Keep in mind that nature has the right idea in the first place; your objective is to return the hoof to its natural state. If you trim too deep, it will bleed, so if you see pink, it's time to stop.

When you have one side of the hoof trimmed, begin on the other toe. Both toes should be even with each other and flat, and the bottom line of the foot should be parallel with the hairline at the top.

I was taught to trim the hoof down even to the pad, trimming the pads as I went. For years, I did just that and had no problems. However, one day one of my heavier does started limping. When I checked her foot, she had a hole in the pad not quite the size of a pencil eraser, which was full of dirt and grass. I cleaned and soaked the hoof, and assumed she had punctured it on a sharp weed stubble. The next day she had a similar hole in another hoof and was having difficulty walking. Another much smaller doe had a similar hole and also was limping.

Fearing something infectious, I took the goats to the vet. His diagnosis was that I had trimmed the hoof shell too short, forcing the goats to walk only on the pads.

By keeping the hooves clean and disinfected and trimming the pads down to the outside shell level I was able to clear the problem up in a few days. I now leave the shell fraction longer than the pad, relieving the pressure (and weight) on the pads.

As you're trimming, check the heel. The heel tissues grow somewhat like calluses, and will grow down between the toes, causing them to spread. Carefully trim away the excess tissue and between the toes, so that the toes stay together. When you're sure you have the foot flat, set it down and see if it is standing flat, without the toes being spread apart. Move to the rear hoof and continue. I start at the left front foot and proceed to the right front, counterclockwise. By always using the same routine on each goat, you never get confused and lose your place should you be interrupted.

Once finished, stand back and survey all four feet as a unit. Each toe should be even on each foot and all four feet even with each other.

When hooves have been left too long and are grossly overgrown, trim as much as what seems safe, and repeat every week till the hoof has been returned to as close as its normal state as possible. This could take a couple months and may never be completed perfectly, depending on how badly the hooves were out of shape.

26

Clipping, Hair Cutting, and Spot Trimming

Clipping the goat is important for his health as well as his appearance.

Goats will keep themselves clean. Cleanliness is usually just a fancy excuse to trim a goat unless you show goats, then it is a requirement, so the judge can feel the hair and see the skin. Goats given room to roll about, clean bedding and a place to scratch, will keep themselves groomed.

They will rub against any fence post or your best fences to free their coats of dirt. To save fences, you can provide the animals with a scratching post in the middle of the pen. An elaborate apparatus for scratching can be made with old pop-bottle caps with crinkled edges. When enough caps have been accumulated, nail the caps to a piece of plywood, approximately three feet high and three feet long. Place the caps two inches apart, with the rough edges out. Stand the plywood (complete with caps) out in the open. The goats will rub the caps instead of the fences.

Another solution is to build the goats a strand of fencing in the pen. I use abandoned and discarded bed springs. By setting the spring on its side and tying it to posts, I have a cost-free (and low labor) scratching place for the goats.

Like all livestock, the goat is susceptible to external parasites such as fleas, ticks, and lice. Clipping the excess hair helps to control the parasite problems and saves the expense of powders and sprays. Shaving the goat is the fastest way to get rid of lice, which are far more common to the goat than fleas and ticks.

Show goats are routinely trimmed and clipped before appearances. This is a habit formed after many years of showing goats, and most dairy goat judges expect a trimmed goat. However, some judges will admit that it is hard to judge the texture of the hair on a finely clipped goat.

Clipping or shaving the udder, back legs, rump, and tail area is necessary for clean tasty milk, and may even save some of your milk volume. The long hairs growing from the udder, around the udder, and inside the hind legs can cause the doe distress when accidentally pulled. Pulling the hair can also mean a loss of milk when the doe kicks over the pail.

Pregnant does should be clipped in these areas shortly before their delivery date. Not only does this serve to produce a cleaner kid, it also makes the delivery process cleaner.

I trim behind the bucks' front legs, stomach and beard to eliminate a lot of odor. Many people do not feel that their buck looks masculine without a beard, but I would rather he lost some hair than have the extra odor. I also trim down the "mane" during the breeding season, and his front legs and stomach. When you are trimming bucks, take great care with the area around the penis and scrotum. It helps to have someone hold the male goat up on his hind legs so you can trim from underneath. Don't do this during the breeding season, though, since a healthy buck is easily stimulated.

Does' beards are trimmed to help make them look more feminine, but this is not a necessity unless you are planning to show your doe.

Most of the hair is generally left on the end of the goat's tail for showing. This hair is trimmed short, except for the last inch or inch and a half. The end is left long and cut square, to look blunt. The tail might remind you of a poodle's without the fluff. Hair should be trimmed on hooves, in a straight line, parallel with the hoof.

Clipping your goat can be as simple as using the scissors to spot-clip areas of unwanted hair, or as complete as using electric shears to trim the entire body. I don't recommend the use of a safety razor, because it takes a great deal of care, experience, knowledge, and a very sure hand. Not to mention a very quiet, patient goat.

The earlier you begin to trim youngsters, the better they adjust to the process of losing their hair.

Always start out fresh when clipping or trimming. Make sure you have all tools clean, oiled, sharpened, and ready before getting the goat. The goat will not stand patiently tied down while you tramp around assembling your equipment.

If you don't know the goat, or you know the animal is high-strung and jumpy, get help. It wouldn't hurt to get help the first couple times, anyway. The sound of the electric trimmers is unnerving to most goats at first. Even the snipping sounds of the scissors sometimes cause the animal to jump. Be prepared and go slow.

Scissors will give a blunt cut until you become more experienced with the texture of the hair and the way it grows.

Some breeds of goats will have a longer growth of hair along the backbone and on the back of the hind legs. Cutting this hair will give the goat a neater appearance.

Also, extra hair may grow longer below, around, and in the ears of many goats, giving them a bushy looking appearance if they aren't trimmed.

Trimming udders can be tricky. While the goat is tied and eating, carefully trim this long hair away. Be careful to watch the end of the scissors. Short scissors may make trimming the udder area less tedious, as the ends of long scissors may be harder to watch.

If you will be using scissors on several goats, it's a good idea to put bandages around your fingers and thumb to prevent blisters.

Electric trimmers are handy, and when in good operating order, can be used safely. Many trimmers have guards to keep from cutting too close and leaving the goat with a shaved look. By trimming against the growth of the hair stroking from back to front, you should be able to achieve a cut that is natural to the way the hair grows. Beginners should take a break halfway through the goat. The goat may look funny for a while, but the job will be easier for both of you.

Start with any area that is comfortable for you. Starting points are not as important as technique and care. Trimming on the facial area, around the eyes and base of the ears should be done slowly for safety. It might prove useful to tie back the ears of a Nubian to prevent them from flopping in the way. Practice makes perfect. If you're going to show a goat, practice on the ones that won't be shown.

It's best not to do a complete trim on a very sunny day. If you do, keep the goat sheltered or covered to prevent sunburn. This is especially true of Saanens and white or light-colored goats. After a complete clipping, allow the goat short amounts of sun for two or three days. Goat coats may be handy if clipping is done in extremely sunny weather. For obvious reasons, goats should not be totally trimmed in chilly weather. They will catch cold easily, and not having their hair leaves them with no protection against pneumonia.

I wouldn't be honest if I didn't say that goats don't have to be trimmed. Parasite products are effective on hair, though they may need to be used more frequently and in larger quantities. A totally clipped goat may have a very odd look to the goat owner who is inexperienced with the gamut of shows, fairs, and sales.

There is one time, however when shaving the goat should not be overlooked. I have found that shaving the goat just before I butcher makes the job easier, neater and the meat better. One of the problems with getting the meat of the goat to taste good is trying to keep the hair from contaminating the meat when the animal is skinned. By shaving a wide line along the same areas where the skinning cuts will be made, you will eliminate any hair on the meat.

The butchering process is made easier, cleaning the meat is easier, and you will feel that it tastes better when you don't have to worry about all the little hairs that could have been missed.

27

Health and Preventive Medicine

This chapter does not replace your vet. Instead it helps save him, you, and your goats undue stress. The education you get will save your vet the headaches of trying to convince you that there really is nothing seriously wrong with your goat.

By all means, don't fancy yourself a vet. I don't. I know my goats, but he knows their problems. When my children were younger and showed symptoms of illness that I was unfamiliar with, I rushed them to the doctor or hospital. I do the same with my goats. On the other hand, if the children's problems were familiar, I treated them myself. This is the goal we need to work toward for goats. Education and experience help, but common sense prevails. When in doubt, get help.

I make it a point never to invest so much in a goat that I can't butcher or sell it, if necessary. I dread the thought of spending several hundred dollars on a goat and feeling obligated to spend a few hundred dollars more if the goat develops serious medical problems. I always advise people to consider all future aspects before paying a big price for a goat. You don't buy a fancy sports car if you can't afford the insurance. It makes sense that you won't spend money on a goat if you can't afford to keep it alive.

For instance, if you spend $65 on a grade doe and have her bred to a purebred buck for $25, you will have $80 tied up in cash. Then add to that, the cost of taking care of her until the kids come. Should she deliver one buck and one doe, with the approximate value of $300 for her and the kids, your cash output drops to a mere $50.

If the goat develops an expensive medical problem, you have the alternative of butchering rather than medicating. The average meat from a full-grown doe would be approximately 40 pounds, at $3 per pound depending on your area which is $120 in meat. You will still have cleared $55 on the doe, not counting care, plus

185

you will still have her kids. I'm assuming that the goat will stay in good health until she does have the kids. This is a gamble with any livestock.

Had you paid several hundred dollars for the doe you would not have had the option to butcher without losing some of your investment. Should your financial situation permit you to invest heavily into goats, you will have gone past the point of trying to raise goats simply on a low budget, which is what this book is all about.

Good health is our top priority when caring for goats. Much of good goat health depends on preventive measures in feeding and cleanliness. No matter how much we study and learn to promote good health, we can't know everything, be everywhere, and prevent all problems.

We are advised to demand health papers when we purchase new animals. I can't say it enough. Papers do not guarantee a healthy goat. They might assure a negative TB and brucellosis test and a goat that "appears" to be in good health.

A parasite problem isn't checked before health papers are issued. The vet issuing the papers has no way of checking a goat's metabolism for low resistance to disease, stress, or management practices. In short, health papers just do not ensure good health. If the goats are going for butcher, health papers don't usually carry a check for the TB and brucellosis, just a "looks good to me" affidavit from the vet.

Stress is a key factor when dealing with goats. It is any condition that causes the goat the slightest upset. This can range from simple feed changes to a cross-country trip. A sore hoof or any population changes in the herd may cause stress. Unseen stresses can be internal parasites and infection. Weaning newborns, changing pastures, changing homes—even a change in schedules can cause stress. In short, a change in the goat's normal habits, behavior, schedules, and health can cause stress. It comes from infection, disease, and any medical problem, and it lowers a goat's normal resistance to bacteria, infection, and disease.

Many goats can handle almost any stress and never show a drop in health or production, while others are so sensitive that a tardy feeding can upset them for days.

The average goat handles simple stresses easily, but simple stresses added over a period may create one large stressful condition. This can lower all the goat's natural resistances to various bacteria attacking their systems.

All health programs begin with reducing stress factors. I'm reminded of a process used on horses. Before giving an injection to a horse, the typical procedure is for the handler to "smack" the skin first. The theory is to stun the area receiving the injection, numbing it so the horse does not feel the injection.

Just receiving an injection causes stress for the goat, but if we were to precede it with a healthy smack, most goats would suffer a dreadful amount of extra stress. Instead, we choose to lower stress factors by keeping the goat calm, distracting it with grain, and giving the injection as quickly and as expertly as possible, and with kindness. The less we interfere with a goat's chosen routine, the less stress we cause.

Once a goat got caught when some decaying limbs she was playing on shifted and trapped her feet and legs. Her cries could be heard all over the area. When I dashed to her rescue I found her highly agitated, scared and nervous, and I couldn't free her. She didn't seem to be in immediate danger, so I sent my daughter after help and sat down with her, wrapping my sweater around her to slow her shaking. She settled down, put her head in my lap, relaxed, and began chewing her cud. By the time help arrived, she appeared to enjoy the situation. She was unhurt and walked back to the herd. It could, however, have gotten her so agitated that she could have gotten sick because stress had lowered her resistance, or she could have fought herself into an early death.

Some stresses can't be avoided. The internal stress of labor and delivery, infections, disease, pain, or loss of blood are going to occur at one time or another, but you can make an effort to keep stress at a minimum and be aware of its presence.

Undue stress can aid in shock, and shock can maximize stress. Shock happens in different degrees. Low-volume shock is caused by a large loss of blood. When the blood loss is too great, the blood left in the system is not enough to sustain life. Neurogenic shock is when the nervous system is upset by pain, fright, or other stress factors. Allergic shock is not common, but certainly not rare. This occurs when blood vessels are upset by a goat's sensitivities to medications, bug bites, etc. Septic shock is caused by infection that affects blood vessels. Cardiac shock occurs when the pumping of the heart is altered.

Symptoms of shock include labored breathing, restlessness, chilling (possibly with cold sweats), weak pulse, and loss of redness, or a bluish coloring in the mucous membranes of the eyes and lips. Body temperature may go down.

Treatment for shock in goats is similar to treatment of shock in people. Steroid injections help to prevent, relieve, or lessen shock. Keep the goat quiet, calm, and covered but not hot. Control any external bleeding. Don't force-feed the animal. It will eat on its own when it recovers. Epinephrine is the common steroid given for shock. It is an injection, and in many cases can be given early when you know you will be upsetting the goat. Disbudding, castrating, minor surgery, etc., are times to keep it on hand.

The goat's normal temperature ranges from 101 to 103 degrees, with over 102 being more likely. Livestock thermometers are available in most places that sell supplies for livestock and should be used any time you need to check a goat's temperature.

The temperature is generally checked rectally. Don't use a household thermometer for goats. They could retain it internally, causing injury. If you must purchase a thermometer, try to get one with a loop or hole in the end. This not only makes storage easier, safer, and handier; it also allows you to tie a string to it and clip the other end to the goat so that it won't be lost in the bedding or grass.

Once you have had experience with a feverish goat, or have frequently checked normal goats, it may not always be necessary to use a thermometer. Experienced mother and fathers of human babies know this. Temperature can often be closely checked by holding your fingers underneath the goat's front leg, up next to the body. Once experienced at this, you can be within a degree of accuracy. If inexperienced, you can use two goats. With one hand on the healthy goat and the other hand on the sick one, you can easily detect abnormal temperature in one of them. Remember, this is never 100 percent accurate, and should not be used when an accurate temperature is imperative for medical treatment or any other aspect of the goat's health. If a regular household thermometer is all you have, and accuracy is necessary, you can come within a few points by putting the thermometer underneath the front leg, up next to the body, and holding it there for a full five minutes.

Since several diseases can run into a lot of cost and problems, I don't become involved with them. Nor do I become involved with expensive goats that I can't dispose of when necessary. This is purely a personal and financial decision which you should consider before you spend a lot of money on a goat.

Preventive measures

I practice preventive medicine. If we know what our goats need and don't need, we can prevent most problems.

Naturally, you know I'm going to start with clean. Feed, bedding, water, milk stands, needles, towels, lots, barns—you always have to keep everything clean.

Knowing that your goats' basic requirements are close to that of a cow or a sheep is really nice, but it many cases, goats need more or less than what sheep and cows do. So following the same feed example for cows or sheep could be cheating the goats, creating a climate for sickness. With the variety of chemicals being used in today's agriculture, our ground is being depleted of many of the trace minerals that keep a goat healthy. Goat farmers may not even know what their goats need. Feeding a mix that is specifically made for goats is good, but can be expensive. Knowing what your goats need, and learning to read labels, is a must.

Having your soil tested to see if the necessary minerals are there to be in your browse helps. The following rundown will only help if you plan to check your ground and your goats for deficiencies.

Magnesium: mainly for bone growth, but aids in muscular health as well. To counteract this deficiency, feed dolomite with vitamin C or top dress with dolomite lime and calcium.
Calcium: aids nervous system, muscular system, heart function, blood clotting, and bone growth. Counteract with calcium fluoride.
Sulfur: contains keratin and copper, important for hair, hooves, horns, and helps prevent lice. Sulfur can be added to feed at l teaspoon a day, or left out free choice. Sulfur blocks or licks are also for sale.

Zinc: aids in a healthy reproductive system. Too much copper can reduce zinc
   levels. However, too little copper does not reverse the situation.
Copper: is needed for overall health, disease resistance, parasite infestation, fungal
   problems, and immunities. Copper can be added in water or feed. Check with
   your feed store for proper amounts and directions.
Red Cell: is an iron supplement and usually sold where horse supplies are. Iron can
   be bought at your feed store in an injectable form.

I strongly advise the soil testing. It is relatively inexpensive and gives you
a complete analysis on what your ground has in it. Then you'll know what your
plants don't have.

Most of us buy our hay, and not always in the same place. We have to assume
the farmer has fertilized with a chemical (although in the South, it is not uncommon for chicken manure to stink up the neighborhood for a few days after it has
been spread on the ground. The guy spreading chicken litter on his fields is the
man to try to catch and make arrangement to buy hay.) If we can't be sure of the
hay we're buying, how do we know if we need additives? We don't. We watch our
goats and hope they will let us know.

Many medical problems aren't too difficult to handle once diagnosed. Diagnosis not only depends on your vet's experience, but your experience as well. For-
tunately, these simpler problems are also the most common; as a whole, most of
them can be prevented before they start. The following are some of the most common diseases in goats and a few less common troublesome problems.

Goat pox

This is generally a mild, though contagious disease, but if ignored, can be a
painful affliction to the does. Goat pox is usually blisters that break out and make
sores on the udder area. If the sores are too close to the teat orifice, mastitis may
occur from the infection. An infected animal should be milked last and carefully.
Nursing kids can break and spread the blisters; so be sure to handmilk the infected
does. Treatment involves a mild antiseptic and treating the pustules every other
day with iodine. Strive for clean barns, clean bedding, clean hands on the milker,
and healthy goats to control the infection.

Foot rot

Foot rot is a viral infection and not merely a condition of one individual
goat's feet. The virus generally grows in wet, dark places and attacks an open sore
or cut on the goat's hooves. Once started, foot rot can infect the entire herd.
Symptoms include lameness, swelling of the feet, and pain. There may be a watery
fluid oozing from the hoof. Treatment includes a foot bath of 10 percent to 30

percent copper sulfate, removing the goats from the infected pasture for 30 days, and keeping the dead tissue trimmed away. Foot rot will not last by itself any longer than 30 days. Preventive measures include keeping lots free of debris. There is a fungicide sold in your feed store to help.

Mastitis

Mastitis is caused by one of two viruses, staphylococcus and streptococcus. To prescribe the right antibiotic for the virus affecting your doe, your vet will need samples of the milk, or you can treat with one type antibiotic one day and another one a few days later. The customary symptoms are high temperature, bad-smelling udder, and an uneasy goat. She will be in pain, and the udder may feel hard. We are told to watch for congestion of the udder. However, the goat can have mastitis for several days with no temperature, and you may not smell anything strange at all. To watch for congestion in the udder, you should be looking for hard knots. They may be as small as the end of your thumb to start; and as large as the infected side of the udder in the progressed stages. Mastitis can begin from any number of causes, including stress. Flies, infection and udder injuries can aid in mastitis, so milk the infected goat last, to prevent spreading the disease to the others. Milk all goats into a strip cup, at least until you know the disease is gone. The milk may show blood, will be thicker, often clots, and the goat won't like to be milked. In later stages, she will walk as if she is bow-legged because her udder hurts when her legs touch it. The earlier mastitis is detected, the less the damage it will cause. The disease progresses very fast so don't wait to see if it will clear up on its own because it won't. Preventive medicine includes lowering stress factors, keeping udders, lots and bedding clean, and controlling goat pox and udder abrasions.

Treatment starts with antibiotics administered as soon as you suspect mastitis. I once caught a doe the second day after she freshened, and after three days of antibiotics, she was cured. It usually takes a little longer to clear up mastitis, but quick discovery makes for a quicker cure.

There is a quick test that you can do at home to help detect mastitis sooner. I start three or four days before the baby is due, and continue every other day until I know she is clean. Squirt one squirt from each side of the udder into separate cups. Separately, mix 4 parts water to 1 squirt of Dawn dishwashing liquid, and slowly stir in the milk. If it thickens to a blob, it is infected.

Early treatment would consist of an antibiotic, gentle udder massages several times a day, and warm Epson salt packs. Alternate antibiotics, because if you don't go to the vet, you don't know which type infection she has.

With mastitis, the doe may not come back into her milk. The sooner you catch the disease, the better your chances that the udder won't be permanently damaged. In severe cases the damaged side of the udder may never regain its full production level.

Milk from infected does should never be used for human consumption, and many breeders don't feed the milk to young kids. I don't feed the milk to a weak or sickly kid, but have had no problems feeding it to the healthy ones when they got out on their own and got to it. Certainly, use your own discretion and that of your vet to decide on this issue.

Hot packs should be as hot as you can stand and left on the udder for as long as you have the patience. Less than 15 or 20 minutes isn't going to do any good, though. Very gentle and frequent massaging, along with the hot packs, should help to clear up mastitis faster.

Caseous lymphadenitis or abscesses, also known as CL

Abscesses are a goat owner's nightmare. Commonly, abscesses are lumps or knots that appear on the animal's lymph nodes. They are usually on the jaw, throat, flank, and even shoulder. Many abscesses are contagious and may be hereditary. There are two kinds of abscesses. One can be cured, and the other can only be controlled to some extent. Since some abscesses are internal, there is no cure. Trying to cure abscesses or control them can be tedious, time-consuming and expensive. Infected animals have to be separated and doctored regularly.

Animals with abscesses may be butchered, and the meat saved, providing there were no internal abscesses on the carcass. It would be best to discard the part of the carcass that did contain the abscess. Abscesses generally surround themselves with very tight little capsules, and unless it is broken, they don't contaminate the meat.

Abscesses are not a problem that the small goat owner wants to handle. This is why I won't bother with an animal that is abscessed. I have seen many animals wasting away while the owner tried his best to cure the problem. It is my solemn oath that if one abscess were to show up in my herd, I would replace all the animals and start over, because it is so hard to control the problem. I wouldn't advise anyone to buy an animal from anyone who has even one abscessed goat. Even if the seller assures you that this particular kid was never around that particular infected animal, don't believe it. But sometimes destroying the one infected animal may control the problem.

If your goats develop an abscess, consult your vet immediately. Have him explain to you, in detail, exactly what the treatment is and what the cost will be. If you still want to keep the goat, at least you will know what you are getting into.

It is important to know that not all lumps are abscesses. I had a doe that developed a lump on her lower jaw and immediately took her to the vet. He could not tell me what the lump was, but he did assure me that it was not an abscess. It did go away, but the next year it returned again for a few weeks. I took the doe to another vet, who diagnosed this as a saliva pocket. As long as it went away on its own, I was not to worry. It disappeared the second time and never returned.

Sore mouth

Commonly called "scabby mouth," it is technically called contagious ecthyma (ORF). This disease is transferable to people and must be controlled immediately. It is more common in sheep and cows, and there is a vaccine for its prevention. The disease may occur at any time on any goat but is most common during dry conditions and on young kids. This disease mimics a pox type infection. The lesions develop initially on the lips, the corners of the mouths, and the top of the hoof line and can be spread to other areas of the body, especially to the top of the hoof line. Scabs may be very tiny at first, but are contagious for many years. Often, the disease will travel through the herd and to man, taking many weeks, months or years to clear up. When treating one animal, treat them all and take the precautions to protect yourself. Do not wear chore clothes away from the goats and wash hands. Due to the severity of the nonbenign cases, all goats should be examined and treated by a vet, as this disease can last from seven to ten weeks, depending on the size of the herd, and how fast it continues to go from goat to goat and back again.

Tetanus

I have been advised continuously by various vets in various locations not to vaccinate for tetanus because of the lack of the disease in the area. Many people, however, routinely vaccinate to be on the safe side. Surely, if your vet feels the need to protect the goats because of a tetanus problem in your area, you must do it. Otherwise, why add the extra expense and inconvenience?

Tetanus in goats is just as dangerous as it is in man and can kill the goat.

Tuberculosis

This is a contagious disease, transmittable to people through milk. Tuberculosis is no longer the problem in goats that it is in cows.

Brucellosis

This rare disease is commonly called Bang's disease in goats and is transmitted to man as undulant fever.

Pneumonia

This is similar to pneumonia in man, except that goats will die much more quickly. Treatment demands that an antibiotic be administered as soon as symptoms appear. Symptoms include runny nose, runny eyes, cough, fever, and listlessness.

I use a lot of "people solutions" as well as the antibiotics. The vaporizer, goat coats, and plenty of nursing care will usually make you — and the goat — feel better.

Prevention is as simple as keeping the goat dry. A goat in good health can handle some moisture unless it is under stress, but a goat that is suffering from any stressful situation will fall prey to pneumonia just from the morning dampness. Making sure goats stay healthy will automatically prevent pneumonia.

Leptospirosis

This disease causes abortion and circling in goats and transfers to people as meningitis. Circling is a situation where animals will go around in circles for no reason and is generally associated with something attacking the brain. Transfer to people results when we come into contact with the urine or blood of the infected animal. In people, it can have no symptom at all, or a range, including fever, headache, chills, aches, jaundice, red eyes, muscle pain diarrhea and/or rash. Consult your vet for the goat's treatment and cure.

Goat polio

Goat polio isn't common. There's reason to believe that a lack of thiamin and too much grain can manifest as polio. Symptoms are disorientation, wandering, and blindness, shrinking head, anorexia, poor feed utilization and weakness. Main causes seem to be high grain content, as in feed lots, and a lack of thiamine (vitamin B-12). Thiamine should be given at first sign of anything going wrong in a goat. It will flush out of the system, so there's no chance of overdose.

Digestive disorders

Digestive disorders are relatively seldom in properly maintained goats, as it is improper feeding and handling that are the main cause. Most problems occur in young kids whose diet is mainly milk, so most problems start with the milk. Temperature is important. If the kids were nursing, the milk would be body temperature. Bottles should be heated to at least 100 degrees. As the goat gets older, the temperature can be dropped a little at a time.

The milk must be clean, along with the nipples, pans, bottles and all utensils. Any foreign particles in the new stomach can cause scouring, constipation, and/or infection.

The goats will adjust to most changes that occur slowly in their diet, but any drastic changes will cause digestive upsets. A sudden increase in protein, a large amount of moist forage, or changes in grain, fiber, or water will cause digestive problems.

Grass tetany

This is a nutritional and metabolic disorder caused by low blood magnesium. It is also called grass staggers, wheat poisoning, or hypomagnesaemia. It is not commonly seen in goats, and usually affects older cows and very young calves, and sometimes sheep. This condition seems to occur in the spring or fall after a cool spell, when the grass begins new growth. Symptoms consist of grazing away from the herd, irritability, muscular twitching in flank, staring, uncoordination, staggering, collapse, thrashing, throwing the head back, coma, and death. Animals on pasture will be found dead for no apparent reason. A urine sample seems to be the only way to diagnose. It would seem that supplying extra magnesium and keeping animals off new grass for a while would be the only preventive.

Bloat

Bloat is caused when there is another reason for the food not to finish the digestive process and the consumed food becomes gaseous. This may occur when overeating tender young grasses or overeating green forage still wet with dew or rain. The animal will show great amounts of distress—kicking, looking at its sides, and repeatedly getting up and lying down. The feed store sells a product for bloat, and cod liver oil will help. Making the goat get up and exercise is good therapy, and ½ cup of coffee may help. Any time you suspect bloat and these treatments don't work, call a vet, because the goat can die.

Indigestion

Indigestion is generally the result of feeding—either too much, too little, or too finely ground grains. Sudden feeding of a new grain, forage or grass can cause indigestion.

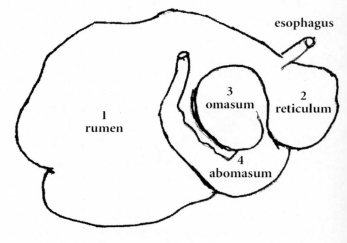

The four stomachs in an adult goat

Impaction

Impaction occurs when the rumination stops. The whole digestive system may also stop. Impaction may be caused from overeating, too much high fiber, poor quality or moldy hays, frozen feeds, lack of water, not enough exercise, and diet changes.

Any stressful condition can cause impaction. There is a loss of appetite, and the rumen feels hard to the touch because nothing is passing through. The animal eventually dies from the gathering of poisonous gases that congested foods produce in the rumen (similar to intoxication). If impaction is caught early, the goat can be drenched with warm water and molasses. However, in advanced cases there is a danger of strangling. Warm enemas may also help with this problem. There are medications available from your vet to relieve this condition.

Constipation

Constipation is the inability to pass normal feces. Droppings may be hard and dry, or there will be none. You will notice the goat straining to eliminate. Plenty of exercise and water are necessary. A laxative feed may help, or a laxative in the amount of one teaspoon of castor oil (or one to two ounces of Epsom salts) to a pint of water for young kids. Increase the dosages according to the goat's size.

Urinary calculi

This is commonly called a bladder infection, or kidney stones, and occurs mostly in bucks and wethers raised in sandy areas. It is deadly. If caught in time, surgery is possible, but this condition can kill a goat in three days. There really isn't a cure, but preventive measures call for ammonium chloride in the feed, always free access to water, and keeping feed and hay off the ground. People raising goats in sandy areas need to monitor their lots closely, making sure the goats are not forced to eat or ingest sand easily.

Founder

Founder is a reaction to eating. Usually the goat eats too much, or eats feed that is too high in protein for the goat's particular condition. Founder occurs as a foot condition. It may occur with bloat. The front of the hooves will grow slowly, and the back of the heel will grow much faster, causing a snow shoe effect. (This condition is called lambinitus in sheep.)

The digestive system in a goat is very complex. The following is a simple rundown of what is supposed to go on in normal digestion.

As the goat bites off and chews the forage, the salivary glands secrete large amounts of alkaline saliva for lubrication to aid in swallowing. The esophagus carries the food to the stomach, which is divided into four parts.

The rumen is a large sac which can hold up to two gallons of wet forage. It is here that all the microorganisms attack the food and break it down into amino and fatty acids. The rumen returns some of these foods to the cud by regurgitation, for further chewing, before they are sent on to the reticulum, where they are pumped into the abomasums through the omasum. Bucks as well as does chew a cud.

The omasum further breaks down the foods and liquefies them before they go into the abomasums. The abomasums is the "true" stomach, and mostly resembles that of humans. From the abomasums, the food goes to the small intestine, where acids are broken down further by pancreas liver enzymes. In the large intestine, more water is taken from the food as it goes to the colon. The colon rids the rest of the liquids and pellets are formed before they are passed out the rectum.

The digestive process takes from 24 to 36 hours. Digestive problems aren't common enough to pose a large problem in goats that are maintained properly. Don't try to be a hero if you suspect digestive problems. Treat immediately and if treatment doesn't work within hours, call your vet when you think you have cause for worry.

Poisonous weeds

Though poisonous weeds don't usually create a problem for goats, I've included a list of major offenders. This list does not include the entire United States, but covers most of the problem weeds in the Midwest.

Most of the weeds are more dangerous to cows, sheep or horses since goats aren't likely to eat enough to harm themselves.

Sweet clover: sheep are less affected
Crimson clover: fresh blooms are the offender
Scotch broom: in large quantities
Black locust: affects mostly horses
China berry: affects mostly sheep
Common cockle burr: affects mostly swine
Horse nettle (berries)
Black nightshade (berries)
Red buckeye: affects mostly cattle
Spotted water hemlock
Castor bean
Redroot pigweed

Eastern baccharis
White snakeroot: also affects the milk and poisons the consumer
Common sneeze weed
Bitter sneezeweed
Poison ivy
Poison oak: Goats only carry this poison to their handlers
Poison sumac
Atamasco lily: affects mostly cows and horses (mostly the bulb)
Stagger grass
Milkweed
Help dogbane
Hellebore
Alsike clover, buckwheat or hypericaums
Cow slips (Dutchman's breaches, dry oak leaves): infrequently affects goats
Rhubarb and a variety of ornamental shrubs
Showy crotalaria: affects goats to a lesser degree
Bracken fern
Mountain laurel and sheep laurel: severely poisonous
Black cherry
Choke cherry
Cherry laurel
Johnsongrass: affects goats during drought, or frost
Yellow jasmine
Pokeberry: rarely affects goats
Jimsonweed
Buttercup
Great laurel
Lantana
Oleander
Bladder pod
Rattle box
Sickle pod
Sesbania: affects cows primarily

Medicines and storage

All medicines, medical equipment and tools should be stored properly. Some medicines need refrigeration. Most need stored away from sunlight and heat. Tools need to be cleaned and oiled, and all equipment should be handy. Follow the manufacturer's directions for storing medicines.

Storage should be away from young children and goats. Many goat owners mount a cabinet with secure latches on the main barn wall.

Since my main barn does not house all my goats and my bucks are frequently on the other side of the property, I find this barn cabinet unhandy. A storeroom in your home, on the back porch, in a tool or utility shed might make handier and safer storage areas. I retrieved an outgrown toy box for the purpose. Not only is it large enough, it has extra room for collars, chains, and an old blanket. It is my "goat box," and a great organizer. Many medicines can't be frozen, so outside locations for storage may not be feasible. My goat box is in a handy spot in the storeroom, or in the house.

Basic supply list

Twelve- to fourteen-inch tube or pipe for giving pills. There is one made of a durable plastic for this purpose.
Four feet of half-inch hose or tubing for stomach feedings. These are also available in supply houses.
A funnel for pouring medicines into tubes. Very cleans bottles, with the bottoms cut out, can be used.
Hoof trimmers, scissors, and hair trimmers.
Calking gun, and other worming equipment.
Tattooing and dehorning equipment, if you will be doing the tasks yourself.
Cotton, adhesive tape, sterile pads, razor and blades, hypodermic needles, plenty of clean rags.
Extra ropes, collars, chains, leads.
Insecticides and containers, rags for cleanup and sponges for application.
Flour and/or sugar, or other blood clotting aids.

Remember, none of your supplies are any good if they are not stored properly. Keep them clean, and in good condition. Replace everything immediately.

Medicines should be adjusted to your situation and your vet's advice. Medicines that one of your friends needs on the other side of the state may be totally useless in your area. This is just a list of basics and should be adjusted to your particular situation.

Isopropyl alcohol, for sterilization
Baking soda
Vaseline
Hydrogen peroxide
Bag balm and other appropriate salves
Epsom salts
Cod liver oil
Combiotic: for cuts, infection, pneumonia. This is a universal antibiotic, though I prefer to go to the vet to purchase a supply of antibiotic that has penicillin in it and can be used more widely, although it may be expensive.

Azimycin: This is a steroid to relieve shock and stress, and epinephrine is sold in
   areas where you can't get Azimycin
Injectable vitamin B-12 with iron, to aid as an appetite and blood builder.
Wound dressings, first aid creams, etc.
Iodine is recommended for dipping newborns' cords.
Worm medicine
Flea, lice, tick sprays and powders
Mineral oil
Udder ointments

   When purchasing medicines get the instructions. Tape them to the container,
and make sure you have the materials needed to administer the medicine properly.
If you don't know what the vet is talking about when he says, "Feed by stomach
tube," ask him. Watch the labels for dates, and never use outdated medicines.
   Always buy medicines from someone you trust. The vet is usually the best bet
but he usually charges more. Reliable feed stores, supply houses, and businesses
that deal directly to the dairy industry can be a great deal cheaper.
   Keep track of all medicine given to all goats, and when they were used. You
may think that you will remember that Blackie got her shot on June 11 and that
Susie was wormed on July 1, but when Mabel has to have stitches and antibiotics
on July 6, and Little Henry catches cold and needs medicine on July 7, you better
have it all down on paper because it's not going to stay in the old memory bank
too well if you're also trying to remember when hooves were trimmed and what
fences need to be fixed.
   A calendar with large squares hanging at your back door will be your handiest
investment. You can record all the daily activities, dosages of medicines, and individual goat's problems as they happen. Then, on a rainy day, or at the end of each
week or month, you can sit down and record all information in the appropriate
book or chart for permanent reference.

28

Parasites

External parasites

Goats are not immune to external parasites. Flies, ticks, lice, screwworm, fleas, and maggots can drive the goat into poor production, poor health, and ill temper.

It has been suggested that any time a goat scratches it's time to suspect parasites. This is not always true, since scratching is a natural method to keep clean. However, it doesn't hurt to check each goat frequently.

Lice generally present a specific wintertime problem when they search out the warmth of the goat for survival. Flaking skin, dry skin, patches of missing hair, and a runny nose are all symptoms of lice infestation. Production can be poor, and the coat will be rough and unhealthy looking. Complete clipping in the spring often rids the goats of their winter guests, as will a very thorough dousing with a reliable insecticide.

Flies are basically a summertime problem, but in the South flies can be a problem on any warm winter day. There may be many varieties of flies, depending on your area. Most of them bite and agitate the goat. If the goat has to spend too much time avoiding the flies, it cannot eat, grow, and produce as it should. Gnats especially fit into this category, as the goat will spend too much time kicking and running and not enough time eating. Flies can carry bacteria and leave larvae and maggots on open wounds. They can cause infection in the eyes and ears. Watch your goats to see that they are eating, grazing, and resting peacefully, without insects distracting them.

Ticks are not particular about their hosts. Ticks don't generally bother a goat, but when that goat is allowed to roam freely in the woods, without protection, a tick will find it, and it usually settles in around the eyes. There is a general theory that ticks don't survive and reproduce in the areas where goats bed and urinate. Most ticks do live in the ground, so the theory may prove true if you were to have your goats on the same ground for two or three seasons. However, as long as ticks are present in the ground, they will cling to your goats. Look for ticks on the udder, under the legs, around the scrotum, under the tail, under collars, in and on ears, and around the eyes. Remove ticks as soon as you discover them, and apply a tick protection.

Ticks suck blood. Since blood is one thing the goat doesn't have to spare, it can't be shared with ticks. Many ticks will leave open sores on the goat, causing infection and a generally poor condition.

Preventive medicine is the first step in controlling parasites. All areas and goats should be kept clean and dry, so as not to attract the parasites in the first place. Drain standing water and keep lots raked free of manure.

Powders, sprays, and dips are available for external parasite control. There are vets and salesmen who will swear that only one product will take care of one problem and that you must have additional products for each additional parasite — one for ticks, another for flies, and yet another for lice, etc. Naturally, this is a very expensive way to solve the problems. On the other hand, if you take the time to look, you'll find an all-purpose insecticide that is safe for goats, handles all your parasites effectively, and costs much less.

I'm not advocating any particular brand of insecticide, as each area has a different name for similar products. Several companies may sell the same products with a different label, and the same product may be available in an assortment of consistencies, with a different label for each. Most products will come in liquid or powder forms. Liquids are often called dips and can either be sprayed or sponged on the goat. When you are using liquids, choose a day that is warm enough for the goat to dry quickly, without chilling.

Be careful not to inhale insecticides. Always apply in an open area, and stand the goat so that any breeze will not blow the product back into its face and your own. Don't spray or powder into or around feed dishes, water containers, or on salt and mineral blocks. Read all labels carefully. Some products are not safe for goats, while others are not safe for dairy procedures because they will contaminate the milk.

Treat every goat on the property. If your neighbors have goats, persuade them to treat their herd or volunteer to do it yourself. One goat left untreated can reinfest the entire herd. Don't forget the bucks, young kids, and wethers that may be out on pasture. When treating the goats, treat their housing as well.

When dusting, spraying or wiping the goat, always make a circle completely around the neck and up as high as you can get behind the ears before you apply anywhere else. This prevents any insects from racing to the head when the rest of the body is treated.

Apply insecticides liberally over the entire body, moving from front to back and from top to bottom. Take great care to get in the pockets under the legs, around the udder, under the tail, and between the toes. Powders have to be ruffled down through all hair, and liquids must soak through to the skin.

Most goats don't mind this procedure, and some actually relish the extra attention. At least they like it until you get to their face and eyes. Working with the head will get the goat agitated, so do it last. Carefully apply the product in and around the ears, though you don't want to soak or stuff the interior of the ear. Brush, spray, or wipe the insecticide over the face, making sure you don't get any in the eyes, nose, and mouth. Check the goat to make sure you didn't forget the chest or stomach, before letting it go.

Repeat the application in two weeks to make sure you get all parasites. Reapply for ticks and flies when necessary, according to the directions and climate. Keep an eye on your goats for a couple of hours, just in case a curious animal accidentally sneaks a taste and becomes sick. Consult a vet immediately if you suspect sickness from insecticides.

Store all insecticide products according to directions and out of the way. Goats are snoopy and will have to investigate anything left within their reach.

Liquids are easier to handle if they're transferred to smaller bottles for applications. Powders can be applied safely in small amounts if put into smaller plastic containers with holes punched into one end. Large salt shakers work well, as do plastic containers with tight-fitting lids to prevent dumping.

Never use a container that has had insecticide in it for any other purpose. Most insecticides do not wash away. When finished, rinse the containers and sponges, etc., and let them air dry before storing them. Label containers so you will only use them for reapplication of insecticides.

You may want to wear rubber gloves when using insecticides, but a thorough washing of the hands and clothing will generally be enough protection for the most widely used products.

Goats can have individual allergies, and one animal may be sensitive to some products. White or light colored goats may show skin sensitivity to some applications. Check out new products on a small area of any goats you suspect might have an adverse reaction.

A thorough application is needed before winter to give the goats a head start in protection against lice.

Since insecticides are so available and affordable, there is no excuse for a goat to be plagued with external parasites.

In the South, fire ants are not a parasite, but they can cause extreme problems for a goat. If you look around your pasture and see clumps of tall grass that the goat has not eaten, you can bet there is a hill of fire ants in the middle of it. Fire ants will attack goats' feet faster than the goat can get away from them. The goat will not stop running, stomping, or jumping until it has freed itself of the critters. Getting rid of the ants is the only cure. Every time you see or hear of a new fire ant control, use it. You need to alternate products every 30 days, and after every rain. You may not kill the ants, but you will move them out. This is a serious problem and needs to be attacked with zeal. Once you've moved them out, recheck every three months.

Internal parasites

There is no doubt among goat owners that internal parasites (worms) are a goat's largest health hazard. Because of the large area of stomach wall, the great amount of roughage consumed, and the variety of internal parasite populations, goats are highly susceptible to an overload of worms.

No healthy goat can be totally worm-free. Some worms have to be present to help the system fight bacteria. An overabundance of worms creates infestation and poor health, so a delicate balance is desired.

A large infestation of internal parasites can prevent conception, cause abortion, stunt growth, stop milk production, and kill the goat. Once goats are allowed an overload in their system, their resistance to other diseases are lowered and they stand less chance of holding their own against viruses and infection.

The hardest management practice concerns controlling worms in goats. The parasite problem is extremely complicated, but I am going to try to simplify the situation. Never forget, however, that the problem itself is never simple.

Parasites consist of a group of animal life that must live in or on another animal (the host). Protozoan is a one-celled animal, such as coccidian, and belongs in the parasite groups.

Worms are ingested by the goat, passed through the feces to reproduce on the ground and be reingested by the goat. Generally, worms do not multiply in their host. One worm larva eaten by a goat grows to become one parasite passed in the manure. Coccidia, however, live and multiply inside the goat as well as elsewhere.

Once dropped onto the ground, the worm larva completes its reproductive cycle, crawls to the tops of the grasses, and is reingested by the goats, where it continues to develop and cause grave internal damage to the goat. The more worm larva the goat ingests, the more damage they cause before being passed out in the feces.

Warm, wet weather aids parasite growth. Cold, dry weather deters reproduction growth. Adult goats are the main carriers of worms and coccidian. Older, healthy, and well-fed goats will build up resistance to a worm population and be less likely to be seriously affected, though they will continue to drop a worm population with their feces. Young kids, sick goats, and those that have not been exposed to worms will show a greater sign of distress and disease and possibly die.

When pastures, feed, and hay bunks are infected, the goats become infested. Therefore, overgrazing low lots and overcrowding must be avoided.

A lack of exercise areas doesn't give goats space to eliminate freely without contamination of feeding and bedding areas and water receptacles.

Worms can go from the bedding to the goat's hair, where they can be reingested as the goats scratch with their mouth and teeth. The bedding should be dry and clean at all times.

Worms can be fatal. As worms feed on the tissue and blood of the goat, they harm its physical condition. Milking does may stop production in the middle of their heaviest peak. Kids will die, or their growth will be stunted. Dry does may not conceive, and bucks may be rendered infertile.

Unfortunately, some goats show no early symptoms except for a slight weight loss or a lack of normal weight gain. Early symptoms of an overload of worms are supposed to be scouring, rough and dull coat, dull, sad eyes, coughing, and a loss of color in the mucous membranes of the eyes and mouth. In severe cases, a drop in temperature will occur and the goat will go off feed. None of the symptoms are accurate, and a goat could easily die without showing any one of the symptoms till the day it dies. Recovery of severely infested goats is slow, up to three months, and the goat may never reach normal adult weight.

Control of worm and coccidian infestations begins with preventive control. Pastures should be rotated every ten to 14 days, and goats should not be over-grazed to the extent that they continually crop the grass too short. When the grass is short, worm larvae have less distance to climb and goats pick them up faster. To control worms, no more than six to eight goats should be grazed on a half-acre of normal pasture in a two-week period. If the land is lush with forage and growth, eight to ten goats can browse until the undergrowth is cleared.

Feed, water, hay, and salt receptacles should never be on the ground or at a level where the goats can contaminate the containers or contents with their drop-pings. I cannot emphasize this issue enough. This is the new goat owner's largest mistake. People seem to think that it can't happen to them and they don't under-stand how their goats could get an overload of worms and die. Since it is harder to build containers to keep the feed and hay off the ground, most people take the lazy way out and throw it on the ground—until they lose a goat or spend a fortune in medicine to save it. Don't take these chances.

Kids should never be grazed with adults or on pasture where untreated animals have had a chance to infest the area. Kids should be wormed early, at two and four weeks and every month until they are six months old. Their systems are not strong enough to handle the worms they would pick up from adults with a normal worm load in the feces.

New additions to the herd should be kept separate for two to four weeks, until treated so you know that they are not passing an abundance of worms.

Treated animals should be moved to new lots fours days after dosage to pre-vent re-infestation, and infested pastures should rest two to fours weeks before goats are replaced. Ponds and marshy areas, where snails and slugs have populated, should be fenced off. The best form of preventive medicine for worm control is keeping track of all the goats' weights. I measure them every week during the sum-mer and wet spells, every two weeks during the cooler periods of spring and fall, and once a month through winter.

If goats show a drop of one-half inch of the tape, I check their mucous mem-branes and make a notation to watch them. If they drop one-half inch the next week, that is a good enough reason to dose for worms.

Also, I watch for young kids to maintain a continuous weight gain each week.

If there is a worm problem, the smallest or the weakest goats will not gain as much as the others.

Worm medicine is a very important part of my worm control measures. Worming regularly is one sure way to prevent the problem and does not harm the goat.

Most species of worms can remain in the ground indefinitely. One vet I spoke with suggested the possibility of a variety of hookworm being on and in infected ground for as long as 40 years. Broadcasting lime will help slow this problem.

A worm program should be developed to suit the size of your herd, your grazing conditions, and your climate. Goats that are kept on a dry lot, and hand-fed in northern climates, may never need a worm medicine. Grazing goats on small pastures in the South may need a monthly worming schedule.

Following is a possible worming program if weather and grazing areas are not infected and worms have been no problem in the past. Changes in this program can be tuned into your specific situation.

Worm all goats when kids are two or three weeks old. Repeat in ten days to three weeks. Continue to worm kids every two weeks till six months. Worm all goats when kids are six months old. Repeat in ten days to three weeks. Worm the bucks and pregnant does one month before kidding. Repeat in 10 days. Worm does again after kidding. Repeat in 10 days.

Worm medicines come in every form imaginable, from injections to pellets that the goats will eat from your hand.

Not all medicines are effective on all goats in all areas, or on all worms. Read labels and ask questions. Be informed about the medicine you'll be using. Every time you worm, alternate medicines and then watch the herd for ten days. I have found that one out of ten goats will not be affected and will have to be treated with another product.

By taking fecal samples to be analyzed you can discover the types of worms your goats have and the intensity of the infestation. Simply gather fresh samples from various goats in the herd, place them in separate, labeled plastic bags, and take them to the vet. You may refrigerate samples until they can be taken to the vet.

Goats will build up immunities to medicines. For this reason, medicines should be alternated. I use a paste medication when worms are strongest and a drench in between. Some worm medicines cannot be used on pregnant does, young kids, or sick animals. Check your directions, and change the medicines when necessary. We now have an injectable for cows that works on goats as well that can also be given orally. I give orally first, because it's easier, then inject the next time, if it didn't work the first time.

Worm medicines are administered according to weight, so weigh or measure the goats. Don't guess.

Injectable worm medicines generally cause the goat a burning sensation and they will act like they are dying, or going into shock, at the very least. Pellets are fed directly to the goat — if they will eat them.

Drenches are liquids that are forced down the throat by a tube and should never be given to a sick or struggling goat because they cause additional stress.

Pastes are relatively simple: the medicine is applied to the tongue, where it sticks until swallowed.

Pills or boluses are available and can be poked into the back of the mouth by hand or pushed into the back of the mouth with a long syringe-type tube made for this purpose. If giving pills by hand, stand beside or straddle the goat and pull the head up so the nose is pointed upward. Force the mouth open with the thumb and forefingers of one hand, and insert the pill to the back of the mouth with the other hand. The pill must be on the back of the tongue, or the goat will move it to the teeth or cud and spit it out. Once the pill is on the back of the tongue, keep the head up until the goat swallows. Stoking the throat downward will induce swallowing. It helps to put peanut butter on the pill so it will stick in the mouth and the goat will want to swallow it.

If worms become out of control and your goats become overinfested, you will have to adhere to strict management practices to keep from losing any animals. Severely infested goats can be saved, even when the vet has given up on them, but it takes a lot of nursing, patience, time, energy and therapy.

I had been assured that young kids didn't need worming until after weaning. I bought two six-week-old bucks, still on the bottle, with the intention of raising them to butcher. Because of their age and my inexperience I did not worm them, nor did I quarantine them from the rest of the kids. Within six weeks, all my kids were heavily infested, and a couple weeks later some of the older does in the adjoining lot were ill. My kids were still drinking milk from the pan, and all my does had been wormed.

Not all vets are familiar with goats or parasite-infected goats. Although I visited three vets, I lost five kids and one adult before the infestation was accurately diagnosed by a fecal sample as hookworms. The first two kids that died showed no symptoms until the day before they died when they developed scours. I treated the rest of them for scouring.

The other goats waited until the last two days to look poor, scour, and become pale in the mucous membranes. A highly respected vet had diagnosed intestinal infection, and they were being treated for that problem instead of worms.

One goat died of pneumonia, due to the rundown condition brought on by the worm overload. This last goat is the one we took to the vet for examination after its death.

After using several medicines, we found one that was effective on hookworms, and the goats showed an improvement in three days. We were not instructed to repeat dosage in ten to 14 days. Three weeks later, we had sick goats again. Every worm medication I have used should be repeated in ten to 14 days, though vets are very lax about giving you these instructions.

Except for one purebred Nubian doeling, all the goats responded well. Delta was not so lucky, despite the added doses, she failed more each day. Saving Delta took three months of nursing care. Several medications were used before we found one that helped. The vet had given up on her and she became so sick and weak that we fed her by hand and kept her on a rug in front of my kitchen stove. Delta was so weak that she lost the use of her legs and had to be hung in a sling from the dining room door until she regained the circulation in her legs. When she finally did walk, it was slow going, for short periods, and even when she returned to the herd, she still came back to the house at night until she had fully recovered. Delta was not big enough to breed during her first season, and on her first birthday she only weighed 69 pounds. There are several factors to remember about this incident.

1. Had one of the vets instructed me to repeat the dose in ten to 14 days, she might not have become so severely infested.
2. I belonged to a goat club, and all the members knew my problem. After Delta survived I told one of the members about this sling and he said he had been through the same situation several years before. He could have given me advice earlier and the goats might have survived.
3. Although I had checked the library, I didn't find the answers in time to save the goats.
4. If I had realized that the kids could and should have been wormed there would have been no problem.

You cannot learn enough about internal parasites. You must know your goats well. Their behavior and health will determine the need for parasite control. Check them often. Weigh or measure weekly during summer and monthly the rest of the time. Check fecal samples and mucous membranes routinely.

Treating coccidian microorganisms can be as simple as treating the water with coccidiostats. Water should be kept in dark-colored containers, because light ones helps bacteria multiply faster. Sunlight will kill coccidia, and copper sulfates will keep the bacteria low, so if you suspect coccidia, place containers in the sun.

Animals frequently react to coccidian in the same manner as they do to worms, so misdiagnosis is possible if fecal samples are not checked. One of the symptoms of an overload of coccidian is scouring with blood. However, this may not always be true, so don't assume that the lack of blood also means the lack of an overload of coccidia. I have never seen blood with coccidia and have had fecal samples come back positive more than once.

All animals have some form of coccidia present in their systems, and many vets firmly believe that one form of coccidia will not go from chickens to goats, or from ducks to goats, and vice versa. However, some vets and breeders disagree. Since the research is still incomplete, I would advise you to take precautions. If you do mix goats with other animals, use coccidiostats in the water of both species to prevent possible problems. It's just best to use them anyway. Treating a problem you don't have is treating one that you'll never have.

I am fully aware that goats are grazed with chickens, ducks, and rabbits. The owners swear that they never have had a problem. When I ask how long they've had goats, their answers are a little vague. It seems that they have not had one goat that stayed for several years at a time, therefore, they don't know if they've had a coccidia problem.

Of all the worms, liver flukes cause the most serious problem. The medicine needed to control liver flukes is now readily available.

Liver flukes start from snails and slugs, so avoid ponds and swampy areas. Copper sulfate solutions are available to spray ditches, ponds and other areas where draining is not possible. It might be easier to fence off the offending area if you know the flukes are present.

Not all snails produce the fluke that is harmful to goats. Take a sample of snails to your vet for identification. Your county extension service can also be helpful in letting you know if the fluke is a problem in your area.

There is a natural way to worm goats, and pumpkins seem to aid in this process. When pumpkins are ripe and ready, cut them into bite-size pieces and offer to the goats, seeds and all. The goats won't eat too much, but you can leave the pumpkin for them to eat at will. The biggest concern is that the pumpkin will turn bad and draw flies. Some goats will not eat the pumpkins, while others absolutely love them, therefore, this is not a surefire worming method. It is, however, one way to slow down the never-ending problems of worms. If your goats do eat the pumpkins, it would be wise to plant extra for use each fall and try to store some back for a winter treat.

Many groups are working hard on creating nonchemical wormers, and I really feel the headway made will be of help to us within a few years.

29

Culling

Culling is the practice by which goatkeepers rid the herd of inferior stock and keep only the goats that will improve the herd. Each breeder has a different purpose and different goal to meet. One may sell his newborn kids and keep the doe that produces two cups a day because that's all the milk he needs and he doesn't need the kids. He's perfectly happy with his goat, and no breeder or writer of goat books can ever convince him that he shouldn't keep that goat. If he were to change his reason for keeping goats and decide to keep the kids (and still have extra milk) he'd either have to buy milk for the kids, or his two-cupper would have to be culled.

Breeders who show goats will often cull a good producer, if its color or spotting is wrong. Experienced breeders have culled for years. The animal that proves to be of least value now may actually be of better stock than the original animal. Someone else's cull may be your choice goat.

Before culling, consider your reason for keeping goats and your goals for herd improvement.

Figure out how many animals you feel you can afford to keep and stick close to that number as you can. I try not to winter more than ten to 12 goats. I may have as many as 25 or 30 goats after the spring kids. I try to cut back to my original number of ten or 12 each fall.

When you breed one goat, you are going to have two or three more in five months. If you breed ten does, you'll add at least ten or twenty kids to your herd. Common sense says that you can't keep them all.

Set up strict culling standards before you expect kids. Make sure your family knows your plans and is prepared for you to carry them out. Kids are not the only animals we cull. When older goats are no longer the best of the herd, they must be culled.

I always ask owners of herds with 20, 30, or 40 goats, "Why keep so many?" Many of the owners have a meat market for their excess stock. Some sell the milk.

Others have bred desirable traits into their animals so they can count on quite an income from the kids born to their business each year.

But over half will say "Oh, I don't know, I'm keeping this one because she's cute, and I want to see if that one will do better next year." And so on. These people end up with 30 or 40 goats in a few years, and drive themselves crazy trying to feed and care for them.

Stick to your decisions about how many goats you can keep or have a darned good reason for changing your mind. If you keep a goat because it's cute or you're attached to it, you better realize that it is going to cost you money.

Each goat is different, so assess each one separately. Don't keep a goat just for its color or breeding or because it's registered. A goat can be registered simply if its parents or ancestors were registered. A strict culling practice reduces cost and leaves room, time, and money for better animals.

Breeding toward your ideal can be a lifelong challenge, and it's always a pleasure to know that stock is being improved upon from year to year.

Some culling decisions are easy, though tragic. The blind, crippled and deformed must be culled if they are indeed crippled. The doe that won't breed, the infertile buck, and animals with abscesses must be removed.

If you intend to follow the breed characteristics and color patterns, so must your goats. Animals whose general conformation does not follow the breed regulation or their purpose must be culled. This applies to lack of dairy character in milk animals and a lack of meatiness in butcher stock.

Animals with physical defects are culled. Undershot and overshot jaws, weak pasterns, and extreme hockiness are the worst offenders.

Serious udder flaws should be eliminated from reproduction. This includes extra teats, even if they are all functional.

After all the easy culling decisions, you will someday have to make a decision about the "so-so goat." Does it go, or does it stay?

Setting sentiment aside may not be easy. You may have had the goat for several years. There is no room for emotional decisions. The goat has to be judged on its abilities, not on your hopes for it.

I frequently make culling plans a year ahead for the older does. If a doe doesn't meet the last year's production, she will be culled immediately after next year's kids. If a doe stops milk production again after four months' lactation, she is also culled. I tell my family why the animal will be culled and allow them time to prepare for it. I can keep the does through another gestation, so I will have the kids in the spring.

It's a good idea to visit a goat show or an experienced breeder before you make culling decisions. Seeing quality stock gives you a better idea of how to come back home to select your own culls. It also gives you a chance to look at your goats and see that they might not be as bad as you thought.

I started with an ordinary unrecorded grade doe. I did not see a goat show until my third year into goats, after I had consistently upgraded.

I was surprised when I saw show stock and realized that I had a couple of goats that could hold their own in the ring.

When making the other culling decisions, there are several points to consider.

1. Is the animal's general appearance worthy of reproducing more stock for your purpose?
2. The animal's background, not just papers or pedigree, but general performance. Has it remained healthy without doctoring? Has the doe had trouble kidding? Has she delivered one, two, or three strong healthy kids? Have the kids from this doe grown well? Has the buck always performed? How do his kids look, especially his daughter?
3. What about past performance in milk and meat? Is the goat easy to handle? Easy to milk? How well does it stand for trimming, cutting, and medical treatment?
4. How old is the goat? Does it have several good years left or are you taking a chance this year?
5. Does the animal hold up well under the extremes of summer and winter conditions or does it require special attention during seasonal changes?
6. Does it eat more than it produces? (That's always a good reason to cull.)
7. Does this goat meet your expectations for future improvement of the herd?
8. Unisexed animals (hermaphrodites) cannot be kept for anything but butchering, or as a pet or playmate for one of your bucks..
9. Since over half of your new kids will more than likely be bucks, they should automatically be castrated and raised to butcher, either for your freezer or someone else's.

I refuse to keep a goat that can't be handled easily. It's not worth my time, effort, or money. You may have similar guidelines in your own culling decision.

You have several choices of disposal. The animal can be sold, given away, traded, butchered, or simply killed and disposed of.

When you've decided which goats go, you also have to decide where they go. Consider the future of each individual cull.

1. Would it improve another herd?
2. Could it be a good family milker?
3. How about a 4H project?
4. Could it survive life as a weed-eater and not require much maintenance?
5. Is it only for butchering?

If selling, check your markets and chapter 33 (on selling).

Giving the goat to a less fortunate goat keeper is charitable, but costly, and the recipient of your kindness may not show the animal the appreciation that it deserves.

Trading a cull will usually result in getting another cull, unless you are fortunate enough to find someone willing to trade other goods for your cull.

Killing the animal and getting rid of it is a waste, the only thing you accomplish is getting rid of the goat.

Butchering your culls is the most feasible method. Besides stocking your freezer, you can relax, knowing that this animal was good for something and did not have to suffer a long life of abuse because it was not a top producer.

A strict culling habit takes practice. You will be called hardhearted. Whether you have one goat or a small herd, you must develop a businesslike manner.

30

Registration

I'm often asked, "Why mess with papers?" That's a hard question to answer. Since papers don't make the goat, why bother?

Ideally, papers should be used for performance, but they are not. Any goats whose parents were registered can be registered, so papers are issued on bloodlines. A goat that is registered simply comes from a long line of ancestors that were registered.

If you breed a purebred doe to a purebred buck, the offspring can be registered purebred, whether the doe was a high producer or not. If you breed a grade doe to a purebred buck, the offspring (does) can be registered as 50 percent American and the breed. That 50 percent American is bred to a purebred buck of the same breed and the offspring (does) can be registered 75 percent American. Again, when breeding the 75 percent American doe to a purebred buck, the offspring (does) are registered as American Nubian or American Toggenburg, etc. Now, when the American doe is bred again to a purebred or American buck, the offspring (does and bucks), are registered as American. Upgrading from a scrub to an American takes years. During this time, none of the goats have to be top-notch quality. Presumably, you would be trying to better the offspring with each breeding.

The ADGA (American Dairy Goat Association) does have rules regarding breed characteristics of each animal registered. This does not mean that the rules are strictly followed.

Here's the trick: As goat breeders, we should use our discretion and not register animals that are from poor quality producers. We are asked never to register an American buck unless he shows outstanding qualities that are desirable for reproduction. At this writing, the herd books are accepting some variations in the breed standards of some of the newer breeds to help increase the numbers and interest in that breed. Oberhasli and Sable have been accepted.

Unfortunately, many breeders register any stock they can, including poor-looking American bucks, just to have them registered. One reason is simply for the

A 4-H club displays signs on a show pen.

prestige of having the papers. Another reason is that these people have different opinions of quality and don't see anything wrong with their goats. And still another group registers all goats as an upbreeding program. Since owners are continually upbreeding and keeping up with the papers, they'll have the papers when they do breed a goat of desirable quality.

They will have the papers for the next descendants. This system would work if the papers of poorer quality goats were not made to sound so important.

On one occasion, I registered some American doelings, only to find that the mother wasn't worth her salt and one of the doelings grew to have a very poor chest and front legs. I sold the lesser doeling and tore up her papers. The other doe did improve her production over her mother and has been kept. The mother, too, was butchered and her papers destroyed.

Any offspring from a poor producer should not be papered unless you have high hopes that the sire will make up the difference. If the offspring don't improve over their dams, cull them and their papers.

If you must sell a young papered animal, please have the decency to tell the buyer the parent's faults. Maybe you could give the buyer tips on mating in order to improve the future offspring. Some people put too much emphasis on papers and are disappointed by a two-cup producer. When they are disappointed, they blame the papers. This is unfair to the good bloodlines in the ancestry.

All is not lost concerning the registration papers. If a breeder qualifies, he can complete a DHIR (Dairy Herd Improvement Registry). In this procedure, the goats are "on test." An official tester visits the herd one day a month without an appointment and takes accurate records on production, particularly quantity and butterfat percentage.

Depending on her production and age, a doe may qualify for Advanced Registry (AR). The requirements for a two-year-old and younger are 1,500 pounds of milk and 52.51 pounds of butterfat, and increases to 1,719 pound milk and 60 pounds of butterfat at five years, on a lactation of 305 days or less.

This gives her a code of *M (star milker) and that is recorded on her registration papers. If her doe offspring qualifies, she receives a *M.

A *****M (five-star milker) means that that doe, her dam, and her grandparents back to her maternal great-great-grand dam all made records that qualified them to AR, or a star — five generations.

If papers denote with an asterisk, it refers to production.

The problem is that going "on test" can be expensive, inconvenient, and a nuisance. Many people with high producers don't have them tested, so they don't have records to vouch for them.

People who can afford to go on test have to make up the money, and they usually add the cost to the selling price of their goats.

For a herd of ten does, you can spend from $400 to $600 and up for a year to go on DHIR test. The fees vary from one area to another.

Your goats are marked and recorded for identification before the test and every doe in milk in the herd must be on test.

The tester measures the amount of milk from each doe and takes samples to compute the percentage of butterfat in it. He will return for evening milking that same day.

If you have told the tester that you milk at 5 A.M. and 5 P.M., that is when he'll arrive. The results are computerized and averaged over the ten-month lactation for a final production total.

If you've bought an unrecorded goat, and it looks good for its breed or it produces well, you can have it "recorded on performance" or "recorded on appearance." This gives you a paper which allows your goat to be shown with the other recorded grades, such as 50 percent and 75 percent. If your animal is recorded on appearance or on production, this by no means helps to hurry the process of upgrading. When a doe is bred to a purebred buck, her offspring will still be recorded as 50 percent American. Goats recorded on appearance or on performance, or as 50 percent to 75 percent, are generally referred to as Recorded Grades.

American stock can be shown and judged in the same classes with the purebred stock in dairy goat shows.

If your show goats place well enough at a sanctioned show, the placements are recorded, and for a small fee, you can receive copies and have the placements recorded on the registrations papers.

Since we live in a red tape world, papers are a part of goats and goat care. Papers are another form of recordkeeping, and we do need all the help we can get in that department.

When mating American does to purebred bucks, I make notations on the offspring's registration papers, designating which generation of American the offspring stand in.

Example:

Does bred to purebred bucks	Offspring	My notation number
75 percent	American A	7/8
A	American B	15/16
B	American C	31/32
C	American D	63/64
D	American E	126/126

By checking my notations I know that a goat reaching 125/126 is eight generations of up-grading. After ten years of consistent upbreeding, you would end up with the remote fraction of 503/504.

Your goat registration club will check to find what generation of American your goat is, should you buy one from another owner who does not know. The ADGA is the largest registry for dairy goats in the United Stated and is very helpful.

Becoming a member is as simple as paying yearly dues. Then, when you register a goat or transfer a title of a goat, you are entitled to membership fees on these transactions.

Each different breed also has a registry for that breed. See what advantages, if any, they can offer.

Any show sanctioned by ADGA will demand that your goat be papered and properly tattooed.

Many buyers are interested in papered goats and bloodlines. The buyers won't even consider buying a goat unless it's registered, so papering your goats may prove to be an investment if you have stock worthy of selling.

Unfortunately, many buyers don't care what papers mean and simply want the prestige of the papers.

If you will be registering your quality goats, there are many times you don't have to apply for registration.

1. No grade buck is allowed to be papered, and should be castrated.
2. American bucks should come from quality parents and show only the desirable traits necessary for reproduction.
3. Purebred bucks not conforming to breed and type should not be papered nor allowed to reproduce.
4. Does (purebred and otherwise) should not be papered if they carry poor

enough traits that can be passed on to their offspring. This includes the two-cup milker.

These restrictions on not papering inferior animals result from individual goat owners honesty and integrity. Too often, goat owners don't follow this honor system.

Poor-quality grade bucks are constantly being allowed to leave the herd without castration. They are bought for pennies, used for reproduction, and continually allowed to pass their poor traits on to their offspring. This applies also to does with undesirable traits. However, does can be bred to better bucks and thereby improve the offspring. At any rate, allowing inferior animals to be registered and reproduce does nothing to improve the goat world, whether in production, meat, and above all, resale market prices.

If you become a member of the ADGA, and I recommend it, or another organization, it will send you all the information you'll need to register your animals. If you choose not to join, you can get registration information from other breeders, the place you bought your goats, your county extension service, or by writing the ADGA.

Goats can be registered at any age, as long as you keep track of their paperwork. Keep all bills of sale, receipts, parents' names and numbers, and breeding slips. If you feel the goat and offspring deserve it, you can have the registration recorded at a later date.

When you sell a papered goat, you do have the right to charge more money for the papers. I charge exactly what the papers cost me. Many people will raise the price of a papered goat simply because it is registered. They will tell you "its dam did this, and its sire did that," which may be true, but you're not buying mom and pop, and you can't be sure the good traits were passed down just because it is papered.

Be honest when you sell your papered animals. One guy told me, "It's not the best goat, but it's not the worst." I bought the goat and have not been disappointed.

The practice is deplorable, but a goat owner will sometimes paper a worthless goat under the wrong parents.

Example:
> Purebred Doe A: kids one doe.
> Grade Doe B: kids two does.
> Both does were bred to the same purebred buck.

The owner registers all three doelings' information as the offspring of Doe A.

You buy one of the 50 percent doelings as a purebred and breed her to a purebred buck. When she has inferior kids the next year, you blame the perfectly innocent buck.

You got cheated. Your doe is being expected to do more than what is genetically possible, and the poor buck probably gets culled for no reason, since he took all the blame. The worst of it is you may never know that you are harboring a 50 percent American instead of the purebred.

An older doe may die, and the owner takes a similar goat and passes her off as the dead goat. The buyer gets cheated, but worse, all future offspring and buyers are cheated, as this is passing off generations of illegal offspring.

The ADGA does not allow any meat goat stock to be brought into the registry as dairy. However, many people with a purebred buck will list a dam that they know perfectly well has meat crosses in it and write it down as unknown. This is also cheating, as it brings a meat cross into the dairy registry.

Cheating is illegal and immoral. You can be prosecuted for fraud, and your reputation is ruined. Don't cheat on your papers. You wouldn't be improving the breeds or your reputation when the goat doesn't produce as well as the papers say is should.

Be very careful when buying papers. Buy only from reputable people, and check goats against papers very carefully. When in doubt, don't buy.

Never put yourself in a position where a buyer might doubt that authenticity of your papered goats.

For various reasons, I no longer worry with papered goats. The red tape and politics got to me, and I honestly just have too many other things to do. Keeping up with papers and matching tattoos takes a lot of time and trouble that I just don't have any more. This is purely a management decision on my part and not any sort of recommendation.

31

Showing Goats

If you've never shown goats, I suggest you visit a goat show first. Talk to the people, ask questions, and watch.

If you arrive early enough, you get to watch the hustle and bustle of last-minute preparations. The goats are clipped, cleaned, polished, and all the does have full udders, each waiting to take its place with its class in the show ring.

Handlers are brushed, scrubbed, and nervously waiting in snow-white uniforms to see how well they and their animals place. Someone is always running around with a fistful of papers, a pen behind his ear, a pencil in his teeth, and a friendly smile or a frenzied frown.

The show begins, the class is announced, and the goats are led into the ring. Many goats have been through this procedure so often that they could go on their own. The judge directs the handler to lead the goats into a circle, then into various lines, maybe another circle, and finally, to stand still. All the while the judge is watching each goat and its handler and checking all the possible faults and good points. You will see that the handlers' eyes never leave the judge and that the handler never places his body between his goat and the judge. When possible, the handler will squat behind the goat, so as not to distract attention from it.

Eventually, the judge will start placing animals in order. Once they are placed, the judge will explain why each goat has been placed in that manner. For example: "I have placed number one over number two because of her all-around general appearance as a producer. Number two is placed over number three because of the capacity of her udder. Number three is placed over number four because of the size of her barrel in relation to her overall size," and so on. (These are not actual quotes from an actual judge.) All judges are trained to explain.

Before you decide whether to show, you have to ask, "Why show goats?" The best reason is to get an objective opinion of your goats and see how they compare with others in the same class. People try to breed the best goat so they can win, thus improving the goat breeds.

If you show your goats, their names and production records will be current, and you can gain some publicity, which will pay off in advertising the sale of your winners. Those of us who only have a few goats wouldn't dream of selling a winner. Many breeders have 30 or 40 winning goats, and selling winners is their business.

Showing goats can prove profitable when your winnings outrank your entry fees, and it can be fun renewing acquaintances and meeting new people. Showing goats is a learning experience.

There are reasons not to show: Transportation, entry fees, traveling expenses, and extra show costs can be expensive.

When you leave to show your goats, someone has to stay behind to take care of the rest of the herd. You may be gone several days, and your help at home has to carry out your directions exactly. You don't want to return to a disaster.

There is a degree of snobbery on the show circuit. If you and your goats don't rank consistently on top, you may find yourself slighted and politely snubbed by some people. But for the most part, goat people are extra helpful. They will be glad to advise you and tell you how they upgraded to attain winning goats.

Showing goats can be inconvenient, time consuming, and a nuisance. It takes a goat-breeder with extra stamina and a long-lasting drive to succeed to compete in the show ring regularly.

You can go down the middle of the road and show your goats locally, in county and state fairs. In this manner, you get all the good of the advice and learning experience and you minimize disadvantages.

Most shows have rules. All goats must have papers and tattoos. Many shows will not allow sick or abscessed animals. If they do, don't show your goats. Go home and write a letter of protest to the show chairman.

Preparing is another job altogether and separate from the wear and tear of normal daily goat care. You'll put much work into show preparations, as you will in your daily goat chores, so your work is temporarily doubled.

If you decide not to show goats, make it a point to visit a show or go to your county and state fairs at least once a season so you will keep up.

It's a good experience to see the show stock, visit with other breeders, and learn about conformation and quality goats. Going home from the show might be depressing, as you compare your inferior animals, or rewarding, when you realize that your goats could have held their own.

Even if you're an old-timer with the show circuit, the following list may be helpful. Should you be a newcomer, this list will give you an idea of what you are getting into.

THINGS TO PACK FOR YOU

A clean set of whites for each show you plan to attend. Maybe a spare set of whites, if you're prone to a goof now and then.

All personal grooming equipment.

Cooler for food and drink, your own coffeepot or teapot with milk and sugar, and drop cords with adequate adapters.

Any snack you crave at 3 am.

Medications you take regularly.

Cot or mattress, bedding, and other nighttime or sleep-time comforts.

Extra comfortable shoes, because you will be up and running most of the time.

Tissues, sewing kits, maps, and directions.

Portable chairs or stools.

Entry confirmations.

All show papers and class listing, goats' papers, goats' ages, registrations, and freshening dates.

THINGS TO PACK FOR THE GOATS

Feed and water pans, extra food and hay.

Hay bags or racks.

Teat dip, insecticides.

Bottles and nipples, if the kids go with you.

A heater to warm bottles.

Clippers, drop cords, and oil.

Brushes, rags, soap, and paper towels.

Scissors and hoof trimmers.

Goat coats, flashlight, and fly spray.

Vaseline, baby oil, or show sheen.

Scour boluses (pills), Combiotic (combination of penicillin and streptomycin), syringes, and needles.

Bedding, wire cutters, pliers, tools, fan, extra collars, show collars, leads, and snaps.

First aid kit.

Classification

The ADGA sanctions a procedure by which a goat can be judged on its own merits.

This system is called Classification. The goat is rated against an "ideal" and given a score that shows how that particular goat compares to the perfect goat.

Though this system is not perfect, it is the best that the goat world has at this point. It allows the goat to be scored on its individual quality to produce and has no bearing on defects resulting from injuries.

Once the application to ADGA has been completed and fee paid, an official classifier is appointed to the herd or area. Classification can be performed privately, or in groups of several breeders and goats. The owner presents the goats to the classifier, complete with registration papers. The classifier identifies each goat with its tattoo, and evaluates each animal individually. The perfect goat represents the idea score of 100 percent.

The areas covered are appearance, body capacity, dairy character, and the mammary system. Each area is rated against the perfect goat and given a score that related to the ideal. The total of all the scores is averaged to produce a classification number.

SHOWING GOATS

Excellent, 90–100	Good, 60–69
Very good, 80–89	Fair, 50–59
Good-plus, 70–79	Poor, 49 and under

The perfect (ideal) goat would be 100; the average dairy goat is 75. Goats can be reclassified later, and many breeders reclassify every one to three years to keep classification current with their upbreeding program.

Many buyers would rather buy a goat classified between 88 and 94 instead of the winner of a class in a certain show.

Classification is a way to have your goat rated officially, on its own merits as a goat and a producer. Since the goat is rated only on physical attributes and not accidental defects, this procedure may prove better than showing competitively in the ring.

Clubs

National clubs are organized for every breed of goat. These clubs specialize in knowing the newest events involving goats. It is to your advantage to belong to at least one club, or to an Internet goat list, if for nothing else but to receive added educational material.

The ADGA registers only dairy goats, but other breeders' clubs register individual breeds, not exclusive to dairy types, such as Angora and Pygmy.

Local dairy goat clubs are generally small groups of dedicated goat owners who have organized to learn, promote the goat, help 4-H kids, improve the breeds, and improve dairy goat research.

By inquiring, you can find out if there is a goat club near you. Your county extension agent will be glad to give you a list of the clubs in your county or state.

Goat clubs are great publicity for the goats. This is the time when groups of respectable people gather to present to the public their product, the goat. By organizing fairs, charities, sales, auctions, and parades, goat clubs have made a slow but gradual improvement in the goats' image. The public is now seeing more of the well-bred, well-mannered goat, and less of the cantankerous old stinking scrub buck.

Local clubs provide the goatkeeper a night for socializing and education at a price that we can afford.

If you join such a club, join with the intention of giving as well as receiving. Too many club members sit on the back row, enjoy the show, cram their brains full of available information, and go home much richer. These people don't volunteer on the committees or donate their time to the activities. The club helps them, but they do not strengthen their club.

Local breeders need support, time, and commitment if they are to succeed in getting the goat up off the scrub pile and back into the public markets.

If there is not a goat club in your area, consider starting one yourself. Following is a series of steps to follow in starting a club.

1. Call the state revenue service and see if you'll need permits or a license.
2. Call the city or county police to see if you need a license to gather as a group.
3. Call the county extension service and try to get the agents' support.
4. Call the local newspaper for advice and space.
5. Call the local vet for support and a list of goat owners.
6. Call all the goat people and see if they are interested.

Once you get to this point, you have to either be an organizer, or know who is willing to give it a try, because once you've found a place to meet, you're on your way.

Put an ad in the local newspaper, with starting time, place, and intentions. Call everyone previously contacted and beg them to attend.

Your first meeting is likely to be a get acquainted session. Someone has to be temporarily in charge. Decisions have to be made regarding dues, where the money goes, club format, election of officers and projected activities.

Ground rules must be laid for the club's intended purpose, the goats, and the club's mission.

There is going to be some petty bickering in any club. Goat people are no different. It's a good idea to make a statement early in the club's life that the bickering must be handled judiciously.

For all the ups and downs of belonging to a goat club, the advantages outweigh the disadvantages. You'll not only be learning, you'll be helping others learn, and in that process, you'll improve conditions for goats and owners alike.

32

Recordkeeping

Recordkeeping is tedious, frustrating, and one big headache. No one likes the chore. Unfortunately, it's very necessary.

Your manner of recordkeeping is your own business, unless you are in business, in which case you have to answer to the taxman or your accountant. As long as you can refer to your records and understand them well enough to get the needed information, it really doesn't matter what system you use. However, to make a job easier you should have some kind of system.

When I started, I made a huge calendar with three-inch squares and hung it on my back door. When I came in after working with the goats, the calendar was handy to jot down exactly what happened. I kept track of which goat received medical care, which goat got wormed, when the herd was moved from lot to lot, and if one of the goats looked a little ill, I made a note to watch it. I even wrote down things to do on that calendar.

At the end of the month I transferred all the information to the right sheet in my notebook. I've changed this system many times, but a calendar is still a big part of my system.

One of my friends jots down notes on scraps of paper and pitches them in a box. She doesn't mind digging through the mess to find what piece of data she needs when she needs it. Her way works for her, and that's what counts.

Records are necessary to keep track of sickness, feed consumed, hoof trimming dates, worming schedules, and daily milk production. Keeping accurate records not only helps you keep track of care and cost, but helps give you an idea of how much of you is invested in the animal so you can accurately decide on a selling price. Twenty years ago, I was caught off guard and sold a pair of disbudded wethers for $5 each to a kindly man who had to have them for his kids and future weed control; then I checked my books. The kids were three weeks old and had been on milk replacer for two weeks. I had invested in medicines and equipment for castration and disbudding. My records indicated that I should have charged at least $7.50. Moral: After you learn to keep records, learn to pay attention to them before you make decisions.

Records need to be kept on every aspect of goat keeping, starting with each individual goat. You need its complete description — tattoo, age, where you got it, parental information — and anything else about the goat that may be of use, including special markings and defects. On this sheet of paper you keep track of breeding dates, due dates, and numbers of kids born. This is where I keep track of the sex, size, and birth weight for reference when the doe kids again.

Once the birth information is recorded on the doe's sheet, each kid gets its own sheet. Feeding and growth should be recorded regularly, plus all health care and any seasonal problems. If Susie's milk production drops whenever there is a change in the herd, it should be recorded as well as the fact that Nancy does not like to be milked by a man.

These records not only help you with your goats, but they also help to inform a prospective buyer of the goat's history. If you should end up buying the same goat back after a couple of years, you can easily refer to your old records to refresh your memories. It also helps to refer to the records from time to time to see if a doe's problems are occurring in her daughters.

Daily milk sheets should be kept, with the quantity of milk being weighed and recorded at each milking. Many people do this in the barn and call them "barn sheets." I have my scales in the house, and weigh and record at the same time as I put away the milk. All my "muss and fuss" is in one spot, and the milk records are kept in a drawer close to the scales.

Any household item also used for goats (Vaseline, first aid cream, laundry expenses, etc.) should be given an estimated value for your expense sheets on the goats. I place these items "miscellaneous." Items generally used for the family can also be used for goats, and some sort of a record should be kept, or the household budget will look as if it's taking a beating.

Your time should be recorded or estimated from year to year to tell if you're improving. My time spent trimming hooves has decreased by 50 percent, thanks to extra practice and added efficiency.

I keep a separate sheet for capital investments. This includes any item that lasts for several years. This includes stacked-up hay, medicines bought in bulk, stanchions, collars, and the value of my goats.

At the end of the year, I add up my total face value in goats, capital investments, and miscellaneous income from the milk, meat, and sales. I then balance the total against all the expenses to see where the goats really stand. My goats always pay for themselves.

The goats and their produce are considered income and always outweigh expenses.

For my own good, I subtract my time at minimum wage. I usually lose in the end, by showing up in the red. It is my ultimate goal to stay in the black after subtracting my time. If I don't make it, I have an extra sheet of records to rely on for consolation. This is the sheet where I estimate the healthful aspects of my keeping goats. This would include the country club fees, if I were to have to play golf for exercise; health spas, if I were to have to use their services; and money saved on jogging and bicycling equipment, if I were to need that outlet for fresh air and exercise.

There are health costs that can't be given a dollar value, such as the milk and butter in our diet, and the natural, chemical-free meat from the culls. I feel this is saving us dollars in medical bills, giving us better health and the possibility of a longer life. The money saved in groceries is tremendous.

I also keep in mind child-care savings. Since we have goats, we are restricted on our own activities. We seldom go out, so we don't have baby-sitting costs, the expense of entertainment and eating out, or the extra transportation costs that could be involved.

The responsibilities my children learn from goat care cannot be taught in school, and the lessons they've learned will last throughout life. I cannot put a price on these items, but I certainly keep them in mind as I keep track of the dollars and cents.

Time heals. Last year's catastrophe does not seem serious now. Recordkeeping eliminates guesswork from year to year, and it's easy to forget that the white goat dried up after three months last year when she delivers three beautiful does this year.

Keeping notations allows you to chart many things regarding the goats' growth and nutrition. For example, I know that Moby measured 15 inches and weighed 12 pounds at one week, and increased to 23½ inches and 35 pounds by the middle of May. Sassy started slower, at 14¾ inches and 11 pounds, but caught up quickly by mid–May. Both goats' original birth weights were recorded on their dam's chart.

Keeping a milk chart allows me to record one doe's milk production for the week or any other given period of time. I can jot weather conditions under each date to see if Bea slowed down production during rainy spells or increased during fair weather. Her beginning lactation date is recorded on her personal chart.

Of course, now we have computers to store records. I've not thoroughly gotten the concept of changing files, instead of turning a page, but we old-timers will never get as used to it as the younger generation. I still keep my clipboard in the barn and my milk records under the scales in a drawer. But a goat's history, due dates, number of kids, and to whom she was bred all now go into the computer.

33

Selling

Selling can be a profitable way to cull unwanted animals or to reap the benefits of breeding top-notch goats. Many people go into business selling goats.

If you, as a small goatkeeper, don't want the goat, who will? Finding the right market for your castaways can be difficult, as small goatkeepers are not usually selling their good stock. Those who are in the business of selling their good stock have to know the markets, because it's their business to be informed. They have advertised and built a reputation that will speak for them. But if you are the ordinary small herd owner who has an extra kid or an older cull every other year, it can be tougher to keep in touch with the markets. The biggest drawback to selling your animals is simple: You won't always know the buyer nor have any control over the goat's treatment.

I've had some disheartening experiences. Goats have been brought back to me sick, dying, and dead, or worse, maimed. Young does have been bred too early and died in the kidding process. Goats have been allowed to run with dogs and have been injured chasing cars. On one occasion, a very good milk doe was left standing at the sale barn for three days with no one to relieve her swollen udder when the buyer neglected to pick her up after paying my price. Kids that have been bought as children's pets have been neglected when the new pet was no longer "new." Since I cannot sell a goat and forget it, I have tried to make it a policy not to sell my culls unless it is for butcher. However, due to the pressure of popular demand, I do relent from time to time, and I have made some guidelines.

I sell only to people I know and can check back with at a later date. I guarantee to buy the goat back if they tire of it, or if it doesn't meet their standards. I never allow an unqualified buck to leave my place without being castrated, so I don't have to worry about someone using one for stud service. I do not sell just one goat unless it will be butchered or the buyer already has goats.

I give the buyer my phone number and offer to be available anytime he needs advice or help. I also offer to help trim hooves and disbud new kids, or at least show them how to do it. This can get hectic, but I don't lie awake at night worrying about the care my goats receive.

I ask a lot of questions. If I'm not satisfied, I won't sell. I have made several people angry, especially the young mother who wanted to buy a young kid for her 18-month-old twin boys. She thought it was a great idea to keep the goat in the house with the babies, so it would keep them entertained.

Some people have pretty offbeat methods of butchering. One method that disgusts me is the process by which an incision is made in the skin of a live animal, and water is forced into the incision (usually by hose) to "loosen the skin from the carcass." This is painful and cruel, and I make certain none of my buyers plan to use it. I always ask how they butcher and pray that they are being truthful.

When selling kids, I give the new owner a slip of paper with the kid's birth date, parents' information, feeding schedules, and suggestions for feed changes necessary for normal, healthy goat growth.

Finding a market is as simple or as hard as buying your goat in the first place. Advertising in the local paper is inexpensive, and you can add the price of the ad to the goat's selling price. Sale barns provide a market, but prices are usually lower, unless the sale is specifically for goats or exotic animals. Goat shows are a great market, providing your stock is of good quality. Local clubs usually have a newsletter and members of local goat clubs are often potential buyers. For the small herd owner, word-of-mouth is usually enough.

If you're charitable and can afford it, you could give the goat to a needy person or deserving child.

However you sell your goat, tell the buyer exactly why you are selling. Be honest about the goat's background, habits, expectations, and physical drawbacks. The buyer may not understand conformation, or even want to, but you must make an effort.

Setting a price on your goat can be as difficult as finding a good buyer. If your animals are registered quality goats, your job may be easier, since each area has an unwritten "understanding" as to market value. By staying competitive with the market, you can set your price accordingly.

It's not so easy if you're simply selling unregistered culls. In many areas, a two-month-old scrub kid is not worth $2. This is inaccurate, considering the dehorning, castration, feed, hay, and care that are involved in a two-month-old kid.

Sometimes the goat can be sold for meat on a price per pound basis. We butcher our excess goats, so I have developed a simple solution to setting a price for my culls.

I figure out what the meat is worth. I grind all my meat, which means that I will receive about 28 percent of the goat's gross weight after it is cut from the bone. If you cut the meat into steaks, chops, and roasts, you can figure total gain at about 36 percent of the gross weight. These percentages include keeping the heart and liver and vary with the condition of the goat.

I value the meat at $1.50 a pound (on the hoof), but you can set your own price. I use this figure because I will not pay any more for processed meat. Often, the price of chevon (goat meat), is compared to the prices of lamb, veal, and venison. It is your budget and your goat, so you can set your own price.

Once you've put a price on your meat, you can set a selling price on your culls.

A 100-pound goat will net me about 28 pounds of meat, making the goat worth about $42 to butcher for our own use. This is before subtracting any cost for the kill or butchering. If you send the goat out to be processed, the cost can range from $10 to $20, making the goat's value between $22 and $32. When I'm selling the 100-pound goat to someone else and we won't be helping the buyer butcher, I do drop my price. It takes me about one hour to butcher and about an hour to clean, grind, and wrap the 28 pounds of meat; so I feel justified in dropping the $42 by $5 to $10 dollars since we won't be doing this processing.

That 100-pound goat is worth at least $34 to me. If I don't get that price, I don't lose a dime by butchering the goat, and putting it in my own freezer. That two-month-old kid that might not bring more than $2 should weigh 30 pounds or more, which is almost nine pounds of meat (28 percent of the gross). At $1.50 per pound, I have $13.50 worth of goat. Even when I subtract $5 for the butchering I won't have to do the goat is still worth $8.50. This still covers the expenses I have, like disbudding and castration. With these prices, you don't make much profit, but you certainly don't lose, either.

If you can use or sell the hides, you are justified in raising the price of your goat to allow for the loss of the hide.

A friend once said he couldn't eat all the culls and it would be too much meat to store in the freezer. This is no problem either. That meat can be traded or given away when I have too much for my family.

If you don't use the meat yourself, check out the meat buyers and markets before your kids are due. If you're lucky, you can sell the young kids for 50 to 75 cents a pound before you put much work into them.

The market for meat kids can be great for Fourth of July barbecues, Easter and June nineteenth celebrations. It might be profitable to save your spring kids and feed them for holiday sales.

If you can't get the price you think is fair, don't compromise just to get rid of the goat. If a buyer finds out you can be suckered into lowering your price once, he will be back year after year. Getting rid of the goat isn't worth losing your investment of time and money. Someone always wants a goat. I have had to tell people no when it comes to selling goats more often than I've had to worry about not being able to sell goats.

Other livestock producers have set standard prices on the produce and most will not drop their price for even best friends and family. Goat keepers should follow these examples and keep prices competitive.

There is a way to figure out the value of an average doe. The following table shows the average figures on one of my grade does. Some goats will do better, some worse. Your feed and management practices may be different, but you can use this table as a guideline to help figure your doe's value.

According to this table, this doe is worth $336 for her first milking, which more than makes up for the expense of keeping and caring for her while she was pregnant and not producing. First fresheners may give as much milk, kids, or manure. Barring accidents, this goat should continue to produce in the manner till she is eight to 12 years old.

Expenses for one goat per year	Amount
Purchase price	$ 50
Three pounds grain per day, 330 days is 990 pounds per year, or 20 bags at $9	$180
Twelve pounds hay per day, 120 days (no hay during browse) 1,440 pounds hay, or 16 bales at $3 per bale (if you get it out of the field)	$48
Misc. salt, vet, worming, etc.	$40
Stud fees	$25
TOTAL	$418

Income from one average doe per one year	Amount
Milk: six pounds per day for 305 days (1,830 pounds, about 228 gallons) at $3 per gallon	$684
Kids about $25	$50
Manure (fertilizer)	$20
TOTAL	$754
Subtract expenses	$418
TOTAL PROFIT	$336

If you keep this goat for 10 years, and production and prices don't change, she is actually worth $3,360 plus the hide and the meat.

I have not subtracted my labor or the headaches involved in worrying about her when she is sick. On the other hand, I have not added the benefits I received from exercise and fresh air while caring for her or added companionship and affection I receive from her.

This particular goat is also a "watch dog." She bellows when anyone comes around, and she talks to the grandchildren when they are playing outside. By listening to her, I have a pretty good idea where the kids are playing, which saves me many trips to doors and windows to check on them, and makes her valuable as a "mother's helper." This same goat can also be counted on to protect the newborn orphans of less motherly does, should I not be present for the birth.

I cannot put a price on her because someone just might be smart enough to pay it. When she has outlived her usefulness as a producer, she will serve as meat in our freezer, which will add more than $50 in meat to her price.

Don't sell your goat short. I keep these figures handy for prospective goat owners when they quibble over the $75 to $500 they may have to pay for a goat.

Season, as well as areas, will affect market prices. Selling a goat in the North in September is difficult, unless it will be butchered. The goat will have to be fed more due to the low browse and produce less due to pregnancy, so prices will be down. April sales are more successful in the North, whereas February sales would be possible in the South. If hay is hard to find, or is expensive, it is harder to sell a goat, and when feed and hay prices go up, the price of the goat tends to drop. Check out all the selling aspects carefully, to get the best possible price.

Regardless of the price you get for your goat, back your sale. Be honest and guard your reputation.

34

Chevon

Chevon is the meat from the goat. Chevon is sold in finer restaurants as a delicacy for huge prices. It's been reported that chevon steaks can cost over $45 on the East Coast, yet many people refuse to taste is when it is served from our kitchen. When properly processed, chevon is comparable to beef or venison. The meat is darker than beef, not as stringy as venison, and there is relatively no fat or gristle on a healthy young goat.

Joe England, who lives near Hope, Arkansas, added a Boer buck to his Saanens in the hopes of having more meat-grade goats.

I cook the meat the same way I cook beef, pork and venison. I do season an older goat with a little more garlic and onion, and a mature doe is ground and seasoned into summer sausage or breakfast sausages.

If your recipe calls for beef or pork, it may help to add one tablespoon of cooking oil or shortening for every pound of chevon, since there is so little fat. I have not included recipes because I feel that special recipes for chevon might mean that there is something different about the meat. There is not.

There are some precautions to take when butchering to ensure the good taste and quality of chevon. If you want the meat to taste as good as the other varieties of meat in your freezer, it must be cared for as carefully.

The prospective goat should be in good health for nutritious meat, though frequently sickly goats are butchered to prevent the total waste of the animals. It is best when the goat has been raised on natural foods, is not overly fat or skinny and, depending on its sex, has been given the appropriate time to recover from pregnancy, lactation, or breeding season.

The goat should not be allowed to run or get excited before the kill. This is true of most livestock. If the animal is excited, the blood is pumped faster through the meat, heating it and causing a stronger hard or wild taste.

We kill only tame goats, and we do it with one rifle shot to the head when they have their head down and are eating. The throat is cut, and the carcass must be hung immediately for fast drainage of the blood. When butchering, choose a season and place when insects will not be a problem. The carcass should be

Boers from the Foreman, Arkansas, 4-H club.

immersed in cold or icy water for quick cooling, and should be thoroughly washed. One hair can taint the meat.

Chevon can be cooked or processed immediately after cooling, but we hang the meat in an extra refrigerator at a temperature between 44 and 48 degrees for two to three days to let it season. Many people advise dropping the temperature to between 40 and 45 degrees.

The meat is then cut or ground and wrapped into packages and frozen. All packages are marked with the date, weight, content and cut (ground, chops, etc.) and labeled "chevon." We do not put "goat meat" on the packages. Who labels beef "cow meat"?

I save the bones and cook them down into broth for soups and stews. The liver is sliced and packaged separately, and the heart is ground into sausage.

Generally, chevon is not thought of as appetizing. Those who have eaten it and found it foul have probably tasted an old buck or goat that was not killed and cared for properly.

The normal healthy goat will not eat anything but good food. Therefore, if the goat is properly cared for the meat will be nutritious and healthful. Improperly handled goat meat is not.

I have kept records on each of my goats and have found that I can feed a goat to butcher weight, using summer browse, for 2 to 5 cents a pound. The only other animal that can boast so low a cost-per-pound ratio is the tame rabbit. Naturally, the more grain, hay, and milk replacer that is fed to the goat, the higher the cost-per-pound will be. This is only one area where your method of management is a large matter of importance.

Goats should never be fed chemicals, and medicine should be used with caution, keeping the condition of the meat as natural as possible.

Epilogue

As I work with my goats each day, I can't believe that it was so hard in the beginning.

But, as I completed this book, there came a fearful feeling that I might have left out some small but important detail.

I've included everything that has commonly happened to me, and my fellow goat owners, and can only hope that I've done my job well enough that I can make your job of raising goats easier than mine was. I didn't realize how much more I knew, and how much more had changed, until I was knee deep into this revision of my original 1984 book. It was a good time to do it.

The goats and I now move easily from day to day and season to season without distressing each other, and without me pulling my hair out in desperation. There's always going to be a new problem and there's always going to be a new book. I hope you read all of them.

I can only add: "Don't give up on your goats. They'll do the best they can for you when they are treated well."

If you have a setback, don't give up on yourself, either. You will learn and be better for it. Never forget who your friends are, and always be willing to bury your pride and ask for help.

Respectfully,
Mama Mary, and her goats, and a lot of friends

Further Reading

Books

Damerow, Gail. *Your Goats*. North Adams, MA: Storey Publishing, 1993.

Jaudas, Ulrich, and Matthew M. Vriends. *The New Goat Handbook: Housing, Care, Feeding, Sickness, and Breeding; With a Special Chapter on Using the Milk, Meat, and Hair*. Hauppage, NY: Barron's Educational Series, 1989.

Luttman, Gail. *Raising Milk Goats Successfully*. Charlotte, VT: Williamson Publishing, 1986.

MacKenzie, David. *Goat Husbandry*. Fifth edition, edited by Ruth Goodwin. New York: Faber & Faber, 1993.

Plumb, Donald C. *Veterinary Drug Handbook*. Fifth edition. Ames, IA: Blackwell Professional, 2005.

Robinson, Ed, and Carolyn Robinson. *The "Have-More" Plan*. Pownal, VT: Storey Communications, 1973.

Smith, Mary C., and David M. Sherman. *Goat Medicine*. Philadelphia: Lippincott Williams & Wilkins, 1994.

Spaulding, C.E., and Jackie Spaulding. *The Complete Care of Orphaned or Abandoned Baby Animals*. Emmaus, PA: Rodale Press, 1980.

Walsh, Helen. *Starting Right with Milk Goats*. Charlotte, VT: Garden Way Publishing, 1947.

Magazines

Dairy Goat Journal: www.dairygoatjournal.com/
Backwoods Home Magazine: www.backwoodshome.com/
Mother Earth News: www.motherearthnews.com/

Web sites

American Dairy Goat Association: www.adga.org/

Fias Co Farm: http://fiascofarm.com/ (Goat health and husbandry, cheese making)

www.hawksmountainranch.com (This site is about sheep, and since sheep and goats are so much alike, you'll find much good information here.)

www.agric.nsw.gov.au/reader/nsw-agriculture (Thorough)

www.rirdc.gov.au/pub/handbook/dairygoats.html (I use this a lot, as do friends in the Home Dairy Goats discussion group.)

Yahoo discussion group: http://groups.yahoo.com/group/HomeDairyGoatsJournal/ (my favorite)

Index